I0007683

SOCIAL MEDIA MARKETING MASTERY 2020

How to Use Social Media for Business

4 Books in 1:

Blogging for Profit

Affiliate Marketing

Instagram Marketing

Facebook Advertising

Michael Robert Fortunate

© **Copyright 2019 by Michael Robert Fortunate.
All rights reserved.**

The content contained within this book may not be reproduced, duplicated or transmitted without direct written permission from the author or the publisher.

Under no circumstances will any blame or legal responsibility be held against the publisher, or author, for any damages, reparation, or monetary loss due to the information contained within this book. Either directly or indirectly.

Legal Notice:

This book is copyright protected. This book is only for personal use. You cannot amend, distribute, sell, use, quote or paraphrase any part, or the content within this book, without the consent of the author or publisher.

Disclaimer Notice:

Please note the information contained within this document is for educational and entertainment purposes only. All effort has been executed to present accurate, up to date, and reliable, complete information. No warranties of any kind are declared or implied. Readers acknowledge that the author is not engaging in the rendering of legal, financial or professional advice. The content within this book has been derived from various sources. Please consult a licensed professional before attempting any techniques outlined in this book. By reading this document, the reader agrees that under no circumstances is the author responsible for any losses, direct or indirect, which are incurred as a result of the use of information contained within this document, including, but not limited to, errors, omissions, or inaccuracies.

Blogging for Profit

A Proven 6 Figure Strategy for Beginners to Make Money With a Blog: How to Create Passive Income From Your Online Business to Generate Maximum Profit and Gain Financial Freedom!

Michael Robert Fortunate

4

Table of Contents

Introduction: What is Blogging and Why it's an Effective Solution to Make Money

Goals are important, and so is having a sense of purpose. When it comes to blogging, a purpose for opening a blog can be different for different people. Plenty of people start a blog purely for personal purposes, but for a handful, the purpose of a blog is for business.

Your reason for choosing this book is ultimately to learn how to use your blog to make money, and that's what we are here to learn. Blogging for business or any kind of endeavor that could bring you money has an extremely pointed purpose- to place your website at a higher rank in Google SERPs, which also means it increases your visibility.

Your business relies on consumers to purchase your products and services. If you are a new business, you can use blogging to help you attract the right kind of customers.

Without blogging, your main e-commerce website will remain invisible, but with a blog, you can constantly add content to make it fresh, competitive, and searchable. When it comes to blogging for business, the sole purpose here is to connect you to your target audience.

The other reason is to boost your traffic and also to bring in relevant leads and audience to your site via your content. The more constant, consistent, and frequent your blog posts, the higher the chances that your website will be discovered and visited by a relevant audience. The more traction you get means that your blog is effective.

Blogging for Business

Doing a quick search on Google about blogging for business, you'd find queries related to making money through blogging. So you're not the only one looking to make money online and using a blog to do that.

The fact that plenty of them are looking for answers shows that not everyone has a definite clue on how much a person can make through blogging. Many of the results will tell you that you need to pay attention to key phrases since Google basically feeds on that. This is true, and a must-do, but there are many more things that you should be doing to make your blog profitable, and we will uncover all of these things in this book.

So back to the question- How much can you earn through blogging?

Let's look at famous blogs and how much they make to give you an idea:

- Bloggers Bjork and Lindsay from Pinch of Yum makes an average of $85000 a year in 2016
- Latasha Peterson of Arts & Budget makes $2,500 to $3,000 a month
- Make Sense of Cents's Michelle Schroeder-Gardner rakes in a monthly income of $125,000
- Harsh Agarwal or ShoutMeLoud.com pulls in $40,000 by blogging

So what's in it for you?

- Blogging is something you can do! If they can do it, so can you
- You need the right idea and the right strategies
- There is no stopping you!

Now that you know how much money bloggers make, this leads us to our next question:

How do Bloggers make money online?

You'd be glad to know that there are plenty of ways to make money using a blog: from banner advertising to affiliate marketing to selling your ideas, your products, or even offering your service. All of these are some of the amazing opportunities to make money.

So what is the best option for you? Well, the answer is- it depends on what you want to do and the kind of industry you want to be in. According to Gael Breton from Authority Hacker who analyzed 23 bloggers and how they make money through their blogs, he concluded that selling your own products or services is by far the most profitable and superior way of making money through blogging. Let's look at the table below:

Business Model	Total Income	Total Expenses	Profit	Profit Margin
Services	$21,508	$2,805	$18,703	666%
Ad Selling	$235,977	$135, 041	$100, 936	74%
Affiliate Marketing	$214,232	$47,664	$166,568	349%
Own Product Sales	$434,004	$113,767	$320,237	281%

Generally, offering services is a little hard to sell, and this generates less revenue; however, the profit margin is excellent. Plenty of top bloggers make a pretty good living by offering services via their blog. Next in line would be ad selling, but these are only because ad sellers need to produce plenty of content and also acquire traffic. While it brings in income, the profit margins are small.

Another great option would be affiliate marketing as this is both profitable and also an excellent way for new bloggers to make quick income. Blogs using affiliate marketing are funded by affiliate income.

If producing, creating, and selling your own products are not something you can do, the options above are great. However, as mentioned earlier, selling your own products generates the most revenue plus it also has excellent profit margins. These margins are slightly slower than those of affiliate marketing, but this is because of the costs involved with processing and shipping products. That said, the higher conversion rates make up for it.

Some people say content is king which means the better your content, the easier you'd get people visiting your blog, and that would mean more money flowing in.

However, in 2019, content alone is not enough. While you do need to create engaging and fresh content, you also need to have a profitable niche and good marketing strategies to pull in a new crowd and retain your existing crowd.

How do you begin?

As with any sustainable, monetizing endeavor, blogging would require some pretty hefty groundwork to be done before you can see cash flowing. You need to be prepared to invest time and effort (which could take months) before you see a significant return of profits.

This is why this book has been created for readers like you who want to take the right steps into achieving your blogging goals.

Let's begin!

Chapter 1: Types of Blogging Platforms

Now that you know that you can make money from blogging, the next step is to choose the right blogging platform. This decision can be a little confusing to make, especially since there are plenty of choices right now in 2019. Blogging platforms have come a long way, and there are different kinds of blogs catered to the different needs and purposes for every blogger out there. In this chapter, we will look at the best (FREE!) blogging platforms that you can earn money from. We look at free platforms because all platforms are actually free to sign up and use at its basic level, or at least free for a trial period.

Once you start exploring and using its features, testing to see if this is something that works for you, you would get a good feel of how things would be suitable for your blogging purposes. Let's get into discussing the pros and cons of each of them. Firstly, here is the list of blogs we will be looking at:

- WordPress.org
- WordPress.com
- Blogger

- Wix
- Tumblr
- Medium
- Joomla
- Weebly

What is a blogging platform?

A blogging platform is essentially a place or a site where you can create an operate your blog site. A blogging software or service, on the other hand, is where you can publish your articles from- it is basically a content management system or CMS. In simpler terms, a software platform that allows you to create your blog post without any form of programming or coding knowledge is a blogging platform. As mentioned previously, there are plenty of blogging platforms out there, but you want something that fits not only your needs but also something that is widely used around the world. Here is a list of the world's most used blogging platform:

- WordPress.org - 48%
- Blogger- 25%
- WordPress.com - 13%
- Drupal- 3%
- Joomla- 2%
- Wix- 1%
- Tumblr- 1%
- Medium- 1%
- Weebly- 1%

The Best Free Blogging Platforms to Make Money

It is essential to choose a blogging platform that is popular as you can get plenty of tips, tricks, plug-ins, themes, and solutions from all around the internet. Also, popular blogging platforms ride high on search engine results.

- **WordPress.org**

WordPress.org is among the best blogging platforms out there, not only in 2019 but ever since blogs started becoming common in the internet space. At present, WordPress currently hosts more than 33% of websites on the internet. The reason for this is because WordPress.org is extremely easy to use. Apart from that, it also has a very helpful and active user community that has plenty of information, guidelines, and how-tos. WordPress.org, a self-hosted blogging platform, and open-source software.

The Pros

- You are on one of the most widely used popular free blogging platforms in the world
- You get to build just about any kind of website you want
- There are thousands of free and premium themes you can choose from for your site design
- Access to about 54,000 free plugins to customize and enhance your site

- It is extremely SEO friendly
- It is also made to be mobile-responsive
- You get high performance with high security
- You also have access to tools that you can develop your theme to fit your needs
- The editor uses a Gutenberg block

The Cons

- As WordPress.org is a self-hosted blogging platform, you need to be able to manage your blog on your own, and this includes backing it up and setting up additional security.

The Cost

- WordPress.org is free to use, but you also need a hosting provider that you can install and start building your blog. Plus, a domain name is also extremely essential. Hosting is pretty standard, and it usually starts about $3.95 a month, depending on the provider you choose. Bluehost or SiteGround is one of the best places to begin as a beginner. Both of these hosting providers are recommended with WordPress.org, and they also put in a free domain as well as an SSL certificate for free. You also have a choice of buying your own domain name as well as hosting provider, and if you do that, then your best option is to go with WordPress.org blogging platform.

- **WordPress.com**

WordPress.com and WordPress.org are two different platforms for blogging. This is something you need to know about the early on-set. So what's the difference? With WordPress.org, the CMS is where you get to develop or host your own blog with a hosting service provider. With WordPress.com, it is similar to other free blogging platforms where you get to create your own blog using their site. Plenty of beginners prefer to begin their blogging with WordPress.com because of its ease-of-use. Blogging is free with WordPress.com, but if you want their premium services and your very own custom domain name, then you also need to pay premium charges as well.

The Pros

- You do not need any kind of setup
- It is easy to use and manage your blog
- You can use the mobile and desktop apps to update your blog site from anywhere

- You own the content on your site which means you can switch it anytime, anywhere

- You also get free Jetpack essential features

- You also get 3GB storage space

The Cons

- You have limited options for customization

- You also cannot run your own ads

- WordPress.com does not allow you to sync Google AdSense

- You can earn money through WordAds

- Your account can be closed at any moment if you violate their terms and conditions

The Cost

The basic WordPress.com site is free, but you also end up with WordPress's very own advertising and banners. However, if you pay for their premium services, you can have your very own domain and get rid of their branding Ads. Their premium costs are $8 a month whereas their business cost is at $25 a month.

- **Blogger**

Blogger is another popular option and a wise one to blog and to make money. It also has a huge collection of themes that you can use for free on your blog. It is also known as one of the best blogs for beginners. Just like the WordPress blogs, Blogger is free, but if you want their premium services, then you need to pay. For bloggers who use Blogger, your domain address would be yourname.blogspot.com, but if you pay for a custom domain name, then you get to customize your domain. This is the right platform for beginners, whether you want to use it as a personal blog or a commercial blog.

You can put in your advertisement so long as you are approved for Google AdSense even if you are on a free plan. This is one of the best free blogging platforms if you want to make money using Google AdSense.

The Pros

- Blogger is a free blogging platform
- It is also easy to use and easy to manage the site- you do not need coding knowledge
- You can use Google Adsense on this blog to earn money

The Cons

- You have limited options to grow your blog
- You do not have access to plugins or extensions to improve your blog's functionality
- While there are plenty of themes, it is not as varied as those on WordPress

- You run the risk of your account closing at any time if you violate their terms and conditions

- As you grow and start making money, you would want to expand your site, but you'd find that it is limited

The Cost

The Blogger account is free; however, it comes with limited options. You need to pay premium rates to have your own custom domain name. If using Google AdSense is your primary goal for your blog, then Blogger is the way to go.

- **<u>Wix</u>**

Wix is an upgraded platform in the world of blogging. Wix started out as an easy-to-use blogging and website option for you to create a free blog or website. You can use this like any other blog or website for free, but like all the other options, you need premium plans for a custom domain. Wix does not allow you to put your own ads in when you are on their free plan however it does offer you so much more capabilities of creating a full-fledged website with plugins and themes to make it professional as long as your imagination goes.

The Pros

- Wix is extremely easy to set up

- It is a great option if you are looking to create a website without any coding knowledge

- It's drag and drop elements enable you to build your site easily using the Wix Editor

- It is also mobile optimized and SEO friendly

- Wix also has dynamic pages which means you can create the same single design for 100 pages

The Cons

- Its free account has limited options

- Wix displays their ads on your website

- You only have one chance to choose a template for your site, and you cannot change it

- Wix does not offer other 3rd party apps

- Their e-commerce options are limited

- It is not an excellent choice to make money, but it is a good option for a website

The Cost

Their most basic plan is at $5 a month, but it comes with the Wix brand ads and limited bandwidth. If you opt for the $14 a month, then you have their unlimited plan. Their VIP plan is at $29 a month.

- **Tumblr**

The world's most popular microblogging site and social networking website. This site allows you to make the blogging experience different from the rest. Tumblr's community is very different from that of the other blogs with its community more into fandom, GIFs, bordering to eroticism, and loads of anime. Tumblr also allows you to use Google AdSense if you have a custom domain name, but it does not allow you to put in your own ad when you are the other on that blogging platform.

The Pros

- Tumblr is easy to use and free
- It also has integrated social networking into the mix
- It allows you to post multimedia from videos to GIFs in a short-term blog

The Cons

- Tumblr has very specific features to enable it to be a microblogging site so if you want to expand your blog; you need to go elsewhere unless you're happy with its microblogging capabilities
- The lack of plugins makes it hard to add in any additional features
- It is hard to transfer or export content from platform to another should you decide to move away from Tumblr and go on to something like WordPress

The Cost

Tumblr is free like the other platforms, but you have to pay for a custom domain name for your blog. You also need to pay for 3rd party apps to be able to use it on your blog.

- **<u>Medium</u>**

Medium is a very popular publishing blogging platform that caters specifically to long-form writing, with a niche audience of writers, journalists as well as story writers. Medium is free to use as well, but for readers, they would need to pay to read articles as there is a membership fee. You cannot put in your own ads unless, like Tumblr, you have your own custom domain. Medium is the long-form version of Tumblr, and it is a great platform to use if making money through writing articles is your purpose.

To become a Medium member, your fee begins at $5 a month, and it can go up to $50 a year, but the great thing is you get unlimited access to the internet's best writers, and you'd also get ideas that you cannot get anywhere else.

Medium charges a membership fee to support its writers the same way Patreon charges its members to support its artists and creative community. The membership fee is distributed among writers based on how engaging their content is with their audience.

The Pros

- Medium is extremely easy to set up and use. In fact, there is little to no setup required

- It has an easy to handle interface

- It is also free to use

The Cons

- The platform's features are limited

- You are not able to run your own ads if you use the platform for free

- If you lost your Medium account, you lose your followers

The Cost

As with all the platforms above, if you want custom features and upgrades, you need to pay for it. It is pretty standard.

- **Joomla**

This platform shares similar features to WordPress.org. It is also open-source, and it has its own Content Management System. It is a platform used commonly by non-profits, small businesses as well as large organizations depending on what their needs are. As of 2019, Joomla has over 2 million active websites. Like WordPress, Joomla also has extensions and plugins, and it is also a free blogging platform. You can also run your own ads on this platform which also means that this is another platform that makes it easy to make money through blogging.

The Pros

- You can work on an open-source software

- You have a search engine optimized out of the box

- They also have awesome design features and functionalities

- Pretty good security

- An excellent option for making money

The Cons

- As it is similar to WordPress.org, you'd be hard-pressed to put your finger on which one is better-making this choice could be hard

- You need to manage your own blog and website similarly the way you would with WP.org

- Joomla's community is much smaller than that of WordPress which means limited support and limited development

The Cost

You need a reliable hosting provider to host your blogging platform. Charges are about the same with WordPress.

- **<u>Weebly</u>**

Not to be confused with Weibo, this is another free blogging platform that is more of a blog site builder. It is one of the best platforms to use if you want to build an online store. You will also need a premium plan if you want to run an eCommerce business. For Weebly's shopping card feature to be added, you need to upgrade your plan to a Pro plan or a Business plan. They have the basic SSL security, and it also comes with 500MB of data storage. On the flip side, it has a subdomain, so if you want to have your own custom domain identity, then you would, of course, need to go premium.

The Pros

- It's an easy setup with simple drag and drop features and interface

- You have plenty of free blogging templates to choose from

- It is SEO optimized

- You do not need any coding knowledge

- The maintenance is minimum

- There are plenty of media and 3rd party integration options when you want to expand the blog's functionality

The Cons

- If you are on the free plan, the features are of course limited

- Since its media integration is robust, you might end up running into limited space the more media you upload

- You are unable to run your own ads to make money. Instead, their ads would be added to your site

- There is no phone support given to basic plans
- Migrating data and content from this blog to another is hard

The Cost

The pro plan comes in at $12 a month, but it is paid annually whereas the business plans are $25 a month, which gives you a free domain and a host of other new features.

Now that we have covered some of the internet's most popular blog sites, the next question to answer is:

How can I start a blog and make money?

Based on the comparisons given above, WordPress.org is by far the most superior and gives you value for your money. You can run ads for free, and you also have more control over your content. You can try and test out the other platforms but take note that in the event you do change your mind and want to migrate your content from other platforms to WordPress- you'd get into a whole load of inconvenience, a waste of time, effort and not to mention money. The more posts you have and the higher the traffic, the more likely you'd need a blog that gives you the added security, the expanding features as well as the necessary support.

So what do you do next to kickstart your money-making business through your blog?

It boils down to these next few steps:

1. Choose a blogging niche
2. Pick a platform
3. Pick a domain and hosting plan
4. Monetize your blog

So which blogging platform is best for making money? It all boils down to your purpose, needs, and of course, budget. If you are not sure, stick to a free plan first and explore the blog's features and then choose the one that best fits your needs.

Choosing to go premium should only happen once you have a pretty good idea of what you want in a blog even if you have the budget to go premium. This is because you would still need to invest time, energy as well as resources to put in the necessary content to see if the blog platform works for you or not. No matter what the decision may be, pick a platform that is easy to set up, reliable, secure, and has good support. All of this will benefit you in the long run and save you money as well as give you more headspace.

Other blogging platforms or websites that you can try are SquareSpace, Contentful, Yola, Jekyll, Ghost as well as LiveJournal.

What are the best blogging platforms for 2019, on the other hand, and which would be best for your business?

We put our money's work on WordPress, Blogger as well as Wix. WordPress.org is ultimately the way to go, and in the next few chapters, our focus will be on setting up a WordPress blog, exploring your niche as well as setting up your blogging business.

Chapter 2: WordPress - The Most Effective Platform to Make Money

Wordpress is an easy yet powerful blog and website content management system on the internet today. Ask any top bloggers what platform they use, and it will most likely be WordPress. This platform is an online-based, open-source blog or website creation tool coded in PHP. But all you need to know about it is that it is easy to set up and start a blog or a website.

Who uses WordPress?

A very valid question and to be honest, anyone can use it for any purpose at all, such as a simple online journal to a vibrant travel blog or even as a news portal or political website. Popular sites such as CNN and Forbes use WordPress, and Fortune 500 companies such as UPS, Sony, and eBay use WordPress. WordPress is the most popular blogging and website CMS because of its many features, stability, and user-friendly navigating.

What's the difference between WordPress.com and WordPress.org?

The one that separates the .com site with the .org site is the hosting service. If you sign up for a .org, then YOU host your own website or blog using the services of a hosting provider. WordPress.org is the software that you can download and install into your web server. For the WordPress.com site, the hosting is done by WordPress, so there's no downloading or paying for additional hosting or managing your own web server.

How do I start using WordPress?

WordPress requires no cost at all, except maybe your time. But essentially, there is no need to purchase anything upfront. It is totally 100% free. Opening a WordPress account is free of course and having a website or blog is absolutely free. However, if you would like to have your online site a specific way or particular color and to have some certain upgrades, then these updates require some form of investment.

Benefits of Using WordPress

WordPress has many impressive features; that's why it the most preferred website and blogging platform. Here are some benefits of using WordPress:

- Easy to sign up

All you need to do is sign up for a WordPress account using your email and password. There is a two-step verification process that users need to follow to confirm. Also, most hosting services support WordPress through a one-click installation option.

- Secure Open Source Network and Vibrant Community

WordPress is used by plenty of people. Therefore, the community itself creates a massive database of free themes and plugins that you can take advantage of for your site. Users can use these freebies, but there are also a variety of premium themes and plugins that do not cost so much and come equipped with excellent support from their providers.

What Kinds Of Websites Can WordPress Make?

When WordPress first materialized on the Internet, WordPress was created for the primary reason to create a blog rather than to create websites. But thanks to changes in WordPress's core coding, this blogging platform has become a massive ecosystem filled with themes, plugins, and tools that enables anyone to create any type of blog or website using WordPress.

Doing a quick Google search now in 2019, you'd see that there are plenty of sites and blogs that use WordPress to power up large commerce and business capabilities. Right now, WordPress is the most popular platform to create stunning and user-friendly eCommerce stores. With WordPress, you can build:

- Business websites
- eCommerce stores
- Blogs
- Portfolios
- Resumes
- Forums
- Social networks
- Membership sites

Monetizing Your WordPress Site

There are plenty of ways to monetize your WordPress site to make money from it but in order to do that, you need to enhance your site to make it easy for people to do what you want them to do you on-site, whether it is to read your content, to purchase your products or to subscribe or sign up for your services.

Apart from those options above, most people also start out with using AdSense ads as well as through affiliate programs. AdSense, which is operated by Google enables you to place your ads on your website and get paid whenever people click on it. Through affiliate programs, especially the ones through Amazon, it allows you to link any product that Amazon carries and you get a commission when there is a purchase.

Making money using a WordPress blog site is possible, but you must know that it does take time, it will take effort, and it will need some form of investment. Once you get the hang of it, once you get things set up, you'd be more of a pro around your blog.

Optimizing Your WordPress Site to Make Money

In this chapter, our focus on optimizing our blog to ensure it is ready to make money or at the very least, making it easier for your customers or your audience to do what you want them to do on your blog.

Making your site Stand out

- **Browsing experience**

The details you put into your site is what sets it apart from a normal website to your very own unique commerce one. Your main goal is to make their browsing experience on your blog as seamless as possible. The way you can do this is to focus your details in the layout and design, which is what most people will see when they visit your site.

- **Hover Link**

Some small details you'd like to look into are things such as the hover link. Most themes feature a distinctive color when the mouse is moved, or 'hovered' over a page or post or link. The side links and categories also change color when the mouse hovers over it. This tells your users that this content is what they are about to click on.

What would your preference be? Would you want it to be the same color? Do you want it to change? Do you want it underlined? These preferences are a personal preference if you would like things to look a little different. These small details are design elements that you can change at any point on your website. WordPress' interface is as easy on the backend as it is on the front end. You may change the header and the footer section, the hover colors, and so on.

- **Experiment with the way your posts will look**

While your site is new, you will not have any traffic (or at least targeted traffic) to your site. So take this time to fiddle with things. Create a blog post to test to see how things look. Check to see how this first post will look on your home page and fine-tune any necessary details you'd like as such as font, font type as font size. Look at the layout and also see how it fits on your site and if it is readable.

- **Utilizing Categories and tags**

WordPress uses a data system called Categories or Tags that can help categorize your posts or related topics together. As more and more posts are added, you will end up creating more tags or categories and don't worry about this because tags and categories are good. Each category will appear either in the footer or sidebar of your page, depending on what layout you've chosen. Archives also act the same way. Your tags and categories should be focused on getting your products noticeable and captured by SEO.

Optimizing Your Appearance Screen

- **Choosing a Theme that fits your niche**

Ensuring that the theme you choose relates to your niche is essential. This is because the theme gives the overall appearance of your blog site, and this is where you bring life to your site. Depending on what you want your site to do, there are several themes that you can use to completely change the look of your site. These themes are designed by WordPress developers and WordPress users, and you can choose from thousands of themes, some free, whereas some are paid themes.

Each theme shown under the Appearance section is built to cater to a particular need for the user. For example, some themes are built to cater to a business type of site whereas some themes are made to feature photographs and pictures; some themes are built to feature fashion and online retail whereas some are built to hold writing and poetry or long articles.

To change the appearance of your site, all you need to do is click on a theme can click Purchase (if it is a paid theme) or Activate (if it is a free theme).

Keep in mind that you would want to align the appearance of your site with the same branding that your business uses. Your online persona has to be the same with all the other marketing angles that you employ for your communications and marketing methods. The same goes for your personal blog.

Planning your Website for your Business

Designing a website or a blog that focuses on making money requires planning, and it needs a robust and strategic plan. Although setting a website or blog through WordPress is free, you'd still want something that is lasting, sustainable, and fits with your business method. You will also want to decide if you would like hosting your own site using WordPress.org or you'd rather use WordPress.com.

Here are a few things to establish:

- What will you do with your site?

- What kind of content do you want on it?

- What business method are you planning to use on your site?

- Who do you want to read this?

- How often do you plan on posting and adding content?

Depending on what your site is supposed to do, you will need to consider what kind of information you are willing to share and post. You would also want to include some contact information so your visitors to your site can contact you-unless you don't want them to.

- **Choosing a Domain Extension**

A domain extension is the three letters after a dot that you see on a website link. This works for both the .ORG or .COM WordPress option.

Usually, when you open a WordPress site, you'll often have your site with a URL such as this: www.mynewsite.WordPress.com. To change this without the WordPress name in it, you would need to register your domain, and this usually means paying for the hosting which WordPress provides.

But before you can choose your domain name, a word of advice- DO NOT attempt to change your site to a fixed domain unless you are very sure of the direction of your site and the content.

Make sure your WordPress site is in the niche you want to focus and concentrate on. Making your WordPress site a functional and revenue-generating website requires critical research on your target keyword pool. Below mentioned are some of the things you need to think about when registering your domain:

- If you want a Business Website- if this site is for your business, then a good domain to register your site would be a DOT COM as in .com site, such as mynewsite.com.

- If you want an affiliate marketing site, make sure your blog name relates to your niche

- If you want a Personal Website- Well it's your own personal site so go with whatever you want, but the most popular is, of course, .com.

- A non-Profit Website- for a non-profit site, the best domain name would be a .ORG.

- Information Website- a .info, of course, would be the best!

There are plenty of domain name extensions, but the most popular ones are .com, .org, .net and .info. And these are easily picked up by Google.

- **Choosing the Right Domain Name**

The domain name and the domain extension go hand in hand. Once you have decided on your domain extension, you need to figure out what you'd like to call your site which will be your domain. Your domain name is what your website's URL will consist of when someone types it in the browser's address bar.

Here are a few crucial points to consider when coming up with your Domain Name:

- Matching Names: Essentially, the name of your site as well as the URL must match.

- Short: So it's easier to remember and can be typed into the browser

- Consistent Branding: Your domain is a reflection of your brand. Keep it consistent and memorable.

- Memorable: Well, a website must be easy to remember and memorable, so you want it to stick the first time when your visitors come to your site.

- Catchy: It must be easy to pronounce and rolls off the tongue easily. Your domain name must also describe what you do.

Includes Keywords: Because you want it to be Search Engine Optimized.

Essentially you want it to be easy to remember and easy to type. Your domain name must correspond with what your business does or what your personal online agenda is for your site.

Customizing and Personalizing

To make your site 100% your own, you can choose to personalize and customize the theme. Usually, customization is done on the fonts, colors, and other simple design elements without altering the layout of the site. To customize the theme you have selected, you can go back to the Appearance section and choose the Customize link. Here, you have the option of doing a variety of things to your site to make it sync in with your branding needs. Usually, most themes allow you to change the logo, colors, and backgrounds, the fonts, the header image, the menus, and widgets.

If you are not experienced in coding, best to leave the customization to the selected options. But if you do know to code and can take your site's customization to another level then go ahead- there is no stopping you and the sky's the limit!

- **Widgets**

You can find the widgets section under appearance as well. Depending on the theme you have chosen, you will have a selection of widgets to choose from. Most widgets are the same for most themes, and some are a few extra special ones based on the type of theme you have chosen. Widgets are preset elements that are added to a site to improve its functions and improve your website's capacity.

Some of the same widgets you will often find in most of these themes are such as Archives, Blog Stats, Calendar, Category Cloud, Facebook Page Plugin, Gallery, Gravatar, Image, Instagram, Milestone, Music Player and Twitter Timeline. Take note that widgets are not Plugins, but they are elements that enhance your website and add more functionality. Widgets help with navigation and also to improve your connectivity to your social media. Widgets are extremely useful so you should add this to your site.

To add a widget, just go to the Widget section, click on the Add a Widget. From then on, you can see a list of several widgets that you can add to your site. Click on the Widget you would like to add and then click 'Save & Publish.'

- **Menu**

You can also change the Menu section of your website. Menus are a crucial element to any website. They offer a means of navigating your site and all of your content. You want your visitors to go through all your captivating content, and how can they do it without knowing where to go and find your content? That is when the menus come into play. If your menus and navigation are hard, your visitors will find it hard to find your content, and this can lead to high bounce rates-which is the number of visitors to your site, how long they spend on it and how many posts they view before leaving.

Menus usually appear on the top of the site (because that's where people look first). Sometimes, you can find the menus at the site or even at the bottom. This is fine as long as you know what you want your visitors to focus on when they first come to your site.

Menus must include pages like 'About' 'Contact,' 'Product,' 'Services' as part of your primary menu. You can always remove or add pages to your menu according to what your site requires. Some menus and their placement on your site very much depend on your WordPress theme.

A good menu has several characteristics which are:

- concise and minimalistic
- represents of all your site's offerings
- very intuitive to use and easy to navigate around your site

Keep these elements in your mind when arranging and working on your menu, and you will be okay.

- **Plugins**

As detailed earlier, Plugins are different from Widgets. Plugins are only available for WordPress.org and are basically pieces of code that are written to perform a very specific function on your site. For example, the sharing plugin added to your site allows you to share content across a variety of social platforms. The WordPress community has developed a variety of Plugins that help in search engine optimization, enhancing the security of your site, maintaining extensive portfolios as well as including contact forms or inquiry forms.

- **Tags**

Tags were similar to categories except these tags are specific to a post. Think of it like hashtagging an image on Instagram or Twitter. These tags aid your site's visitors in finding specific information and content on your site more easily.

- **Your Profile**

Oh, how can we ever forget to talk about your profile page! Setting your WordPress profile is really easy, and one of the most natural things to complete when creating your website. You can always edit and change information on your Profile by going to your 'Edit your Profile' section found on the administrator screen at the top right corner of the screen.

Here, give yourself a short description and also add in your social media links.

In the profile image, all you need to do is upload an image of yourself or your Logo, and this becomes your Gravatar account. Under this section, you can also manage your billing information- if you want to purchase any paid Widgets, Plugins, or themes, and you can also decide on the security for your site. WordPress gives its users the option of generating a strong password so that your site is secure.

Bottom Line

Just start already! Sometimes the best way of learning about WordPress is through trial and error. We all have many inhibitions when starting something new, but all these things are just opening up doors to failure.

Creating a website and generating revenue or getting your content out there in the fastest way possible is no small feat. It takes a lot of hard work, marketing, and publicity to get people to know about your site and to get your products or services or just read what you have to say. But with WordPress, this seemingly hard task is made simple. For the next few chapters, you'll find more tips and tricks to get your website up and rolling and bringing the revenue.

Chapter 3: Setting up and Securing Your WordPress Blog

As with anything that you set out to do, you need to understand the basics of blogging or at least the basics of WordPress. With WordPress, learning the basics is straightforward and easy. While this chapter is not going to into a step-by-step guide on how to set up a WordPress blog, it will, however, focus on the important aspects of setting up a WordPress blog, particularly where security is concerned.

To get you started, there are a few things to learn about the Dashboard. Think of the Dashboard like the command center of your website. This is where you can change the look and feel of your site, decide who can post things, who can comment, you can modify the way the site looks- everything! Firstly, WordPress is built with an easy user-interface which means blog and website owners can update page content and operate their blog quickly and effortlessly. However, before you start posting or editing or customizing your site, here are a few basics to go through:

Logging In

Begin by logging into your dashboard, which is the back end of your website. Think of the backend as the backstage area of a stage production. The backend needs to be working properly before anything upfront can operate correctly. Your login can be accessed via the WP-ADMIN. You can also type in www.WordPress.com and include in your log in details which are your username and password.

View Site Link

Upon logging in, you will be at the Administration screen, which is also called the Dashboard. This is the control panel of your site where you can change, edit, delete, add, and alter things. This is where you organize your whole site.

At the top of the screen, you will find the toolbar. To view your site, all you need to do is click on the link that shows you Site name. This will take you directly to your WordPress site-whatever name that you have you given it. Look at it and see what you like about the layout and the colors, the navigation panel. Don't worry about changing it now, though- you can always do this anytime.

Trying out your WordPress Site

Now if you are new to WordPress, take your time to look at your site before changing anything and trying to figure out how everything works. It is always good to test out the basic site, so you know what the difference is between posts and pages, menus, and widgets. The layout for your site is how your website will look in appearance. Usually, the layout will correspond with the theme you pick for your site. As mentioned earlier. Most layouts will contain these basics:

Header

- Footer
- Menu
- Title & Tagline
- Links
- Titles

Posts

Most posts will have a title, and the title will come with a date of when the post has been published. In the layout of the post, there will be a body where most of the content will go on. There will also be some tagging that you need to include, which is called post metadata. This usually contains information about the post that can be quickly picked up by Google, so each time someone searches for something on the internet and your post has a tag related to the keyword, it will show up in search results.

Pages

Pages differ from posts. Pages are more static, and this usually is things like About Us, Contact Us or Sign Up for Mailing List. These pages, while static is still editable down the road. But make sure the information you put on these pages are things that you want all visitors to your site to read so they must be consistent and correct. Page titles describe the information you want to share on your page.

Sidebar

At the sidebar on your website, you will generally see all the sections of your website. You will find things like Recent Posts and Recent Comments, Archives of course as well as the Categories section. You will also find RSS feeds and the logout link. People will use this to move around your site to find different things on your site. You will need this, and this is important not just for finding information on your site but also, so your site appears to be one of the top five on Google's listings.

User Profile

When you click on it, the screen will bring you to a list of users that are using the account. There could multiple users assigned to the site, but there can only be one or two administrators. Multiple users for a site mean that more than one person has access to the site. However, as the administrator of the site, you will be able to control what other users can or cannot do. You can assign roles such as Contributor, Author, Editor, Administrator, or Follower. Each of these titles has specific roles. The Author can only accept and edit content but cannot change the appearance of the site. The Administrator can do all of the above and have total control of the site. As the website owner, you get to decide who can have access to what segments on your site.

Hosting and Securing Your WordPress Website

For a website to be successful and cater to the large influx of visitors, it needs proper hosting and security. Now that you have familiarized yourself with the backend section of WordPress and the various ways in posting, managing and customizing your site, it is now time to look at an often overlooked but highly essential element of a website- hosting and security.

Web Hosting

A good hosting system will and can improve your SEO as well as drive up sales and site visits. WordPress offers various types of hosting options such as Free, Shared, VPS, Dedicated, and managed WordPress hosting. So what hosting would suit your website needs? Here are some excellent tried and tested hosting providers that you can use for your site:

- BLUEHOST

This company is one of the oldest web hosting companies on the net, starting way back in 1996. BlueHost is a brand that comes up whenever there is a need to host a WordPress site. They can be considered the official WordPress recommended hosting provider. BlueHost offers free domain as well as a free site builder that comes with existing templates that you can choose from. Many WP beginner users prefer to use BlueHost as it also comes with a special offer.

- HOSTGATOR

HostGator is also a very popular web hosting company, and it hosts over 8 million domains. HostGator offers and easy to set up one-click WordPress installation, and it also comes with 24 hours support.

- DREAMHOST

Been around the industry for 18 years, DreamHost is very well known for its hosting simplicity. You get a custom dashboard and a one-click WordPress installation as well as frequent automatic WordPress updates to keep your site in top condition. It also has unlimited space and unlimited bandwidth and free SSDs, which makes your site 200% faster to access and navigate. There are no set up fees, and they also offer domain registration for free.

INMOTION

InMotion has been known to offer superb and reliable performance, especially for business websites. It has an award-winning technical support team with 99% uptime. InMotion's hosting capabilities and packages cater best for very active bloggers and offers immense scalability for the blogger's growth.

Securing your WordPress Website

Malicious attacks on your site are frequent, and plenty, especially when you collect and store sensitive information that is why securing your site is important.

There are many ways of dealing with malicious attacks, and most experts will tell you that there is no ONE sure way of doing it and in fact, the best way to secure your website is by employing several methods and strategies. Just like how you lock your gate, secure your home with CCTVs, and even have access codes and alarm systems for your home, the same thing works for your website.

Sometimes you may experience malicious attacks, but most of these attacks may be things that you never realized were happening. So in this section, we will talk about enhancing the security of your site. Take note that you do not have to do all of it because it very much depends on what you put on your site.

A) HIDING YOUR SITE'S LOGIN PAGE

If your site allows user logins, then malicious login attempts are unfortunately unavoidable. Your login page needs to be easily found on your website so that your users can access it easily. However, you can do other things to protect against malicious attempts which we will discuss later on. But for not, we will focus on hiding your login page because this is one way of cutting down on the malicious login attempts. A virus that cannot find your login page will not be able to log into it.

If you are not keen on hiding your login page, then you can also place in other security measures such as using a Captcha code verification. This requires installing and configuring an excellent security plugin. Obscuring your login page is a valid security measure, especially when it is used as part of a combination of security strategy. Here's how to hide your site login page:

Strategy 1- Installing WordPress its own Directory

Back up your site and store it someplace where you will not accidentally modify or delete it. Next, install the WPS Hide Login plugin. This plugin allows you to safely and easily change the URL of your login page to almost anything that you want. This plugin does not rename or change any files in your system; neither does it rewrite any codes. All this plugin does is intercepts page requests, and this can be used on all WordPress websites. By using this plugin, the WP-Admin directory and the wp-login.php page becomes inaccessible to anyone except you. Create a URL that is unique but easily remember only by you. If you deactivate this plugin, this will bring back the login page to the same exact state that it was before.

Strategy 2- Using WP Hide & Security Enhancer

WP Hide & Security Enhancer is also plugins that help find the fact that your site is running on WordPress. The reason why you want to hide the fact that your site is on WordPress is so that you can create custom login URLs while completely disabling the default URLs. Apart from that, this plug also boasts over 1000 active installs, and while this isn't an overwhelming number, it is actually a large enough sample size that can be used for user reviews. Ratings have been solid and consistent, thus making WP Hide and Security Enhancer a good plugin to have.

Strategy 3- Cerber Limit Login Attempts

Another popular plugin for enhanced security would be the Cerber plugin which essentially limits login attempts. Currently, it is actively used on over 10,000 sites and has a rating of 4.9 out of 5 stars by its users. Apart from limiting login attempts, this plugin can also hide the standard URL so you can use a customized one instead. By far, this is the safest and easiest option favored by the WordPress community with more than 700,000 active installs.

B) WEBSITE LOCKDOWN AND BANNING USERS

Another way of securing your site is by adding a lockdown feature, especially when there have been failed login attempts. Most online banking systems do this. Lockdown features solve a major problem which is to minimize or altogether stop continuous brute force attempts. If there is a hacking attempt by using the wrong passwords repetitively (at least 3 times), the site immediately gets locked down, and you will receive a notification of unauthorized activity.

One such plugin that enables this feature is the iThemes Security plugin which has been around for quite some time and is favored by the WordPress community. Not only does this plugin offer the lockdown feature, but it also enables you to specify the number of failed attempts, and then the plugin also bans the attacker's IP address immediately, so you do not have to worry about this hacker again.

C) TWO FACTOR AUTHENTICATION

Nowadays if you notice, even email services offer two-step authentication processes such as the one employed by Gmail and even Facebook. Called the 2FA, this is another excellent security feature. The user wanting to log into a site provides the necessary login details for two different elements. The website owner decides what these two different components will be. Usually, it will be logging in the password and then answering a secret question or a code or a set of characters.

USING YOUR EMAIL AS LOGIN

Using your email may seem like a less secure way, but in truth, it is actually more secure. Usernames are much easier to predict, whereas email IDs aren't. Also, opening a

WordPress account requires a unique email ID; thus, logging in via this identifier is much more secure.

D) ADJUSTING YOUR PASSWORD

Changing your password once every three months is recommended for all kinds of login system, especially your banking online accounts and sites that you frequent all the time. If changing it totally isn't ideal for you, then play around with the password by changing it to lowercase or uppercase, adding numbers or special characters if your site allows it. No idea what to use as a password? Then try a password generator!

E) SECURING YOUR ADMIN DASHBOARD

The most engaging part of a website for the hacker is the admin dashboard because here, the hacker gets to control your site! Dashboards are usually the most protected section of the entire website, and it will be the hardest to get through for the hacker. To enhance the security of this section, here's what you can do:

- Protecting the WP-Admin directory

   If this part is hacked, then your entire system can be compromised and damaged. One way of preventing this from happening is by password protecting your wp-admin directory. This means that the website owner or main administrator for the site can only access the dashboard via a two-step authentication process. One password protects the login page whereas the other protects the admin section. The owner of the site can also unblock certain parts so other users may have access to it via a one password system, but the owner can lock the rest of the site which stores more sensitive information.

- Using SSL to encrypt data

  SSL refers to Secure Socket Layer, and you can implement the SSL certificate to ensure a more secure administration panel on your website. SSL enables secure data transfer between browsers as well as servers, thus making it a challenge for hackers to infiltrate a connection or spoof sensitive info. Getting an SSL for your website is not a hard thing to do. All you have to do is purchase one at a dedicated company, or you can also check this with your hosting firm who can hook you up with a service provider. Most often, SSL certificates are included as an optional item in most hosting packages.

F) CHANGING THE ADMIN USERNAME

One of the most vulnerable things you can do to weaken your security is by using 'admin' as the username for the main administrator role for your website. This is because it is a pretty straightforward and easy to guess username that hackers will no doubt use. All they need to know now is your password and then get their hands on your information. Again, you can use the iThemes Security plugin to stop malicious login attempts because this will immediately remove any IP address that attempts to use admin as the username.

G) MONITORING YOUR FILES

Monitoring your website activity is crucial. You may want to install a plugin such as Acunetix WP Security or Wordfence that can help you monitor the changes to your websites' files. Also, all of your site's information and data is stored in the database, and here are a few ways that you can take care of it:

- Changing the WordPress database table prefix- WordPress has a wp- prefix that is used exclusively by the WordPress database so to enhance the security, change it to something unique such as mywp- or wpnew- or wpnewsite-. Plugins can also do that for you, such as the WP-DBManager that helps you change your plugins into something unique with just a few clicks.

H) BACKUP YOUR SITE REGULARLY

No matter what security enhancements you have and how secure your site is, it will never hurt to make room for improvements. So try backing up your site at least once a week or daily if you must at an off-site backup which is the best solution. Having a backup will enable you to restore your WordPress site to a working state at any time, especially if there's been a hack or damage. VaultPress by Automattic is a great plugin that can help do this for you. This plugin backs up your site at 30-minute intervals so you can restore pretty easily should anything bad happen. Restoration just takes one click, and it also checks your site for any malware and sends an alert if it detects anything fishy.

I) SETTING UP STRONG PASSWORDS

Your main databases require an extremely strong password and as always, use a combination of characters, numbers upper and lower case alphabets. Try to think out of the box and use items or locations or things that have absolutely no connection with your site. For example, you can use a password combo of your favorite food, music, perfume, band name, or even a place you visited before. Special characters such as the asterisk mark or the exclamation mark make for strong passwords.

J) PROTECTING YOUR wp-config.php FILE

This file extension holds all the crucial information about your WordPress site, and as a matter of fact, this is the most important element in your site's root directory. Compromise this, and you lose plenty of things on your site. By protecting the php file, you are protecting the very core of your WordPress blog. When you protect this core component of your site, you are then making it extremely difficult for hackers to break the security of your site because the wp-config.php file is impossible to access by them.

Do you think this is hard to secure?

Think again. Securing or protecting your file is really very easy. All you need to do is change the location of your wp-config.php file by taking it and moving it on a higher level than your root directory. Will the server be able to access this if it is stored somewhere else? Well with the all-new and improved WordPress architecture, the configuration file settings have been programmed at the highest priority listing so even if this php file is stored one level above the root directory, WordPress and only WordPress can find it.

K) BAR ANY FILE EDITING

If your site is a multi-user site, and if another user has administrative access to your WordPress dashboard, then they can edit, change, remove and alter any files that are part of your WordPress installation which also means deleting or adding plugins or changing themes. So to prevent this from

58

happening, you need to disallow file editing. By doing this, if a hacker has somehow obtained admin access to your WordPress dashboard, they will still not be able to modify any kind of file.

L) CONNECT YOUR SERVERS PROPERLY

You should only connect to your server via SFTP or SSH when setting up your site. SFTP is the most preferred way over the traditional FTP because it has better security features and none of these can be found in the standard FTP file. Connecting your server using the SFTP way ensures secure information and files transfer. This is also an optional feature in most hosting packages.

M) SETTING DIRECTORY PERMISSIONS

Setting up wrong directory permissions can cause serious problems for your site, especially if you are working using a shared hosting environment. In this case, changing directory permissions and files is definitely a good move because it secures the site right at the hosting level. You can set the directory permissions to 755" and files to '644', so you protect the whole filesystem from directories to subdirectories and even individual files.

N) UPDATING YOUR SITE REGULARLY

Finally, one of the main things to do is to regularly keep your software products updated. Developers usually release updates and bug fixes and these updates are meant to patch up any security loopholes. If you do not update your themes or plugins, this will make it easier for hackers to attack your site, simply because they are relying on the fact that people couldn't be bothered to update their themes and plugins, making their jobs so easy. Hackers also exploit loopholes and bugs that are outdated and have not been fixed.

So if you are using WordPress, update your system regularly.

Another good thing to do would be to remove the WordPress version number. This will prevent hackers from identifying the version of WordPress you are using so they are unable to build an attack. The security plugin mentioned above, such as iThemes can help hide your version number.

Final Points

Security is a very important issue, and this is something you must always take into consideration whenever you are building a new site and collecting and storing information such as bank account numbers and telephone numbers. Once your site is compromised, it will not only be a problem for you, but it will also decrease customer trust in your site, thus affecting revenue.

Chapter 4: How to Make Money with WordPress

We know you're itching to get started on making money through blogging and that's great! Enthusiasm is a good thing to have and just remember to keep this energy throughout the whole process of setting up your blog, creating your content, marketing and promoting your site and bringing the right audience to site.

But before you start looking at the money aspect, there is still quite a few things we need to fine-tune and focus on which is why in this chapter, we will look at the fundamentals of blogging for profit and strategies to monetize your blog. Take note that this is a general guideline based on the overall money-making business on your blog. Making money from a blog is not as hard as you may think, but it is also not as simple as you may think because it is going to require plenty of:

- Time

- Effort

- Persistence

- Hard work

All of these elements combined successfully will see your blog paying off. None of this is going to happen overnight either if that's what you're hoping.

Great things about using your blog to make money:

- You don't need to fork out huge sums of capital upfront

- You don't need to be a whiz or a genius that is an expert to get started

- You do not need coding information to create a blog

- Anyone from any field can get started making money from a blog if they know the right way to do it.

On the other hand, there are things that you need to be aware of:

- You would need to be consistent with these efforts and persevere, especially when it seems like things are not moving fast enough, or not moving at all.

- Blogging is a competitive field. Yes, it is competitive because there are literally thousands of blogs online, and the numbers just keep growing every year. It is easy to get lost in a sea of blogs and never get yours noticed unless you're equipped with the right strategies to do so.

- To make money from your blog, you need to be in it for the long haul.

On your journey to make money from your blog, there is one thing you need to not lose sight of, and that is don't ignore the fundamentals of online marketing. Because making money from your blog at the end of the day, is about how well you market your blog. Once you're ready to start making some serious cold hard cash from your blog, there are going to be five rules of blogging that you're going to need to keep in mind if you want guaranteed success.

These rules are the fundamentals to blogging successfully, and if they're not taken seriously, it is going to be almost impossible for you to successfully make money from your blog and you'll just end up very disappointed. The five fundamentals of blogging successfully if you want to make an income from your blog are:

- **Deliver Content of Quality** - Nobody is going to be interested in your blog if the content is mostly frivolous. Quality is key to keeping an audience, and blogs with the highest audience traffic are going to have the best success rate in earning an income from the blog. Think about creating content that adds value to the user, and you'll have a higher success rate to monetize your blog.

- **Deliver Content of Value** – Tied closely with quality; your readers need to find your blog valuable. The best way to add value to your readers is to create content that is informative, with video tutorials where possible.

- **Be Focused** – It is of the utmost importance that blogs be focused on. Do you have a specific niche or topic that you're really good at? If you do, make that the focus of your blog. Blogs work best when the author knows what they are talking about, and that is how you garner a loyal following. If you are not already focusing on a niche, you should be, or you'll risk losing your audience, and that will do nothing towards helping you earn an income from your blog.

- **Be an Authority** – Similar to having a blog with a focus, a blog with authority is what is going to help you monetize it quicker. Are you an expert at something? Or well-known in your field? That could be a huge advantage to your blog if you are, and it will help to drive traffic much faster towards your blog. If you already have authority, all you would need to do is the leverage that to your advantage to generate an income stream from your blog eventually.

- **Be Engaging** – Does the kind of content you produce on your blog entice people to spend time on your blog reading it? A blog that generates little engagement has very little chance of monetizing the blog. Each content that you produce on your blog should be able to engage and capture the attention of the audience you are targeting, especially if you are selling a product or a service because your audience will be more likely to make purchases from you that way.

Strategies to Monetizing Your Blog

Like with everything else, the secret to success when it comes to monetizing your blog lies in the kind of strategies you employ to help you reach your goals. Here are some excellent strategizing methods that you can utilize to help you make the most out of your blog, which we will discuss in further detail in this book:

- **Email Marketing** – One of the best ways to make money through your blog is email marketing. Email marketing is done through building a list of subscribers which can be added to your email list and using this list to alert them as to what is the latest that is happening on your blog. Building a list can help monetize your blog by keeping those who are already interested in the know, so they can be the first ones to pick up on any offerings on your blog.

- **Google AdSense** – The easiest way to explain how this works is, you make money by putting ads on your blog. You earn from Google AdSense based on impressions (which depends on page views) and based on the number of clicks (based on how many views click the ads on your page). How much you make on AdSense would depend on the volume of traffic you get to your blog and how many viewers are willing to click the ads that are on your blog.

- **Affiliate Marketing** – This is simply another form of performance-based marketing. This works by including links to a product or service which is offered by another business through an affiliate program on your blog. When choosing an affiliate program, only promote material that is relevant to your niche, products, or services that you have personally used and would recommend. Also, do not forget to add a disclaimer to your site.

- **Offer Courses or Services** - Another great tool to generating an income out of your blog would be to create a chance for your viewers to get an exclusive one-of-a-kind opportunity that they may not be able to score elsewhere. The earning potential here would depend on how much people are actually willing to pay for the courses or services that you are offering. It's a great way to generate traffic to your blog.

- **Paid Reviews and Banner-Ads** – You will also be able to generate an income from your blog through paid reviews, sponsored posts, and banner ads. Blogs that generate enough online traffic are more likely to be approached by businesses who would be interested in sponsoring your blog.

- **Securing Sponsorships for Your Blog** – To be able to garner sponsorships, your blog needs to be generating a high volume of traffic to successfully make a significant amount of money. Sponsorship is a great tool for making money if you are using it right. With sponsorship, always be upfront with your readers and audience and be as transparent as possible, so you are not misleading them in any way.

While there are more ways than one to generate an income from your blog, the methods listed above are among the core methods that will see the fruition of all your hard work.

Chapter 5: Making Money Through Advertising on Your Blog

Among the most effective and commonly used techniques to bring in money is through advertising. When it comes to blogs, advertising is done through banner ads, sidebar ads, and pop-up ads, and these are all ways that you can make money with your blog.

Types of Ads that you can use on your Blog

- Pay-Per-Click
- CPM Advertising
- Pay-Per-Action Ads
- Personal Sale Ads

What to consider when adding an Ad Network to your Blog

The main reason you join an ad network is to make money. There's no other reason people would want to do it. But before you join or sign up for any ad networks, this chapter will talk you through the elements that you need to be aware of, the pros and the cons of ad networks and how to sell with ads.

1. **Find out the CPM rate:** Your main goal with looking for the appropriate ad network is the

guaranteed CPM rate they can offer you. There are plenty of ad networks out there are they all try various ways to guilt-trip and entice new or struggling bloggers with promises of great returns, but remember that if an offer sounds too good to be true, then it probably is.

2. **Find out if they have contracts:** Whatever these ad networks say, demand for an agreement. An agreement in black and white is always the way to go, and if an ad network is reluctant to offer you a concrete agreement, that is a big red sign to walk away from it to avoid finding yourself getting stuck in a bad situation.

3. **Find out the extent of your control on ads:** Essentially, the ads that are going to be featured on your blog should be in sync with the content that you are writing or selling about on your blog- your niche. You don't want an ad that is in contrast to your content because it is going to send mixed messages to your readers, and your blog runs the risk of losing credibility among your followers. When signing up with an ad network, get it in writing that you have the right to request any ads you deem inappropriate for your blog to be removed without issues.

Like everything else in life- there are pros and cons, and the same thing goes for ad networks. Ad networks basically work like advertising brokers, whereby you offer available advertising space on your blog for purchase, and they will do their part trying to sell the space for you for a cut of the sale.

The pros of working with an ad network are:

- There is less effort on your part in the sense that you're not stuck being a one-man show doing all the legwork selling and setting up your advertising. By joining an ad network, all you have to do is sign a contract and place an HTML code on your sidebar, and you're set.

- Ad networks can sometimes earn more than private advertising can, although how much you make would vary depending on several factors.

- Ad networks do more than just sell ads since they work with multiple bloggers and have more connections. They are able to attract a bigger pool of prospective clients, some of which may have big advertising budgets they can work with, an opportunity that may otherwise be harder to score if you were working on your own.

And now, the cons of working with an ad network:

- You may not have as much control over the ads as you would like. Ad networks are often reluctant to relinquish control over the ads that get displayed to the blogger, although there are some exceptions. Do not work with an ad network unless you are prepared to give up control and let them have full run of the kind of advertisements that show up on your blog.

- It may be difficult to secure an ad network to work with. Getting in with a network could require up to months of pushing and persistence. Having connections and contacts in this instance would definitely give you a leg up. Otherwise, it can be a challenge getting in immediately with these networks, and very often you may find yourself waiting for months before an opportunity shows up.

How to Sell More Sidebar Ads

Average advertising is easy enough and noticeable. It is the sidebar ads that very often go unnoticed in most blogs. But sidebar ads also have earning potential for your blog, so they should not be ignored. One great thing about selling sidebar ads is that you have complete control over the ads that get displayed on your blog at all times, which may not necessarily always be the case with regular advertising through an ad network.

So, how do you get the most out of your sidebar ads? By following these simple rules for monetization:

- **Focus on making your ad placements obvious—** If an advertiser is looking to advertise on your blog, they may not notice that there is an option to advertise on your blog unless you make it loud and clear to them, plain and simple. Make it clear that you have advertising spots for sale by putting an advertisement tab in your header, for example that will link advertisers to your advertising page. Remember a lot of these advertisers are most likely very busy people who simply do not have the time to comb and sift through your blog, wondering if there is any advertising opportunity available. It is up to you to make it obvious.

- **Be as clear as possible on your ad page** – Once you have directed advertisers to your advertisement page, make things even simpler for them by being as detailed as you possibly can. Typically, the kind of information that advertisers would be after include page views and unique visitors to your blog, what your blog's demographics are, and what are the advertising options and prices they can expect. And if you have any testimonials from former advertisers who have worked with you before? Even better! Throw that into the mix, too, because it adds credibility to your blog. List down every compelling reason you can think of as to why advertisers should choose to work with you and you'll be in business in no time.

- **Make sure to offer special discounts** – Nobody can resist a good discount or a bargain. If you want more advertisements to sign up with your sidebar ads, offer them a deal that they simply cannot refuse. For example, offer your sidebar advertising rates at 50% off the original price. Limited time offers are a great gimmick to entice these advertisers to sign up for your deal, and they will be a lot keener to take up a sidebar ad subscription on your blog if they feel that they are getting a bang for their buck.

- **Make sure to offer sales and offers**– Companies love feeling like they are getting the most out of their money, and sidebar advertising is a great opportunity to make the companies who work with you feel special. Seal the deal with your new partners by offering to mention the company on your Facebook or Twitter accounts, for example, which is, in a way, a free form of publicity for the company. You could even offer to write a free blog post for the company if you love what they are selling and you're comfortable promoting their products or services to your readers.

- **Never leave blank spaces** – If your sidebar ads are empty, it gives the impression that your blog space is not quite up to par yet for people to want to advertise on your blog. This could be the kiss of death for your money generating attempts, so avoid leaving blank ad boxes even if you don't have any ad deals signed up. Fill those spots with affiliate ads or work with friends who run their own blogs and give them free advertising, for example. Anything to keep up the appearance that your blog is interesting enough to advertise upon, and this will, in turn, attract other advertisers if they see there is already an interest built on your blog.

Chapter 6: Making Money Through Product Creation

One of the most lucrative and sustainable ways to make the most of your blogging journey is by offering products and services on your site. Plenty of popular bloggers all started with dishing out things that they knew readers and their audience could not get anywhere else. These products and services ranged from financial advice, templates, digital content, event services, organic cosmetics, coffee even and bamboo brushes, for example.

When a product or service is offered exclusively on your blog, your earning potential increases because readers will only have to come to your blog to get what they want. Even better if you are an authority in your field, and they know that what they are paying for is going to add value and be well worth it. An example of how to make the most money out of your blog would be through creating and selling online courses, selling products or services, and organizing giveaways.

Here are some ideas for products and services you can offer:

Idea #1- Creating Online Courses

What it is?

An online course is a platform in which an individual can provide information or tutorials on a vast array of subjects that he or she is either has a passion for or experience. This can range for a variety of topics from culinary arts, music, software, fitness, gardening and soon on. Contrary to popular belief, you do not have to be an expert in your field to come up with an online course. You just need to have more knowledge on the subject than most people. While some individuals have shared their knowledge through books and online videos, creating an online course and marketing through your blog is a great method of generating income. Many people have made tons of money through their online courses over the years, and according to global industry analysts, online learning will be a $240 billion-dollar industry by the year 2021.

How much money can you potentially earn?

The average worker in the U.S makes an average of $25 per hour. With an online course, you stand up to make $1,000 per hour. This happens because after completing most of the initial work upfront on your online course and blog, this content can continue to generate revenue every time you sell a course over the course of the next few months or even years. And the more courses you create and sell, your revenue or hourly rate keeps multiplying.

Idea #2- Online Consultancy

What it is?

Online consultancy is a very broad terminology, to begin with, and it covers a huge number of topics and roles. The need for online consultancy usually stems from market demand. Some of the fields that usually require online consultancy are: -

- Accounting
- Advertising
- Auditing
- Business
- Business writing
- Career counseling
- Communications
- Computer consulting
- Editorial services
- Headhunting

Organizations are known to look for online consultants due to the following reasons: -

- Consultant's experience and expertise
- A different outlook and solutions to the issues being faced by the organization
- The temporary overhead for a short period of time

Honestly, everyone with decent knowledge on a particular topic can become a consultant on it. You can write about your expertise on your blog and offer your expertise with specific rates. While you do not need to have many years of experience on your topic or niche, you should not resort to unethical practices when providing your knowledge and insight on a particular field or topic.

How much money can you potentially earn?

Here is a couple of top online consulting sites below will show you the range of how much do online consultants charge for their services: -

- Clarity – the minimum hourly rate of $60. A site for upcoming entrepreneurs and consultants are usually seasoned experts.

- Maven Research, Inc – the minimum hourly rate of $25. Consultants for a variety of subjects.

In 2013, the market size for online consulting was estimated to be around 39.3 billion, and it shows no sign of slowing down. In 2013, 42% of organizations planned to hire more online consultants, and another 5% planned to increase their budget to spend on online consultants.

Idea #3- Develop Design Elements

What is it?

If you have a talent for design, and you've got a talent for technology, developing design elements and selling it on your blog could be a great potential source of income for you.

As a designer, you have the flexibility of options to increase your business without having to feel like you're piling up on your workload.

What's great about generating some income as a designer is that it reduces your dependence on clients to get paid. When you work as a freelance designer especially, it can be stressful constantly trying to search for clients, pitching your ideas, hoping they like your proposal and then going back and forth negotiating on the terms of payment.

Developing design elements that you can put up for sale on your blog platforms and online marketplaces, on the other hand, cuts out the bulk of your workload. You just need to design the content, put it up for sale, and anyone who's interested can purchase it immediately.

How much money can you potentially earn?

How much money you potentially stand to earn from this would depend on the type of content you're selling and how often your content gets purchased. Another factor that is going to affect your earning potential is the rates that you charge. More experienced, reputable designers have the luxury of charging slightly higher prices than those who have recently joined the scene. Design content can start anywhere from as low as $5 to $10 per content, and even be as much as a few hundred depending on the quality and intricacy of the work involved.

In the case of making passive income from developing design elements, the money you'll be earning is going to come repeatedly from the sale of one job. Recurring income is what makes it passive since you're no longer having to invest even more time working on developing and designing new content.

Idea #4- Selling T-Shirts Online

What is it?

If there's one item that is universally accepted by men, women, and children everywhere, it's t-shirts. These items are stapled that everyone (no exaggeration here) owns at least one, if not several. Take a look in your own cupboard and count how many t-shirts you own. Whether their worn in the summer, underneath your jackets in the colder months, or for lounging about the house in t-shirts are a constant in everyone's wardrobe, and that is why selling t-shirts online is a great passive income idea. You're selling something that everyone needs, how could you go wrong?

How much could you potentially earn from this?

Now, how much profit you stand to make per t-shirt is going to depend on what your initial cost is, and which platform you're selling your t-shirts on. For example, if the cost of your t-shirt was about $12 on average, and you wanted to sell your t-shirts on Amazon. If you log into Amazon, you will see that the suggested selling price for a t-shirt is $19.99. This means that you could potentially earn around $8 in profit from just one t-shirt alone. Depending on the volume of t-shirts you sell, the more you sell, the more you earn.

Is selling t-shirts online a good passive income idea? Yes, but this opportunity is not necessarily suitable for just anyone. The ones who are going to benefit most from selling t-shirts online as a passive income option are people who love being involved in sales, artists, illustrators, and designers because they've got the creative advantage of being able to design their own unique t-shirts without having to outsource that part of the business, and anyone who is willing to commit the time and effort to sell t-shirts online as an extra income stream.

Idea #5- Develop WordPress Themes

What it is?

What better way of utilizing your WordPress blog than to create WordPress themes for people to download and use! WordPress.org has a huge database of these themes in their directory. Each theme has a specific layout, feature, and design. You can then select one that fits your website from these directories. Since there is a market for various types of WordPress themes, many developers have found a way to generate income by selling WordPress themes.

You do not need to be a web developer to create WordPress themes because these themes aren't limited to those with web design knowledge. Creating a WordPress theme that suits your specific requirements is relatively straightforward. And it doesn't require a lot of technical knowledge or experience with web development.

How much money can you potentially earn?

ThemeForest is a platform designed for selling WordPress themes, and in 2008, they recorded around $280,000 worth of transactions just on WordPress themes alone. According to Vivek Nanda, a creator of PaySketch, developers are making around $200-300K per year on selling WordPress themes. But he also warned there are any that don't even make any income from the themes they have designed.

Chapter 7: Making Money Through Affiliate Marketing

The idea behind affiliate marketing is that you promote someone else's products or services using an affiliate network. When doing so, you earn a commission if any products are purchased thanks to your marketing. The mechanism behind affiliate marketing is revenue sharing. Say if you have a product or service that you want to sell more and reach out to a bigger audience, you can offer financial incentives to promoters using an affiliate program. If you have no product and just want to make money, then you can be the promoter of the product that you feel has substantial value and can earn you an income as an affiliate marketer.

There are 3 components to affiliate marketing. They are:

1- The Affiliate

2- The advertiser

3- The Affiliate network

What is an affiliate?

The affiliate is the individual that does the promoting or the one that owns the website. Anyone can build a website nowadays that is suitable for the business that they are in;

however, when building a website for marketing purposes; consideration should also go into marketing said website. In this website, you will find details or reviews about a product or service that is sold on the advertiser's website. The affiliate's website cross-links to the product page of the advertiser using a link known as an affiliate link. This special link tells the advertiser what is the link's source.

What is the advertiser?

The advertiser refers to the business that sells a product or service. It could be an individual, a company, an organization so long as there's an online commerce site.

What is the affiliate network?

The affiliate network refers to the tracking cookie that is dropped into the buyer's browser when they visit an advertiser's website. This cookie is dropped when a buyer clicks on any affiliate links on the affiliate's website. This cookie is the reason that makes affiliate marketing possible because they send the payment to the affiliate. Still not sure how affiliate marketing looks like? Let's see it in action.

Let's assume that Jane is an affiliate. She has a website that showcases products about woodworking. She even has a blog that she shares videos of her latest woodwork as well as images of the crafts she has made and the places she visits to purchase her materials. She also provides in-depth information on the best and worst places to get resources for woodworking.

Her information provided also gives reviews with links to the advertiser's website where the recommended woodworking supplies can be purchased. The key to this is that the link included is no ordinary link. An ordinary link would like: janewoodworks.com/best-wood-supply-store

In actual fact, an affiliate link would like:

janewoodworks.com/best-wood-supply-store/affiliateID112783

If a visitor goes to Jane's site and decides to purchase a product from a store after reading her reviews about what places to go to buy the best supplies, then Jane as the affiliate will be rewarded with a commission for referring a buyer to the advertiser's site. No matter when a buyer decides to purchase a product from the advertiser's site, maybe in a week after reading the review or in two weeks, the affiliate will still be rewarded the commission simply because of the cookie that was used on the affiliate network that remains on the browser.

How much can you earn from affiliate marketing?

Your income will depend entirely on a few massive factors, such as:

1. The reliability and efficiency of the affiliate network you are working with.

2. The conversion rates and commission levels of the advertisers you work with.

3. The level of commitment you invest in.

4. The depth of willingness and knowledge to learn all you need to know about your niche to succeed

These commissions and networks vary widely. There will be new affiliates that can take over a year just to make their first sale but with the right training, acquiring knowledge as well as persistence, you can earn a lot of money. Through affiliate marketing, you can easily make some pretty impressive earnings. Top earners earns multiple millions of dollars a year.

Creating A WordPress site for Affiliate Marketing

Turning your WordPress site to make it optimized for Affiliate Marketing is easy. It is essentially a regular blog but one that is filled with good quality content and linked with affiliate links. A high-quality blog means high sales volume-it is a quick reaction. What does a high-quality blog require? Here are the essentials that you need to do to tweak your WordPress for affiliate marketing:

Make it Easy for Users to Find Info

Remember that it takes only 3 seconds to make a first impression online, so make it worth it. Messy templates and an unorganized site will also get your customers frustrated and lose interest in what you have to sell. They also will not be coming back because they have associated your site with all things negative. You want to provide a nice online shopping environment, easy navigation, and overall pleasant experience when customers browse your site-much like how you would be providing a nice space to shop if it was a regular shopping store. When you build your site, keep these things in mind. Even if you like shopping at a website that provides easy access. So when designing a website, you need to answer these questions:

- Is it easy to navigate?
- Is your website easy to find?
- Is your website easy to find the section?
- Does it highlight the products?
- Are there clear calls to action?
- Is your website simple enough to find information?
- Is your website responsive?

Your site does not need to have flashy graphics to attract users. It just needs to be intuitive and simply enough to be interactive and easy to navigate. Identify what you want on your site, what products you want to display, and the content you want to have on your site. Make sure that your website also personifies the kind of products you are selling.

- **Posting consistent, relevant and high-quality content**

High-quality and updated content on your blog is an essential part of affiliate marketing. Heck, it is an integral part of any kind of marketing. Users nowadays are very used to high-quality images and content so having low-resolution photos and poor descriptions only damper your ability to sell. This rookie mistake is a major problem that is very often overlooked. Content is important in marketing and no matter what your site is made out for, whether it is comparisons, product reviews, blog articles- all of these contributes to your online sales either directly or indirectly.

Do not make the mistake of posting up content that has no actionable item or is not insightful. When writing a piece of content, always make sure that there is a solution or a purpose. Put yourself in the shoes of your potential buyers and imagine what kind of content they would be interested in. You want people to get hooked on stories and cool facts, not random ramblings.

Good content alone is not enough. You must also ensure that you churn out content on a regular frequency. When your users are interested in what you have to say, they will be expecting some form of consistency in terms of your uploads- they want to know more, and you have the job of getting them consistently engaged.

- **Tracking the performance of your website**

Knowing how your website is doing is an integral part of understanding success. Of course, the amount of money you make is a tangible indicator, but tracking performance enables you to understand your user's browsing habits- what they click on, where they click on, how long are they on your site (whether they read your content) and what buttons attract them. Part of marketing is optimizing your data and tracking it. You want to see the cause and effects that happen when you do tracking, so you know what works for you. You can use various tracking tools such as Google Analytics, Hubspot, or Sprout Social. The website you choose to host your content should also be able to give you plenty of analytics for you to see.

- **Stay Ethical, Keep things Legal**

It is important to protect yourself as well as the information that is collected on your site. Depending on where your business is located, you are bound by the terms and conditions and legal issues related to affiliate marketing. In the US, for example, you need to disclose that your link is an affiliate link. The affiliate disclosure must be part of the link or as close as possible to the link itself and not at the bottom of your posts. Not disclosing this is an accident waiting to happen and whatever you have earned may end up going for legal fees if you do not do your business ethically and legally. It may seem tedious to do, but it will save you time and money in the long run.

- **Cloak your links**

As an affiliate, you want to create links that are not confusing and also easily searchable on search engines because if you look at some poorly created affiliate links, most of them are very messy with all sorts of numbers and words. Getting custom URLs for your products or cloaking them helps you gain visibility and credibility as well. Use Pretty Link Lite to cloak your affiliate links. It's free to use, and once you've done this, it is easy to find your affiliate links and also, with cloaked links, your content is less spammy. People will trust your domain and are more likely to click through your links.

- **Weave in links expertly**

When you do affiliate marketing, you have a choice of your involvement because your involvement determines your profits. Do you want to go all out and provide excellent, quality content in return for high profits or do you want average or low involvement which also translates to low profits? This choice is yours, but when you do promote products and services, you want to masterfully recommend these products in a way that is non-spammy.

When you provide content that is not spammy, your users are more likely to believe you and trust what you are saying. If you want to make money with affiliate marketing, content, and context are key. The affiliate links you use must make sense in your post. Randomly dropping them in your content is not very helpful.

- **Add affiliate links to your popular posts**

Updating content and marketing them is one way (and an easy way) of staying fresh. You can freshen up your posts but updating them with affiliate links and adding new content in them. Keep in mind NOT to over-link your post though. You can also try linking your top-converting blog posts with affiliate links. Tutorial posts, best of's and cheapest kind of posts really work in this avenue. You do not need to make complex articles just to add links- updating what you have sometimes goes a long way.

- **Resource Pages**

Your resource page gives you a wealth of links. You want to create a resource page that lists all the products you recommend. Say, for example, if you are a makeup blogger, then there can be a page full of makeup products you love. You can even make a list out of makeup products that are vegan and cruelty-free or best makeup for skin color or best makeup for traveling. Get the idea? There are plenty of ways you can add your link, and the resource page is one of them.

- **Target audience**

One of the best ways to make sure you get profits and reach your 10k target is to make sure your target audience and your niche are aligned. What are you promoting? To Whom are you promoting it to? What problems are you solving for them? One reason why you may not get the kind of money you want through affiliate marketing is the misaligned audience and niche. You are probably recommending a product your target audience does not need. Say, for instance, you are a vegan blogger.

What would your main source of income come from? It wouldn't be on kitchen gadgets, would it? It would probably be on the recommendation on vegan food guides, vegan travel tips, vegan restaurants, and vegan products.

This is because your target audience is just like you- people who are foodies but want vegan alternatives. To be successful in affiliate marketing is to keep your audience needs in mind. Always think- how am i solving my audience's problems today?

- **Experiment with different styles**

Affiliate links come in many different formats and styles. You do not want to stick to just one even if they bring in the most traffic for you. You want to diversify so you can reach a wider audience. Use product images, simple links, coupon and discount codes as well as cleverly placed banner ads. You also want to play around with your content format and recommend products in different ways, from lists to photos, stories, and videos. You may want to choose both formats (write up and video) if your product needs it.

- **Newsletters**

Getting users to your blog and getting them to subscribe to your newsletter is another way of getting your content to your audience right into their inbox. Through you newsletters, you can include your affiliate links too. You can also send out newsletters on affiliate products that you love but make sure to include them in a good way such as in an email challenge or a social media giveaway. Also, make sure that all posts LINK BACK to your blog. We all know how hard it is to build an email list and get active subscribers, so do not let this go to waste. Use your email marketing as best as you can.

Chapter 8: Making Money Through Consultancy and Coaching Services

- Are you an expert in a certain field?

- Do you have relevant years of experience in a specific topic?

- Have you been part of a project for a decent time to know all you need to know about it?

- Do you want to share things you have experienced, learned, and explored?

No matter what the niche or industry or even topic you are interested in, if you feel the passion in it and you want to share it to people and also make money out of it, consultancy or coaching services could be something you can explore and expand on your WordPress blog.

The thing is, many people think that coaching and consultancy are always business-related or money and finance related. In actual truth, as long as you know a significant amount of information on a topic, you have the experience, and you can convey this information in a succinct and easy-to-understand format- you can coach and consult.

What makes coaching such an in-demand thing is that your readers will inevitably be facing all sorts of challenges at some point in their life. Everyone has their own challenges that they need to overcome, and coaching is a positive way to help your readers through that period in their lives when they may need it the most. And that is something they would be willing to pay money for.

Coaching and consultancy can be anything, such as:

- Sustainability
- How to Dress Well
- Public Speaking
- Toastmaster
- How to Live Zero Waste
- Juicing
- Photoshop and Indesign
- Creating Intuitive Presentations
- Social Media

Coaching is a great tool to use on your blog if you're serious about making money from it. It is common for bloggers to dabble in online coaching these days, and coaching is a great way to nurture a loyal audience following. Why would your audience be keen on coaching services if you were to offer them on your blog? Because of the results that they hope to achieve through that coaching. As a coach, your focus should be on helping your readers to deal with the challenges in their lives in a positive and constructive way to help them overcome the hurdles that they may find impossible to do on their own without a little help.

Using your WordPress blog for Coaching & Consultancy

Coaching is for some, a way for them to help others and in the process, sharpen their skills at solving a problem while building their reputation as the person to go to if someone were to have a similar problem.

Coaching on your blog is a great way to strengthen your relationship with your readers, who in turn, could draw in more potential readers to your blog, which equals more traffic. More traffic at the end of the day means more advertising opportunity, which in turns helps your blog become a money-generating machine in the long run that can churn out money for you even while you're sleeping. If your readers like what you are selling, they will buy from you, there is no doubt about that.

Coaching helps your readers, but it also helps you as a blogger at the same time. The whole point of starting a blog in the first place is because you have a passion for something, and a desire to share that information and knowledge (especially if you're an authority on it) with the rest of the world.

Blog posts and articles are speaking to the general audience, but when you offer to coach, suddenly it becomes much more personal, and if your readers already like what they have seen on your blog thus far, they will not hesitate to pay for any coaching programs you offer if they feel they stand to benefit from it.

The best part about coaching through your blog? Your earnings aren't limited by your geographical location. Because it is online, you have the potential to reach people from across the globe, which means your earning potential is skyrocketed just like that. If you're good, people will be willing to pay.

How to Get Started with Coaching on Your Blog

- Make it Obvious that You Offer Coaching Services

The first thing you need to do is to establish the niche you are coaching for. A coaching program that a reader is going to be most enticed towards is one that highlights the aspects of a situation that the reader is going through, and they need help with. To do that, the coaching program offered on your blog needs to be specialized in solving specific problems that your readers have, only then will they be willing to pay money for your program.

- Create a coaching program that can be accessed by anyone, anywhere

A successful coaching program that is going to help you generate an income from your blog is important, and to do this, you need to identify what kind of coaching structure you are going to go for. Are your sessions going to be solely blog based? Would you offer a live video session on your blog that your readers can tune into? Is there a schedule that participants would need to stick to?

Would you be holding your coaching sessions in person in a specific location? Either method you choose, your readers should only be able to sign up for your coaching sessions through your blog, because that's how you will be able to generate an income from it.

- Create a consultancy or coaching program that is ongoing

Create a coaching program that is ongoing or at least one that has plenty of date options so your readers will always keep coming back to your blog. An ongoing coaching and consultancy series has a lot more earning potential than a one-off program. Remember to make your coaching sessions educational, informative, inspirational, and most importantly, offer insightful tips that your readers can employ to their own problems. Create content that is of value to your readers to keep them coming back for more. Teach your readers how to achieve their goals and overcome challenges with constructive tools and advice, and your coaching courses will become a hit in no time.

Chapter 9: Making Money Through Sponsored Posts

Sponsored posts are a very common thing in the blogosphere, and it also one of the quickest methods of making money from your blog. Sponsored content is content that you are being paid to write or come up with by a company or a brand, or even another blogger. The content you create will have to be promoting a particular brand or service offered by the company in question, and you will be paid for it!

Introducing your readers to new products or services that they may not already be aware of is one way of providing value to your readers, but the trick is here to create content that is top-notch and honest at the same time without compromising the credibility of your blog.

Be savvy and be smart and selective about the kind of sponsored posts and campaigns you want to take on and limit the number of brands you commit to at any given time. Even though your content is being paid for by the sponsor for you to spin some positive light on it, it should still hold a genuine voice to it and not come across as fake to your readers. Before you hit the publish button, ask yourself if you were reading your post from a third-party point of view, would you be convinced enough?

How much can you make through Sponsored Content?

You need to know what your blog is worth. Earnings from a sponsored post can vary depending on the company and brand in question, but it is also important for you as a blogger to know what the value of your blog is. If your blog has been around for a long time, for example, and has developed a strong following with hits on the site every day, you have more bargaining power which will allow you to negotiate a better deal for your sponsored content.

Why Sponsored Posts Are An Awesome Revenue Generating Tool

What makes sponsored posts so great is that you don't have to invest too much time of effort into it. Sponsored posts are easy; sometimes all a company needs is a link or a mention of their product or service on existing blog posts or an upcoming blog post that they could pay to be mentioned in.

In contrast with affiliate marketing, one of the most exciting things about sponsored posts for bloggers is that they are paid immediately, more or less. This may vary depending on the sponsor in the question of course, as some sponsors will prefer to pay upfront and others may opt for payment only after you have published a post on them. Still, it is a lot faster than affiliate marketing and advertising, and the pay here can be pretty good depending on how popular your blog may be and how much traffic it generates on a daily basis. A quicker option to monetizing your blog compared to a lot of other monetizing efforts.

How to Secure Sponsored Posts on Your Blog

- **Be specific about what brands can expect when they work with you**

When presenting your pitch to these companies, be specific about what the company or brand can expect if they decide to work with you. Tell them your ideas with enthusiasm and give them as much detail as possible to really show it is going to be well worth their time and money to secure a sponsored post on your blog. Tell them what you plan to write, who your readers are, and what they want, how much traffic your blog generates, be as specific as possible and spare no detail.

- **Show of your creativity**

Do not be afraid to show your creativity when trying to convince companies and brands to work with your blog. Creativity shows that you think outside the box, and you're all about ideas and its ideas with a creative spark that is going to drive interest towards a product or service. Show the companies or brands that you hope to work with what you can do for them, and they'll be more than interested in teaming up with your blog for a sponsored post or two. Maybe even more.

The Types of Sponsored Post Options to Work With

The types of sponsored post options that bloggers would have to work with are sponsored posts that have access to the readers, and sponsored posts which are just a link on the blog or website. The type of sponsored content would depend on the company or brand's preference and what they think would work best for them.

Sponsored content that has access to readers would depend on the type of influence your blog has. The more influence a blog has, the more likely the company is to decide on this route to take when it comes to posting sponsorship. Sponsored content that works with just a link would depend on how much authority a blog's domain has. The higher the domain authority, the more opportunities your blog will have. Which is why it is important to pitch as many details as possible about your blog to the company or brand you hope to work with so they are able to make an informed decision and get the most out of their sponsored post collaboration with your blog.

Chapter 10: Making Money Through Email Lists

If you are a blogger with an e-commerce store selling a product or service of any kind through your blog, an email list or a newsletter subscription is an integral part of your marketing arsenal. Why? Because it is a powerful sales tool that can drive your business and engagement. An email list is a direct way to keep your subscribers updated about the products and services offered on your blog, and more importantly, alert them about any new products or services that are now available.

Optimizing your email lists and the type of information you send out to your subscribers is easy enough. Remember that the people who are reading your emails are people who could possibly be potential customers if they aren't already, and if you're serious about monetizing your blog, you are going to need to make your customers your lifeline.

When your readers read your email list, they want to feel that whatever you have put down in there is speaking to them directly, and not just a generic email blast with no specific group or target in mind. Readers like to feel exclusive and special, so make them feel that way and construct your emails like you would as if you were speaking to your readers face to face instead of over the internet. Make your reader feel important like you have specifically tailored your product or service to meet their needs, make them feel special, and they will keep coming back to your blog for more.

And the most important thing to remember is to always respond to any of your readers who reply to your emails. Always.

Building an Effective Email List

With the right strategies in place, you could have your email list up and running in no time. Remember an email list means more blog traffic for you in return, especially if your readers subscribe to your list and keep visiting your blog each time they get an update about something new that is happening on your site. To really maximize on your email list, the following methods will help you give your subscription numbers a boost:

- **Pop-Ups** – Pop-ups are annoying yes, but on some level, they actually do work, especially if the reader is already showing a keen interest in your blog and is a frequent visitor. Many blogs incorporate the use of pop-up encouraging readers to sign up for their newsletter or subscribe to their blog. You've seen it if you've visited other blogs yourself. Annoying at times, yes, but there is a reason many blogs are using this. Because they work.

- **Freebies** – People are sometimes reluctant to give away their email address for fear of being spammed annoying in their inboxes by unwanted emails. Unless there was a good enough incentive and reason for them to do so. Everyone loves to receive a little gift for free, so why not try that tactic to entice your readers to sign up for your newsletter when they visit your blog? Depending on the nature of your blog, try to provide a giveaway that is going to be something of value to your readers, something they would be excited to receive in their inbox. Perhaps a discount to one of your products or services, for example.

- **Subscribe Pages** – Your readers can't subscribe to your blog if there isn't a subscribe page available. To be effective with your subscribe pages, it is a good idea to include multiple sign-up boxes for your readers to choose from, and provide the readers with as much detail as possible about what they can come to expect when they subscribe to your blog.

- **Promote Your Blog on Social Media** – It is highly likely that you have your own social media accounts, but are you using these platforms to market your blog? If you aren't, then you should! Social media is everywhere, there is no escaping it, so imagine the huge audience potential you are missing out if you're not leveraging this platform to your blog's advantage. Use your social media account to highlight the exciting features on your email list, updated regularly, and update often so your social media followers have no chance of forgetting it.

And then we come to the million-dollar question.

How to Monetize Your Email List

- **Directing traffic to your site**

Do you have AdSense on your blog already? Then you're going to want to tap into the email list potential to get readers heading your blog's way. An email list is an indirect way of monetizing your blog, but you should grab every opportunity you can to link back to your site or even link to a post on your site that has the potential to generate money on its own, then that is what you should do. The more traffic that gets directed to your site, the more potential there is to earn an income from your blog.

- **Using Affiliate links**

The second way is using affiliated links. Do you have a product or service that you are happy with and you have written a shining review about on your blog? Include them in the email that you are going to send out to your subscribers. If your blog has been around for a while, there's going to be a lot of posts and content in it, and sometimes readers just don't have the time to sift through all of that before they find what they are looking for. Why not make things easy for them? Include the affiliate link in that email along with your review, and if your review on your blog is enough to convince them to buy that product or service, you'll get a cut of the sale. Money in your pocket, all thanks to your blog and email list. You're going to be glad you've got an email list on hand when you want to promote a new book, a new product or a new service because this is one of the best platforms to start building up interest among your subscribers before the launch of the new product or service takes place.

Chapter 11: Making Money by Giving Reviews

With online platforms available to anyone who wants to create a profile, it has given people a new channel to voice out their opinions, give feedback, and seek answers. People are quick to channel their happiness as well as grievances with a brand on social media. Love a recent hotel you stayed in? Let's review them on TripAdvisor. Don't like the service at the Italian restaurant down your street? Let's review them on Yelp. Checking to see if a certain brand of vacuum cleaner works as advertised? Check Amazon reviews.

Reviews are a major source of information for plenty of people to judge whether a product or service does what it says or delivers its brands' promises which is why blogs and websites such as AliExpress, Amazon, and Ulta have a review section on their sites.

But what if you want more personal answers? Well, some people have turned to review fashion and beauty products on their own blog platforms and managed to amass a huge following of fans who want to hear and see what they have to say.

Your blog can be that platform to create reviews in forms of videos, posts, and even images, and you can link these media back to your social media platforms. YouTube for videos and Instagram for images. Of course, your blog hosts the majority of the information in long-form such as links, more detailed information as well as where to purchase these items.

Giving fashion and beauty product reviews is a lucrative income stream because there is a guaranteed following already.

Who is it for?

It is for anyone who is purveyors of fashion and beauty products who knows what works and what doesn't. If you love anything fashion and beauty and you see yourself purchasing a fair bit of products, you can definitely start giving your reviews as well. Users of today prefer hearing first-hand reviews of products as they feel there are better credibility and greater transparency of a product or service.

How much money can you potentially earn?

On an average basis, you can sign up as testers and reviewers at places such as FameBit or CrowdTap or even Modern Mom where you can see yourself earning about $50 to $75 for the reviews you make. Some people have even gone to their own social media channels to make videos telling their audience what they think of a product, and as their audience grows, brands take notice and request for their own products to be reviewed. The reviewer can then charge them a certain sum for the number of views the video receives.

How it works - Step-by-Step

So how do you get started on writing reviews? If you are not a fan of increasing your audience on social media, you can start creating your foundations as a reviewer on sites that pay you for writing reviews.

- Firstly, you can check out sites such as SwagBucks, Inbox Dollars, or Vindale Research.

- Next, you need to open an account with them. Follow the steps to sign up and provide the necessary verification information. Each site will have different verification as well as a rewards system. Swagbucks, for instance, provides its members with free gift cards and cash for daily things that they already do online.

- Depending on the reward criteria, you need to shop online or watch videos, or search the web, or answer surveys to redeem your points.

- When you have collected enough points, you can redeem these points as gift cards with online merchants such as Walmart or Amazon. You can also opt to get cashback from PayPal.

Chapter 12: Finding the best Niche Topic for your Blog

While the best niche would be something you love writing about, you still need to put in more thought into its profitability, readership as well as how niche it is in your industry. There are plenty of things you can create a blog about and how much profit you get from your blog depends on the kind of business you want to do with it.

For example, is your blog being used for coaching, or is it used for affiliate marketing? Are you using it to sell products and services, or are you just starting it off as a personal blog and see where it goes? You may have plenty of topics, products, and services that you are interested in, and it can also be overwhelming to find a niche, but it is not as hard as you think.

Here are some methods that you may want to try in looking for the right niche:

Tip #1- Brainstorming

Brainstorming is always effective for practically anything you need to work on- ideas, solutions, methods, and finding the right niche. To begin brainstorming ideas for your niches, meet up with your like-minded friends who know you and will be able to help you or someone you trust.

When you meet, one of the things to think about is the items that you or your friends have bought online or recently purchased. Write these things down, even if it perplexes you. There will be tons of niches that are profitable, but that does not mean you should rush to make a decision.

Tip #2- Research, compare and evaluate trends

eBay is one of the places to check if what you want to do is to sell items on your blog, whether using an affiliate marketing method or just to simply use it as an e-commerce site.

Once you get onto eBay, one of the things you want to research is to identify the products in the different niches in the higher-priced bracket, the ones that are expensive so it can be anything like $50 or $200 or $500 depending on the product. When you get your search results, allow it to show 'completed listings.' Completed lists shows items in red or green, red being the item did not sell and green is sold.

Look at the items only for the products you are considering to niche in- it is okay to go over this list a few times until you identify about 20 products within your niche that sells out almost always- at least 10 units a day.

From here, request for price lists from various suppliers, get shipping quotes from customs brokers as well as storage capacities for a product.

Tip #3- Decide if you should choose passion or money in a niche?

It really depends on you. To some people, starting a blog to turn it into a business also means that they can work on a product or do a business that they love. Whereas to some, they find motivation, the more money they see in their bank account, and they don't care what they sell or how they make that money.

The truth is, you want to make a profit for any kind of venture or business you are in. So you will most likely look into a balancing act of pursuing your passion and creating a successful profit line.

Having said that, you still need to have some kind of interest into the niche that you want to focus on because it will keep your motivated to explore, to expand and even to contribute to the industry you are in. When it comes to pursuing your passion, it doesn't necessarily mean that you'd be successful immediately, but passion can lead to a more sustainable and long-term business endeavor. You could even become an expert in your industry when people feel your passion and becoming an expert would lead to more opportunities above and beyond blogging.

So how do we balance the two?

Passion does lead the way. Finding profitable niches to things, items, and products that you are passionate about not only makes your bank account healthy but also it makes you have fun and love what you do.

To help you discover your passion, if you already have not, let's take a look at niches that are based on your passions. Here are some questions you can ask:

- What kind of blogs and websites do you interact with and visit the most?
- What kind of pages or accounts do you follow on social media that you enjoy?
- Which online stores do you usually purchase from?
- What do you think are your biggest obsessions?
- What kind of products do you usually collect or buy most frequently?
- If you had $1000 to spend on any product you *want* (not need), what would you buy?

Now answer these questions to create a shortlist based on your passions.

Next, if you want to choose a niche based on how much money you can make, then you might want to ask yourself these set of questions:

- Which products are the most popular right now?
- Which products have the highest profit margin?
- Which niches hold the biggest audiences?

Trending Products Blog Posts

Another thing to look out for is updated product lists. Oberlo is one such company that regularly shares updated product lists to ensure that they are always at the forefront of today's most popular products. These lists can also help you determine what you want to niche on. Apart from that, keep an eye out for blog posts with lists such as:

- 20 of the best gardening tools to have in 2018
- 30 Fail-proof Business ideas to make money in 2018
- Best Buy Beauty Products for Summer 2018
- Top 10 Polishes To Get your Car Shining like Brand new

Wikipedia's List of Hobbies

Wikipedia's list of hobbies is a great way to find a niche of practically anything that you can think of from hobbies to passion, from crocheting to baton twirling, resin art to golfing, furniture restoration and terrariums- you will be surprised to find an extremely extensive list of both indoor and outdoor hobbies. Look into the lists if there are any hobbies that compliment your passions or look into researching to find profitable niches that are within these categories. Some are hobbies are popular enough to have a large market of followers so you can actually build an entire store dedicated to selling these products or the items that help these hobbyist work on their passions.

The amazing thing about hobbies is that you will like-minded people join groups and spend the money to pursue their hobbies. This itself gains you an audience you can immediately sell to. Some of the hobbies on the list that you can build e-commerce stores for include:

- Jewelry making
- Astrology
- Do it yourself
- Fashion
- Flower arranging
- Gardening
- Magic
- Pet
- Various fitness niches
- Baking

Google Trends

Yes, Google Trends is another tool you can use to discover your niche. What you want to look out for are niches that have a stable growth, no matter how slight. Here is a list you can check out- Google Trends.

Do you need to be an expert in finding your niche?

You do not necessarily need to be a niche, but some experience will help you a long way. It may be slightly harder to build a successful brand without having some kind of niche experience, although it is not entirely impossible.

Alternatively, you can also fake it till you make it. This means that you can just find the right target audience through Facebook ads as well. You can also engage influencers using the power of Instagram to build an audience as this can lead to sales. Having some idea about the niche you are getting into will also help you create content that resonates with your audience. No experience may render it harder to reach them and bring that traffic to your store.

On the other hand, you can also outsource these blog writing tasks to ghostwriters or someone equivalent. But most entrepreneurs do this, especially when starting out to keep costs slow. As mentioned previously, getting into selling a product you somewhat like and having some expertise in the niche can help motivate you, in the long run, to sustain your business, especially if the money isn't hitting the profit margins like you want to.

BONUS: Bloggers Making A 6 Figure Salary and What You Can Learn
From Them

As we come to somewhat the end of the book, one of the takeaways to have profitable and sustainable income from your blog is to keep it active and relevant and for that to happen, it requires a full-time endeavor. This entails posting up quality content, writing relevant posts, engaging with your audience on social media as well as doing research to find ways to write better content.

Many of today's successful bloggers have found ways to turn their passions and hobbies into lucrative forms of income, and you can learn from them too, by understanding what makes the main source of their income and how it can work out for you too.

1. Creating Valuable Content

Abby, the author and blog owner behind Justagirlandherblog.com makes a total of $31,000 a month.

Her site is 6 years old, and her niche is on DIY, Home Organization as well as Home Decor.

A majority of her content focuses on DIY crafts, and home decor and a whopping $10,000 comes from her <u>Framework</u> e-book and course. She's so successful because people trust her tips and tutorials, enabling her to sell this content at a price that people are willing to purchase them.

Of course, not all her eggs are in one basket. Abby second successful venture is through her Webina bundle that brings home a total of $8,700, whereas her affiliation with Bluehost earns her about $8,600 a month. All she has to do is direct people to the website with some guidance on how to start their own blog, suggesting Bluehost as a reliable hosting provider. For each signup, she gets $65.

What you can learn from Abby:

- You can start a business of promoting a web hosting affiliate just the way Abby has done

- You also need to pick a niche to talk about in your blog

- Sign up as a Bluehost affiliate through their <u>affiliate program</u>

- Focus on creating content that ranks high on Google's search engine so people looking for a hosting provider or blogging tips can see your content in the first page of the SEO results

- Promote your content effectively

- Rinse and repeat

2. Making Money from Direct Ads

While the content on Justin's blog is also valuable, he's site differs dramatically from Abby's by way of the type of content. Justin focuses entirely on Internet Marketing as his niche. His blog started in 2011 and rakes in $28,636. The vast majority of his earnings come directly from ad revenue, and they are direct ads from various media companies catering to the niche he blogs about.

What you can learn from Justin:

- To sell ad space on your website, you need to give advertisers a reason to advertise on your site, and the main thing would be to focus on a niche

- Make it easier for advertisers to reach out to you. Ensure that your contact page directly calls out to advertisers with a simple 'To advertise, contact:'

- Consider a blog post specifically addressing advertisers. You can even use your email list or newsletter to your subscribers about your desire/venture.

- Join an ad network

3. Focus on your promoting your niche

When you decide on a niche topic, make sure you go all out to promote this niche and work with industry players to rake in income through ads and affiliate marketing. Dom from HumanProofDesigns.com focuses specifically on web design and affiliate marketing. He pulls in $17,000 a month maintaining a website that focuses primarily on affiliate marketing and churning out articles related to how-to in web design as well as blogging about internet marketing. His niche also caters to providing ready-made sites that you can purchase directly from his website in a package bundle that also comes with video tutorials.

What can you learn from Dom:

- If you have a niche that has a market and you would like to sell this to your audience- then you should

- This is especially for those with products to sell and services to give and works great for people who are content writers, web designers, and other cyber-expertise

- Create a blog that matches your product and the niche you are in

- Be honest with your clients about what you are selling and where to buy them. Additionally, don't shove it down their throats. If your audience is interested in purchasing, they will click to learn more.

- Offer special deals- a free welcome pack or a discount here, and there would be extremely useful in your sales strategy

- Listen to what your audience wants. Keep doing what they like but also find ways to explore new and different ideas and approaches.

4. Becoming an Amazon affiliate

Sharon, who runs **DigitalNomadWannabe.com**, earns $8,337 from her blog alone. It may not be a 6 figure salary like the rest simply because Sharon uses this blog as a digital resume more than a money-making site. Here, she posts how-to guides and posts articles she writes for other publications. Sharon's other focus is an Amazon affiliate program as well as sponsored posts.

What can you learn from Sharon:

- Becoming an Amazon affiliate is easy, and as Sharon puts it, 'One of the best things that she has ever done.' Becoming an Amazon affiliate does have a monetary impact, and you can do it too

- You can **Sign up** on the Amazon site, where you would need to open an Amazon account as well as connect your blog or website.

- From here on, it all depends on your niche and what you want to focus on as an affiliate.

- You can also create sponsored posts talking about your niche to bring in the money

5. Make your blog visually outstanding

Will, the owner behind **TravelBlogBreakthrough.com** writes about his passion- travel. The blog is cool and image-heavy, making it a pleasure for the eyes, and it also makes browsing fun. His content is cool too- it focuses on how he makes travel money making passion. Will makes over $5,090 a month. The topics he writes about ranges from travel tips to tech support- there's a little bit of everything. He also promotes the idea of Ambassadorship where it is all about a brand reaching out to you, to work on larger and more personalized campaigns to represent their brand. You become their digital spokesperson.

What you can learn from Will:

- Becoming a sponsor or brand ambassador means that your blog pulls in the attention of a public relations manager who sees the potential of working with you to further their brand image among the more specific audience and in a personal way

- You can also reach out on your own to a PR manager to pitch your blog and idea to work with them

- Use social media to promote your blog and link them to the articles and content you write about with the brand's products that you use

- Use ads to make money once you become their brand ambassador and start writing reviews about these products or services

Bottom Line

There are many bloggers out there that make 6 to 7 figures on a monthly basis, and there's plenty of takeaways from each of them. But one thing is for sure- all of them put in extra effort on a consistent basis to get to where they are from. Whether they followed a specific niche or a passion, time, money, and effort have been invested in ensuring that they get the following they want. Blogging for profit is not a get rich scheme, nor is it a monumental task to make money. If these bloggers can do it, so can you- all it takes is effort.

Conclusion

You've made it to the end of the book! Congratulations. Now that you know all (or at least the most important things) there is to know about blogging for profit and gaining financial freedom, you still need to do one thing and that is to create a personal mission statement. Gaining the necessary information about this method of making money is not enough unless your head and heart are in it because it takes effort and discipline to gain sustainable and profitable income.

Write your personal mission statement by answering these questions:

- What are the goals you want to accomplish with your blog?

- What do you want to teach and share with people?

- What do you want people to gain from reading your blog?

- What are your values and beliefs?

Once you've written down the answers to the questions above, post it somewhere you can see every day- your mirror, your journal, your phone, heck even on your own blog (but make it a private page).

Your next step is to write down clear steps on how you want to achieve these statements, information which this book already provides such as how to select a niche, how to optimize your WordPress blog to get money, the various ways in which you can make money from your blog as well as choosing the right kind of blog to work with.

Good luck!

Affiliate Marketing

A Proven Step by Step Guide for Beginners to Learn All the Secrets to Make Money Online Using Paid Advertising from Low Ticket to High Ticket Programs!

Michael Robert Fortunate

Table of Contents

Introduction

Congratulations on purchasing *Affiliate Marketing: A Proven Step by Step Guide for Beginners to Learn All the Secrets to Make Money Online Using Paid Advertising from Low Ticket to High Ticket Programs!*

Marketing has taken different faces in today's world but affiliate marketing is still one of the most hyped ones. There are countless success stories about affiliate marketing that you will find on the internet. Every internet marketer in today's world aspires to generate a sustainable and regular flow of income but can affiliate marketing provide you that? The answer is yes but there are some conditions attached to it.

Firstly, you need to have a well-structured business plan that will guide you in the right way. For this, you need to fully understand the dynamics of the world of affiliate marketing and have all of it under your grasp. Secondly, you also need to know how you can leverage the influence of social media in order to drive in more sales and thus, bring home more profits. And that is exactly what is covered in this book.

The aim of this book is not only to provide you with a comprehensive guide on how affiliate marketing works but also to educate you on all the key factors that are necessary to keep in mind while framing a successful affiliate marketing program. With this book, you will become a pro at the various strategies of paid advertising from both low ticket and high ticket programs.

Every effort was put into compiling this book so that it can serve fruitful to every aspiring affiliate marketer.

Chapter 1: Why Affiliate Marketing Is the Best Way To Start Off Your Internet Business?

Do you dream of making some sustainable passive income? Imagine a day where you can make money while you are still asleep in bed! Sound great, doesn't it? Well, it is easier said than done. You will need a solid plan in order to move forward with affiliate marketing and build a stable career with it.

But first, you must have a clear idea about what affiliate marketing really is. The main idea of affiliate marketing is solely based on revenue sharing. The idea is that when you are promoting a product, which actually belongs to someone else, over an affiliate marketing network and someone ends up buying that particular product, you will earn a commission. Simply put, you will get an incentive every time someone buys a product that you have promoted.

But to break it down to the basic level, affiliate marketing has four different parties involved in it and each one of them has been explained below.

- **The Merchant:** The merchant can be anyone who is responsible for the creation of the product that you are promoting. It can be a brand, an individual, a vendor, a seller or even a retailer. It can be a content creator selling online courses about photography or it can be a big brand like Mitsubishi manufacturing air conditioners. An affiliate marketing program can have anyone as its merchant starting from solo entrepreneurs to the biggest companies there is. But the merchant does not require active participation. All it has to do is possess a product that can be sold.

- **The Affiliate:** Also referred to as the publisher, the affiliate too is not limited to any specific entity. It can be a company or it can also be an individual. The affiliate is the person who is responsible for the promotion of the products. He/she can promote as many products as they want but their responsibility lies in acquiring the attention of potential customers and convincing them to buy the product. This is mostly done through the establishment of a review blog which the customers can read and end up buying products they like.

- **The Consumer:** The consumer definitely holds an important position in the entire cycle of affiliate marketing. This is because the concept of sustainability resides on the fact that there are some actual sales and without consumers, there will be no sales. So, there will be no commissions and no one will make any profit. The affiliate approaches the potential consumer through various methods. It can be done through social media, a blog or even through digital billboards. But whether or not the consumer is made aware of the fact that the product is part of an affiliate marketing system lies entirely in the hands of the affiliate. But since these days, transparent affiliate marketing is being encouraged and it is also one of the strategies for gaining the trust of the consumers, the affiliates usually choose to let the consumers know. Despite the product being a part of an affiliate marketing system, the consumer is not charged anything extra.

- **The Network:** This is the fourth component of affiliate marketing. Although the network is not always considered as a component by everyone, it should be. This is because the network is what serves as the intermediary between the merchant and the affiliate. But the presence of a network is not something mandatory. You can promote someone's product directly and develop a direct arrangement with the merchant regarding your share. But in some cases, in order to be able eligible to work as an affiliate for a certain merchant, going through a network is mandatory. In that scenario, the network also acts as a database apart from being the intermediary. Currently, the biggest affiliate network is owned by Amazon. With them, anyone can become an affiliate by signing up and then they will be given a custom affiliate link. The affiliate will earn a small commission every time someone buys a product through his/her custom affiliate link.

So, affiliate marketing is one of the best sources of passive income and also perfect for starting your online business. All you need to know is how you can drive more traffic and also use effective strategies to convince the customers regarding the potential that each of the products have. Only then can you make some meaningful income out of it.

If you are feeling confused and thinking that it is too much to take in then don't worry as this book will make all of it seem way easier. And this chapter is all about why you should choose affiliate marketing at all when it comes to starting your own business online.

Here are some reasons why you should start affiliate marketing today!

Reason 1 – It is Quite Affordable to Start

Of course, a start-up might seem all fancy but have you considered the costs associated with it? In most cases, it is huge and requires a lot of funding. On the other hand, starting an affiliate marketing business requires a meager amount of investment as compared to the other modes of online business. The best thing is that most of the affiliate programs that you will find on the internet are all free to join. Moreover, the product that you are actually promoting is manufactured by someone else and so you need not worry about that cost as well. So, there are practically no start-up costs associated. All you need to do is adapt some effective monetization methods on your own website. All you need to invest in is for setting up your own website. You will have to pay for your website domain and hosting services.

Reason 2 – You Will Get an Assured Commission

There are definitely a lot of ways in which you can earn money online but do all of them reap 100% guaranteed profits? No. But with affiliate marketing, with every sale you make, you will get an assured amount of commission. No one can take that away from you. It is completely genuine. But you do need to come up with some quality content that will grab the customer's attention and make them want to buy the product thus resulting in sales.

Reason 3 – There is an Endless Amount of Professional Independence

One of the best aspects of doing approaching affiliate marketing as your online business is that you will be your own boss. There will be no one to tell you what you should do or how you should do it. Everything will lie in your own hands. You can decide the hours you want to work for and you can even work from any location in the world. The only thing you would need is a stable internet connection and you are good to go! Every poll on the internet shows that online marketers who are doing affiliate marketing can earn anywhere between thousands of dollars yearly to even millions when you have set up your business properly.

Reason 4 – The Sales Performance Can Be Easily Measured

The scalability of any affiliate marketing program is another of the reasons why it is perfect for a beginner. The entire process is very transparent and you will not have too much on your plate. This is extremely helpful especially for beginners who cannot handle complex matters of business. In case you ever feel like the work is becoming too much for single-handed operation, you can always hire some additional people and yet invest much less than other businesses. This is because you are going to save a huge amount of money on office space as a business in affiliate marketing does not necessarily require you to have a physical office space. Measuring the performance of your sales is much easier in businesses dealing with affiliate marketing.

Reason 5 – You Will Have the Freedom to Sell What You Want

With affiliate marketing, you will never be pressurized or forced to sell or do anything that you do not want to. So, with professional independence, you can also choose the brands with whom you want to work with. Thus, your integrity will remain intact and you will have the opportunity to remain honest to yourself. Nobody will have the right to push products to you that you personally think are not worth it to promote. You will get to speak about only those products that you believe in or would have bought yourself. That's the beauty of affiliate marketing. Just think about it – you will be earning money by promoting products that you actually love. How cool is that!

Reason 6 – Affiliate Marketing Generates Commission Per Sale

Although the rate of commission generated differs from one affiliate marketing program to the other, but hey, look on the bright side! You are actually getting paid for every product sold. But when you end up working with companies, they can give you a fixed rate of commission. With affiliate marketing, the amount of money you make will progressively increase with the number of sales.

Reason 7 – It is Perfect For Those Who Always Love to Be Amidst Competition

With affiliate marketing, you always have to deal with tons of competitions. Your site metrics might not be the same every month. Moreover, there will be several affiliate marketing sites that pop up from time to time and some of them might even be good enough to take away your audience. So, audience retention is a huge aspect and something to be mastered if you want to do well with affiliate marketing. There are several marketing strategies that you can apply and we will talk about them later on in this book. But with each change in your strategy, you must always look out for any development in your metrics. You must also keep an eye out for any negative development. If any strategy is not working out in your favor, you need to stop implementing it. So, coming up with newer strategies to stay on top of the competition ladder is one of the things that you have to be good in. So, affiliate marketing is definitely the perfect option for those who love some eternal competition.

Reason 8 – You Might Even Get Sign-Up Bonus

Some affiliate marketing programs can even grant you an instant bonus amount for signing up with them. Are you wondering about why are they giving you a bonus? Well, it is because if you are just a beginner, there will be some time before which you earn some commission through your first sale. But the bonus is meant to give you a headstart and will also keep you motivated.

Reason 9 – No Hassles of Customer Support

With affiliate marketing, you do not actually have to deal with the customers as you are only promoting the product. But with companies, the scenario is completely different. The hassles of customer support are pretty real. When after making a purchase, a customer is unhappy with what he/she received, they can put the blame of the company and then the company has to come up with a proper grievance redressal mechanism. But you do not have to worry about customer satisfaction. Your only work is to link the seller with the consumer. All the complaints from the side of the consumer will be dealt with by the seller.

So, now that you have got a basic idea, you should know about some basic facts about affiliate marketing that would push you further towards starting it right now.

- The power of affiliate marketing is now being leveraged by 84% of publishers and 81% of brands in the United States every year. This statistic is not going to decrease any time soon but is only going to increase further.

- It has been calculated that the United States notices a 10.1% increase on a yearly basis in the spending towards affiliate marketing. So, the estimate states that if this continues at the same rate, then the number would rise to $6.8 billion by the year 2020.

- According to the stats, the costs generated in content marketing are much lesser and amounts to about only 62% of the costs that are required for the schemes of traditional marketing. Moreover, out of all the orders that are placed online, 16% comprises those made through affiliate marketing.

- The structure of the Amazon affiliate program was changed in the month of March in 2017 after which the passive income of creators dramatically increased because the rated provided by the company were raised to the range of 1-10%.

So, if you are just starting with your online business, affiliate marketing would be the best way to go about it. There is no shortage of products and you can even create your niche. If you are someone who is passionate about sports gear or photography gear, then you can expand on that same niche and create a blog or YouTube channel around it. Or, you can also create a website whereby you will be reviewing products belonging to different categories. There is no right or wrong way to do it and that is the best thing. You do what you feel would work for you. But cultivating an audience should be your first step because, without an audience, you are nothing. You will make money only when someone takes your recommendations and makes a purchase. You can even choose to make it personal by establishing yourself and proving your credibility in your niche. With time, you will be able to establish your blog or website and you will become an expert in the eyes of your audience. It is true that affiliate marketing will not fetch you money overnight. But when you stick to it and continue doing it for a long time, you will get success.

Another term that is not consequently used with affiliate marketing is the concept of influencers. When you become an expert and gather an audience, people will follow you for making their own decisions. The hyper-focused niches of influencers are now getting more priority and thus more traffic. The audience that they send to the various websites is highly credible and also shows much higher conversion rates.

So, if you are indeed planning on diving into the world of making money online, affiliate marketing would be the one that will not require too much investment and you can start straight away. Gain control of the life you lead and the income you make and you will see how your entire life changes. Although your skills will play a very crucial role in your success as an affiliate, with a consistent and intelligent approach, meeting your income goals is not something difficult. Read this book and you will learn about all the tips and tricks you need to know to excel in this field. Get higher engagement rates and convert your audience faster with these strategies. If you are not feeling confident enough, then you can always start with affiliate marketing as your second job and then gradually, when you seem some considerable income growth, you can make it your primary source of income.

Chapter 2: How And Where To Find The Idea About Which Products To Sell?

Doing well in an affiliate marketing business is every marketer's dream but first, you need to carve a niche for yourself. This means that you need to find the right type of affiliate products to sell. Affiliate marketing definitely seems incredible but everything can go wrong if your products don't sell. Making a living completely based on affiliate marketing can be tough and this is proven by the statistics which states that 90% of the total sales and conversions are achieved by only some of the affiliates amounting to less than 10%.

So, now let's dive into the topic of how you are going to find the best niche for your business.

Step 1 – Research and Find Your Niche

For those who are not aware of what a niche is, it is basically a market or category of highly specialized items. For example, organic shampoos. Normal shampoos have a vast market but when you think about organic shampoos, the market automatically becomes smaller and so does the competition. Moreover, there is also a smaller audience who are specifically interested in organic shampoos. This way, you can target them easily and focus better on your conversion tactics.

Here is one thing that you can do to figure out your niche. Search on Google with the keyword 'Top 100 websites' and there will be several websites that list the real-time data displaying the traffic that each of these websites receive. From these lists, you can figure out which sites receive maximum audience. You do not have to emulate the content but you can find out the niche.

Some of the evergreen markets in the world of affiliate marketing that usually appear higher up in the search results are health, romance and wealth. Some of the major markets in the health niche include weight management, fitness supplements, smoking issues and so on. Products related to diabetes are also on the top ranks because diabetes is now a growing problem. The primary reason why you should get started with a health niche is that people are concerned about their health more than anything else and so there is a chance that you are going to get big spenders if you use the right strategies.

Romance niches are mostly about online dating, sexual wellness and attracting someone of the opposite sex. In today's world, people are always on the lookout for a life partner or a companion and so you will get an audience that is willing to learn more.

The wealth niche comprises of topics like employment, gambling, Forex and so on. People are always looking for information on how they can make more money and so this niche is truly evergreen.

But these major markets have sub-niches too and you should choose something that you are passionate about. To develop the smaller niches, you can go to Quora and put the broader niche as your search term. You will get to know about a variety of topics that people are really interested about.

Step 2 – Check the Monetization Options

Don't start with any niche straightaway. If you have decided on a particular niche, you must also check what monetization scope it has. Starting out with affiliate marketing will do you no good if you cannot monetize your niche. ClickBank is one of the best places to search for monetization options.

When you visit the website, there is an option 'Affiliate Marketplace' on the top panel. Click on it. You will find the search bar on the next page and you can enter the category of your products which will help you narrow down your search. But the website also has some already curated lists which are shown on the left-hand side of the screen. Select the category you want and then search for your respective niche. When the results are displayed, you might find it a bit overwhelming if you are a first time user. Each search result that you see is something that the page is suggesting you to sell.

But to make the entire thing easier, you must sort your results by 'Gravity'. The main purpose of this metric is to let you know how well a product in a certain niche sells. Once you get the search results, look at the products and then decide for yourself whether they will be easy to sell or not. The search results will even show you the average income you can make from selling those products.

Step 3 – Check With Google AdWords

Checking the cost per click of keywords is another crucial step while selecting a niche for your affiliate marketing business. If you want to make more sales, you have to drive in more traffic and traffic is directly related to the competition in a particular niche. The Keyword Planner of Google AdWords is the best place to start. You should search the keywords based on phrase or category. So, select the respective option for that and then type the keywords related to your niche. Here, you should type in related words to your niche as well so that the search results can be diverse.

Once you have entered the keywords, click on 'Get Ideas'. Here you need to check the competition, average monthly searches and suggested bids. You will come to know about the traffic that these keywords get on a monthly basis. With the competition stats, you will understand the difficulty level of these keywords and how much effort you have to put in order to rank high in them. The suggested bid column simply gives you the data to signify whether or not this keyword is worth spending your time and money on.

Click on the column of 'Suggested Bids' and your results will be automatically listed in an order having the niches that pay a high amount for a single click on top. Now, inspect the results and see if there is something that suits you and then you can go back to ClickBank and do some further research on that niche in order to come up with better results.

Step 4 – Start With Virtual Products

There are both physical and digital products in the world of affiliate marketing and you have to make a choice regarding which ones you want to sell. Virtual or digital products include things like e-books, software and music but on the other hand, physical stuff includes a variety of things like gadgets, furniture, cosmetics and so on.

If you are just starting off, virtual products would be easier to deal with. Virtual products are instantly delivered to the customer once they pay the money and so there is no hassle or delay in shipping. So, if the customer needs something on an urgent basis, for example a book, they might opt for an e-book rather than a physical book. Moreover, with virtual products, you can reach a wider audience. Shipping is not always done to all parts of the world and so that is exactly where the virtual products come of help. Also, there will never be issues like products being out of stock as there is not physical product involved. So, even if you don't have to deal with the customers directly, you do have to depend on constant sales. But at the end of the day, the decision will always be in your own hands as to which products you want to sell.

Now that you know all about how you can find the products to sell or how you can figure out your niche, it is time for you to figure out where you can get these products. Finding the best affiliate programs is also important when it comes to generating handsome commissions from sales. So, here are some of the major websites when it comes to the best affiliate programs and you can find a wide variety of products to sell from them.

Amazon

Amazon is not only the biggest website in terms of affiliate marketing program but it is also the go-to website of every person willing to purchase some item. There is not a single product that you cannot find on this website. It practically has everything. Here are some reasons which will convince you to join the affiliate marketing program of this website –

- People have their faith on Amazon and they trust the website because they that the delivery of their products is guaranteed.
- As already mentioned earlier, Amazon is known for listing everything, even the weirdest products in the world.
- The upsell capability of Amazon is outstanding and this means that you are going to get some good commission too. This is because the commission is not only valid for the product you referred them to but also on all other products they buy from Amazon.

- The rates of commission at Amazon start at 4-5% and the more sales you make, your rate will become higher and higher.

ClickBank

ClickBank has over 500,000 members across the world and it also has an endless list of products that you can promote. This site is one of the major sources of all types of digital products. You should use ClickBank because –

- The pool of products on this website is quite huge.
- They will also provide you with real-time review reports which will help you to analyze your performance by monitoring, sales, refunds and cancellations data.

Rakuten

This website was previously known by the name of LinkShare. Its affiliate marketing service is quite well-established. The main characteristic of this website is that they generally work with those companies who operate on a large-scale basis and have aspects like annual sales and marketing budget. Rakuten is popular among affiliate marketers because of the following reasons –

- You will get an updated report on your performance as an affiliate.

- Both long-term and short-term marketing goals can be catered with the help of this website.
- Their affiliate marketing service is easier to work with form affiliates because they operate on an enterprise level.

ShareASale

From business services to organic products, ShareASale has everything that you need. But you must know that they will charge you a small sum as their signup fees. They also charge a small amount of money for every sale you make. This is mainly because their range of products is vast and they already have a strong market. But some of the reasons why people choose ShareASale are as follows –

- Different types of ads are supported by the website like pop-ups, image ads and so on.
- They keep a track on your progress and they also send reports from time to time. You can access your progress statistics anytime you want.
- They even provide different types of documentation and training videos to its affiliates as a part of the membership.
- If you are stuck in a problem, the website has a dedicated support team to help you navigate through anything you want.

- They work with a wide array of merchants and publishers belonging to different sectors.

eBay

Being one of the oldest stores online, eBay is still highly popular today. With over 5 million sellers and 162 million shoppers, the website has millions of products that you will find relevant to your niche. Another great thing about eBay is that it is open worldwide to about 13 countries at present. So, if you are planning to tap into global customers, eBay can be the door to success. Here are some more reasons why you should consider joining the affiliate program of eBay –

- You can access the database and so personalization of your feed is possible and easy.
- eBay gives you the opportunity to come up with links for every single listing and so you can share them on your social media.
- Their customer services are available in five different languages in the different countries.
- All the latest tips and trends that circulate in the world of affiliate marketing will be sent to you by eBay.
- Their reports and analytics are quite user-friendly and easy to decipher even for a layman.

So, if you want to start your journey as an affiliate, these websites can serve as your starting point and then you can continue sreading your reach.

Chapter 3: How To Create The Right Type Of Website To Drive Traffic?

Not everyone has an idea of what they are doing when they create their first affiliate marketing website. As an affiliate marketer, a large chunk of your time will go into creating promotional content, building strong and long-term relationships with brands and also pushing yourself to walk the extra mile in order to make your content stand out from others. Creating a website that can drive in profitable sales is not all about SEO. There are a lot of factors that you must take into consideration.

The golden rule of being a successful affiliate marketer is to know the tricks of marketing yourself well. If you want to become a full-time marketer, you will have to attract thousands of visitors to your site and for that, you need to be fully aware of the hacks of promoting yourself to the world. This does not happen overnight and takes a lot of dedication.

You can start your website on WordPress because it is not only cheap but also way easier to handle. If you are not yet familiar with how WordPress works, don't worry because this guide will teach you everything that you need to know in order to set up your website. The services of WordPress are completely free but there are two important things that you need to purchase and those are – domain name and web hosting.

Domain Name – The URL people enter for reaching your website is the domain name. To get your website's own unique domain name, you will have to get the registration done with a domain registrar. Now, the terms might seem intimidating but the process is not.

Web Hosting – A web host serves the role of making your website visible to the rest of the world. In simpler words, you are basically paying rent to a web server.

These two are the most important things that you need to take care of for building a successful affiliate marketing website. Now, there are several places where you can avail these services for free but if you are serious about affiliate marketing, it is always advised not to approach the free services. This is because in some cases, the site that you approach for these services might even hold a certain portion of the right to your content. That doesn't sound good, does it? Thus, to put it in a simpler manner, the business that you are spending time to build might not even be yours completely. Alternatively, when you get your own website, you will have control over everything.

So, if you are not sure where to start, here is a step by step breakdown of the entire process to make it easier.

Step 1 – Choose a Good Domain Name

Choosing your domain name should be done with considerable thought because it has to be something authoritative. Your domain name, if not chosen correctly, can even limit your website's potential in the future. For example, if you choose something like topaudiogadgets.com then your niche automatically gets narrowed down to audio gadgets and you wouldn't want that for your website. If in another couple of months, you want to review an air conditioner, you wouldn't be able to do so just because your website name says audio gadgets. But something like thetechadvisor.com can open a lot of doors for you as you can review any tech-related products. Long-term thinking should be your first priority if you want to make your business a success in the future.

Here are some tips to keep in mind while you are choosing the domain name for your website.

- **It should be easy to type** – The more the number of words in the domain, the more difficult it will be for your audience to remember it. So, you should keep it short and simple and yet catchy so that they can remember it after just a single glance. Multiple spellings are another problem that can meddle up the brains of your audience. For example, some people may write the word 'express' in their domain name as 'xpress'. Now, this may seem cool in the first instant but it won't be so cool when your audience is unable to remember the correct spelling and hence, ends up landing at some other website.

- **The name should have appropriate keywords** – There are several ways in which you can churn out ideas for names that will fit your website. For starters, why not come up with something that is directly related to your business or the category of products you write about? Or, you can also simply base your website on your own name. But the presence of a strong keyword would definitely play a big role. The implementation of keywords in a domain name is very smart. There are tons of SEO benefits to it. Ranking your website higher in the results of search engines is the ultimate goal and putting keywords in the domain name will only help that dream come true faster. Also, when you use the potential keywords in your domain name, any visitor to your site will instantly get to know what your niche is and what your website is about.

- **You can use a domain generator** – In case you are out of ideas, you can always leave the task of brainstorming to a domain generator. But you can only take those names which have not already been taken. For example, you cannot name your blog thewirecutter.com because the name has already been taken.

- **Avoid the usage of hyphens and numbers** – While you are coming up with ideas, avoid using hyphens and numbers at all because they often create misunderstandings. For example, if you say your website name is top10products.com, someone listening to you might think it is toptenproducts.com and then they would not be able to find your website.

- **The domain name extension has to be chosen carefully** – The extensions at the end of your domain name also have a role to play (.com, .net, and so on). The most popular one out of all the extensions is the .com one but getting a short and catchy name in a .com extension can be tricky as it is usually already taken. Here are some of the other extensions that are usually used but they also have their own meanings – .me (for personal sites and blogs), .org (for nonprofits and organizations that are non-commercial in nature), .net(for websites related to tech-based subjects), .info (for websites that are mainly informational) and .co (that is generally used as an abbreviation for a variety of words like community, commerce and, more popularly, company).

Step 2 – Buy Your Domain Name

Once you have finalized the name of your domain and made sure that it is available, it is time for you to finally make the purchase. There are a wide range of options for you to choose from when it comes to companies from whom you can buy the domain. Some of the major accredited domain registrars are HostGator, GoDaddy, A2 Hosting, Bluehost, Pantheon and so on.

Choose any website you want and then enter the domain name that you have selected in their search panel. You will automatically be show whether that name is available or not. If it is available, then you have to proceed with it and make the necessary payment after which the domain will be yours. But you will also have to enter some details as you are literally getting the domain registered to your name. Once you have bought the domain, the next step is to get web hosting.

Step 3 – Choose a Good Web Hosting Company

Creating quality content may not yield fruitful results if your web hosting is not right and so you need to take web hosting seriously. Your web hosting will determine how responsive your site is. James Lyne, who is a Forbes contributor, had stated that every day, over 30,000 websites are hacked. And do you know the reason behind this? They all made wrong choices when it came to web hosting. Of course, there is no perfect solution to this problem but you can always be a bit more careful in order to prevent such mishaps from happening with you. Whenever you choose a web hosting company, you can stay assured about the fact that they update their database from time to time so that they are ready to deal with any potential threats.

But if you want to make the right decision while choosing your web hosting company, here are some essential tips for you.

- **Decide on the type of web host that would suit you best** – Your web hosting options can easily be narrowed down if you start analyzing and understanding the specific needs of your business. For example, if you are going to open a review website with all the affiliate marketing links that also has high-quality videos, then your hosting will definitely need to be with someone who can provide high responsiveness. Moreover, if you are going to open a website that is going to receive a high amount of traffic, then you cannot do so on a shared server. Shared servers are suitable only for websites that have a fixed list of demands.

- **Choosing the appropriate hosting package is important** – Many beginners start with shared hosting packages because they are much cheaper and thus affordable for someone who doesn't want to invest much. But they also have greater risks. The biggest problem that these shared hosting packages have is that they will provide you with a way slower website response time. This can drive off your audience who do not have the patience to wait eternally for your website to load. On the other hand, VPS or Virtual Private Servers can provide much better performance.

- **Read the reviews before settling for a company** – Just like any other product, settling for a web hosting company before reading any of the reviews would be a big mistake. Reviews denote how reliable these websites are. While reading reviews, you might even uncover complaints from past or present users and you can even check whether or not the company puts any effort to solve these problems.

- **Choose the right bandwidth** – When your website is new, it is obvious that it won't require too much bandwidth. But you must always go for a bandwidth amount that leaves space for future growth. Moreover, you should also check whether the web hosting company provides flexible options regarding upgrading your hosting plan later on. This way, you can always go to the higher rung on the ladder when your business demands you to.

- **Don't get tempted by a lower price** – When you are just starting off, it is easier to fall to the temptation created by certain companies by offering hosting services at a cheaper rate. But you should not fall for that trap. Don't ever get fixated on the price. Always remember that these companies are not doing anything for free. They are charging less and so they will also give poorer service. It can be anything like a slower server, constant downtime, unresponsive customer support and so on.

- **Don't skim through the Terms of Service** – Always remember that this is your own business and so don't just sign up with something where you don't even know the terms. Think of it as an investment of time towards reaping the benefits in the future. It is true that everyone skips through the part where you have to accept the Terms and Conditions but don't do that, at least not with this. Moreover, you should also keep an eye out for any type of refund policy which these web hosting service providers sometimes have.

- **See whether they have a backup plan** – You should always be assured of a Plan B in case everything goes south. Ask your web hosting company what measures they take in case all your data on the site is lost. In case they give an answer with which you are not satisfied, don't avail their services. It is always better to be safe than sorry.

- **Enquire about security features** – Security breaches can happen at any time and to anyone and so to stay on the safe side, you need to be sure that your web hosting company has taken all the necessary precautionary measures. Enquire about their security features and how do they intend to protect the private information of their customers.

- **Avoid new companies** – There is nothing wrong with new companies but you will have to think about your own good. New companies who have just entered the market might provide you with amazing deals on their packages but they do not have the experience to handle growth. So, if you rely on them for web hosting, it might happen that your site will suffer later on.

Thus, it is always advisable to get web hosting from an experienced company.

- **See whether they provide extra features** – In case you need extra features like an SSL certificate or email hosting, then you need to check with the web hosting company beforehand.

No matter what company you are choosing, make sure your hosting plan supports WordPress. This is because it is the easiest website builder and as a beginner, it is the platform you should use to build your website.

Step 4 – Create Your Essential Website Pages

In your arsenal of affiliate marketing, your website is the strongest tool you have. So, it needs to be comprehensive and all-encompassing. Once you have completed your website hosting, it is time for you to start creating your website. Now there are some pages which form the skeleton of an affiliate marketing website and your first task would be to construct them. They are as follows –

- **About page** – This page should have a personal touch. This is the page that would give your visitors an idea about who you are and why you are doing this. But the popular belief states that the About page is entirely about the author or owner of the website. This is not at all true. The About page should also focus on how you can be helpful to your readers and how your content is unique and reliable. The goal of an About page is not about telling your life story when it comes to affiliate marketing. Rather, it is more about converting your audience.

- **Home page** – This is the page that will open to your audience the moment they come to your website. So, the importance of this website is completely transparent. It should be engrossing. You can choose a variety of themes on WordPress in order to come up with an attractive design for your Home page. You can even make it an amalgamation of some of the latest reviews you have on your website.

- **Contact page** – This page is crucial too as this is how various brands will reach out to you for collaboration. This is also the page your readers will use in case they have something to ask about. This page can get you some seriously potential leads and so no mistake should be tolerated while constructing this page. Moreover, it should be easy to navigate. You should also keep your social media links on this page in case your audience wants to follow you there. Moreover, the link to your Contact page should be prominently placed in the Navigation Menu of your website so that the visitors do not face any difficulty in finding it.

Step 5 – Write Your First Post

Once you are done with constructing the basic pages, it is time for you to write your first post. Regardless of the niche that you have chosen, there are certain types of posts that are popular in the world of affiliate marketing. You can start with any of them.

- **'How to' guides** – These are one of the most popular blog posts. You, as an affiliate, can construct an informative blog post showing your readers how they can use a certain product or how they can do something within a budget. It can be something like 'How to build a smart home under $100'. You can either write an article like this which will combine a variety of products or base your articles on a single product and give a complete guide on it. But make sure that the chunks of information you include are easy to understand and have proper readability. You should also anticipate the questions that your audience might have and answer them in your guides.

- **Simple product reviews** – If you want to start off with something less complicated, then product reviews are exactly what you should choose. The rating system you use should be understandable and simple. The content must be well-researched and every aspect of the product should be discussed. Make the review honest because only then will your audience develop faith in your opinion. Most importantly, don't back off from giving negative opinions because they are equally important.

- **Product comparisons** – These are another type of popular articles as they address the dilemma that everyone faces while purchasing an item. The focus of your article should be placed on providing every single detail about a product that a viewer could ask for. Your writing style should be more educational and less promotional. It should add value to a customer who is trying to choose between two competing products.

- **Best of lists** – These are basically articles that deal with a particular category like the 'Best Lipsticks of 2019'. These should inform the audience about products that are currently at the top of their category and what specialties do they have which makes them unique.

You can also consider making you first a video rather than a written article. Videos grab more attention mostly because people enjoy watching something rather than reading about it. Moreover, it will also have the potential to reach a wide range of audience.

So, these were the steps that you should follow in order to construct a website that can bring in a lot of traffic every month and thus generate sales.

Chapter 4: How To Leverage Social Media Sites?

Leveraging your social media sites will give you a high amount of traffic if done in the right manner. According to the statistics given by Nielson, users of the internet that spend their time on social media amount to 23% and among those users, 70% engage in online shopping. So, these statistics alone are enough to prove the importance of capitalization of your social media platforms.

So, here are some ways in which you can make the best use of the social media sites at your disposal –

Step 1 – Choose the Right Social Media Platform

Careful consideration has to be done while you are making your choice regarding which social media platform you want to use for your affiliate marketing business. The choice you make is important because of the following reasons –

- When you choose the right platform, you will have access to the right audience who will be genuinely interested in the products you promote. Thus, driving in more traffic would not seem much difficult. Moreover, social media will also help you to expand through likes, shares, and follows.

- Making the right decision will allow you to make the best use of your resources. Thus, improved sales and increased web traffic are guaranteed.

But, if you want to make the right decision with respect to your social media platform here are some tips that you should follow –

Refine your goals with audience demographics – You will have website visitors from a varied number of sources. The audience demographics are the metrics that will help you to categorize your audience. The basis of categorization includes a variety of factors like gender, income, age, location and so on.

Now you must be thinking how audience demographics can help you choose the right social media platform. Well, the answer is simple. With these stats, you will know where exactly does your audience socialize and secondly, what is the type of content they prefer the most.

There are two different ways in which you can use the demographics of your audience.

- *Use Google Analytics.* The data acquisition part is the most important step. You not only have to track where your audience is from but you also have to study their behavior on your site. For example, if you notice that most of your visitors like to share your content on a certain social media platform then you can use that information to your advantage. This will also help you narrow down your options when it comes to social media.

- *Use this data and compare it with the social media platforms.* Once you have acquired the data from Google Analytics, your next step would be to approach the known social media platforms and then compare your data with their demographics. General demographics like gender, location and age can also be used. In this way, you will find the social media platform which best matches the type of audience you have.

No matter what strategy you use, statistically-obtained data is always the best when it comes to studying your audience and increasing the returns on your campaigns.

Your choice should be in line with your business goals – Whatever choice you make regarding your social media, it should completely be in line with the goals you have in business. But if you are not sure how to do that then here are three basic steps that you should follow –

- *There has to be a main goal.* This is the goal that determines what result you want out of your social media campaign, whether it is expanding your reach or building your traffic. So, from there you can move forward with the rest of the process.

- *Build an action plan.* Once you have selected your ultimate goal, your next step would be to frame the path you want to follow. For example, if traffic building is what you are aiming at, then coming up with a lot of clickable content should be on top of your list. But if you want to expand your reach, then coming up with content that is shareable is what you should do.

- *Find the medium for your actions.* If you are preparing shareable content, then the two best mediums are Facebook and Pinterest. But if you want to drive in more traffic to your site, then you should aim at Twitter while on the other hand, Instagram can come in quite handy when it comes to expanding your reach.

Know the limits of your resources – Of course, unlimited resources are something what every business owner could have profited from but sadly, that is something not present with everyone. So, you have to do an honest assessment of the time, commitment and money limitations that you might face. Your platform selection should be done only after you have done a full assessment of all the limitations you have. Here is a two-step process that you can follow to make things easier –

- *Uncover all the possible limits you have in all aspects*. Every social media campaign requires some amount of time and effort from your part. So, it is your job to determine beforehand how much of those factors can you truly devote to your campaign.

- *Choose the platform that aligns with your limitations*. This will become clearer with an example. So, if you want to churn out the best possible results out of your social media, then Facebook can be handled with around 1-2 posts on a daily basis, Twitter's best performance can be achieved with 10-15 posts and 5-10 on Pinterest will work perfectly fine. But one of the most important things that you should keep in mind is your budget. This will ensure that you make the right decision and receive a decent amount of ROI or Return on Investment.

What you must understand that even if your resources are limited, it does not necessarily mean that you will have a poor social media campaign. You just have to play it smart.

Step 2 – Build a High-Quality Following

Creating your account on the right platform of social media is just the beginning of a long journey. The next steps are when all the hard work begins. And you should know that there is not shortcut to this. You cannot acquire thousands of followers overnight. You have to interact with the people following you and build your credibility so that they can put their faith in you. According to statistics, it has been noticed that 17 per cent users of the internet feel more reassured about a brand when they see their online presence. So, here are a few tips that you can keep in mind if you want to build a quality following –

- *Follow people in your network.* One of the first steps of growing your following is to follow other people on the social media platforms who are somehow related to your niche. Surround yourself with positive vibes and people who are likeminded. This way you will also stay updated on the different hacks others are using in their affiliate marketing business.

- *Keep up with the consistency of posts.* You should post your content once in a while. You have to be consistent if you want some real results. The best way to maintain this is to make a schedule. This will keep all of your posts organized and you don't have to be worried. Moreover, concentrate on one platform at a time. If you keep juggling between the various social media platforms, you will not be able to see any positive results. Make a content calendar and everything will start falling into place. The key to maximizing the engagement on your posts is to time your posts so that you do not have to do that in real-time. Also, don't repeat your content. Make it unique and it will receive all the love they deserve.

- *Provide some real value through your information.* Your posts must be informational. If you are reviewing a certain product as an affiliate, your post must be detailed and unbiased. Only then will your audience rely on your before taking any final purchase decision. If your audience finds your posts relatable, they you can assume the role of an authoritative person in that niche. Your posts should concern the real-life problems or any questions that your audience might have when they buy the same product. This will, in turn, increase the number of shares and retweets of your posts.

- *Don't forget entertainment value.* Humor can popularize your content in a great way. Moreover, it plays a crucial role in humanizing your brand. People are attracted to light-hearted discussions rather than something which is grim and serious. Your content should discuss serious matters but in a friendly and smooth manner,

- *Be responsive.* Always stay on alert once you have made a post on social media. Your audience needs you to be present for every query they have. Respond to the comments they leave. If your audience has some additional question on the product or service that you have just reviewed, don't back off from answering those questions. Working that extra bit shows that you really care for your audience and that they can turn to you for any help they want.

- *Your focus should be on helping and not selling.* Sales are obviously important otherwise you will not be making any revenue. But concentrating solely on the selling part will not earn you any real following or audience on social media. If there is some specific problem that has been buzzing your followers, take the leap and make some content surrounding it. That content will spread like wildfire because it is something that you audience has been craving for.

- *Be social and don't just concentrate on numbers.* Your social media following is just a number but your aim should be building a solid relationship with your audience. It is always better to have a handful of 1000 followers who are highly active and engaging rather than 100,000 followers who do not care about you at all. Realize the beauty of social media which gives you the power of making friends from all around the world. Don't be arrogant. Be open-minded and embrace everyone with a big heart.

- *Post video content too.* Video content is now spreading faster. Moreover, Live videos can bring you way better engagement than normal posts. So, don't simply stick to text-based posts and expand your horizons.

Step 3 – Build an Effective Posting Strategy

Now that you have discovered the platforms that work best for your business and the ways in which you can build a following, it is time for you to construct a posting strategy. Successive ads are not the way to go about it. Remember that social media is your virtual family. So, imagine if someone in your party keeps blabbering about how they are so cool and how their work is so amazing, do you feel attracted to that person? No, right? Instead, what happens is that you feel least interested and tag that person as an obsessed and self-centered human. The same things holds true for your different social media platforms.

Your posts should have a diversity in them. There is rule of posting that is followed widely and is known as the 4-1-1 rule. Read on to find more about it.

The 4-1-1 rule stands for –

- 4 – sharing four relevant, new and unique posts from others in the world of internet who are quite established influencers themselves
- 1 – re-sharing one content from someone who belongs to the pool of audience you have
- 1 – one post that is action-oriented and self-promotional

The rule should be followed diligently and you should not mess with it in any way if you want good results. Arrange your promotional calendar accordingly and keep one-month worth of content ready beforehand so that you do not have to stress about anything at the last moment. Most importantly, don't make the mistake of repeating content! This is extremely important otherwise your audience will lose interest in you and turn to someone else who can give them more unique and updated info.

Now if you are wondering how does the 4-1-1 rule work, well then read along and you'll find out.

- Firstly, the rule demands you to share content from other influencers who have already built their credibility. When you share their content, people will form a perception about you as a thought leader. Consequently, you will start gaining credibility too. In the eyes of your readers, you start gaining that authority which the influencers (whose content you are sharing) already have. But what you must be careful about is choosing the content which you share. The content should align with the type of content that you produce as well.

- Secondly, the rule involves re-sharing your audience's content. Now, this step will help you form a strong bond with those present in your audience and deepen your engagement. When you share their content, they will become more encouraged to share your content in return as well.

- Now, once you have completed both of the above-mentioned steps, you can release one self-promotional content. By this point, your audience will take the self-promotion well because you have already established your base. Now when you post this self-promotional content, it should be addressing your audience's concerns and not solely be based on you or what you think about it. Your views are obviously important but you must also think about the several questions that could crop up in the minds of your audience and answer all those questions beforehand. This way, your audience will find your posts comprehensive.

- You should also give some call-to-action posts from time to time. These posts should develop a sense of scarcity in the minds of your audience. For example, you can release a promo code for your audience or you can give a discount on a certain product after collaborating with a brand. But make sure these discounts and codes last only for a certain amount of time so that the audience is pumped up to take action now! You can also build reciprocity in your audience by promising them a small gift along with the purchase they make with your affiliate link. You can also ask them to write a testimonial for your affiliate website so that it can produce a social proof of your credibility to others. You can then, in turn, post those testimonials on your website and social media and gather newer audience.

Don't get disheartened if you don't see any fruitful results at first. It is totally natural as achieving success on social media is a step-by-step process and takes time. Implement the tracking parameters and keep a regular analysis of your growth because this will help you understand which strategies are working best for your case. If you maintain a disciplined and regular approach, building a strong foothold and creating your own tribe online is possible. The greater your following and reach, the more commissions you will earn.

Chapter 5: How To Use Paid Advertising To Make Money Faster?

One of the very initial dilemmas that almost every affiliate marketer has to face is that whether they should move forward with paid traffic or just stick to free traffic. Well, free traffic might definitely seem alluring because of the simple fact that they are free but in the long run, free traffic would not help you to reach a wider audience especially with all the new algorithm trends coming into the market. There are tons of content creators all over the world and everyone is trying in some way or the other to sell their content. So, if you stick to free traffic, it will be years before you witness any real growth.

Free traffic would require you to have outstanding SEO skills and that is something you will be able to utilize in your business. But a little bit of paid advertising never hurts.

So, before we get into the details of how you can use paid advertising, you need to know the benefits of the process so that you can get motivated into using it for your affiliate marketing business.

Thus, here are few of the benefits that you can enjoy from paid advertising –

- **Faster growth** – As already mentioned above, free traffic is good but if you want to climb the ladder of growth faster, paid advertising can really benefit you from that sense. If you are still skeptical then analyze the competition present and you should do this comparison with the other long-standing websites in the same niche. Check who has a stronger domain authority as compared to you and the process of narrowing down will become easier. Getting constant free traffic is a cumbersome procedure especially because of all the factors that play a role in it. And so, if you learn the tricks of paid advertising, you can establish your base faster.

   Why wait for years when you can start making something fruitful out of your affiliate marketing effort right from today? Once you start optimizing, growth will become prominent instantly and PPC advertising or pay-per-click advertising is the best method to target the right audience. See your posts rank higher than before once you implement the right strategies of paid advertising.

- **More targeted reach** – When you use only SEO techniques in your growth process, you may not always be reaching the right audience, or let's just say, the right target audience. Thus, you might not be attracting the right type of visitors who might actually buy something. Take this for an example. You have a blog post on a certain brand of sports shoes that you have affiliate links to. Now, once you publish that post, you will be getting views and traffic from different sources and organic Google search as well. Does this sound amazing? Well it is until one day you realize that all this traffic is not doing you any good as these people are not really buying any stuff. But the main aim of affiliate marketing is to make your audience click on your affiliate link to buy the product or service. So, what went wrong? It is simple – the target audience. When the traffic was organic, it was also disorganized and not specific. But to actually make it work, your target audience is, suppose, men belonging to the age group of 20 to 30 interested in running. So, that is something highly specific and paid advertising can help you reach that kind of audience. This will not only generate traffic but also turn them into loyal readers of your blog if your posts are captivating enough. And the best part is that all of this can be achieved within a very short time span if you use paid advertising.

- **Convert your traffic into sales** – Writing a blog post doesn't really take that much amount of time as compared to the time that you have to spend towards the design and promotion of that post. Now, as you must have heard already – time is money so don't waste it in something which is not going to be fruitful. Then, what is the solution? Well, for starters, you can divulge in paid advertising. This is because, all that experimentation and testing that you do in order to make your affiliate marketing business work is a lot time consuming, so why not make the best of the time you spend? If you depend on SEO alone, it will be years before you finally realize a sizeable income. You will spend all those months on the grind just to make yourself visible to the eyes of the world especially with this much amount of competition all around to deal with.

On the other hand, when you use paid advertising, you are showing your content to those targeted people who might actually be interested in buying the product. Thus, in simpler terms, paid advertising will increase your conversion percentage which is directly equivalent to more sales.

- **You don't actually need a lot of investment** – One of the greatest myths of paid advertising is that it costs a lot. You know what, it doesn't! All you need is a few dollars to initially get started with the paid advertising that is present on the different social media channels. With that small amount of money, you can start targeting a specific group of audience and see if that works out for you. With a few such hit and trial experiments with advertising, you will come to know which type of audience is actually worth putting your money in because they are going to fetch you some good return. When you are just starting out, try split testing. This means, you need to divide your marketing budget into different ad campaigns and at the end of a specific time period, say 15 days, analyze which of those campaigns is performing the best. This will make the entire process of converting your audience into potential leads much easier. Just to give you an idea, an amount of $10 is enough for a solo entrepreneur to invest in his/her ad campaign per week and that will bring them quite good returns.

Now that you know about the several benefits that paid advertising can fetch you, it is time to know how you are going to do it. For starters, here are some practices that you should know about as they form the basics of paid advertising when it comes to content creation for affiliate marketing.

Tip 1 – Target the right audience

This point has been reiterated time and again in various chapters and for good reason because your audience is everything. Affiliate marketing is solely based on traffic and conversion rates. So, the first step of paid advertising will be finding out the right audience for your business. It is true that ad targeting doesn't involve a lot of steps and thus, people tend to rush along the process to save time. But this is not the place to think about how much time you are putting into it as this will literally determine the success of your business. You should devote as much time you need to pin-point exactly the audience that would be interested in buying the product you are promoting.

You might be having a great advertisement but still not making enough revenue. This is usually the case with those who do not spend the time that is required in the targeting phase. Yes, you might even have to spend hours in experimenting the different target audiences and whether they bring you returns or not. But if you think that something is off, don't step back from making adjustments and tweaks in your targeting audience because that is exactly what you need to do until and unless there is a right fit.

But if you are too afraid to take up all of this by yourself or maybe you do not have the time to do all the research required for marketing, you can set aside some budget for hiring an expert consultant on this matter. This way, you can even figure out the more profitable targeting faster.

Tip 2 – Perform a complete keyword analysis

The keywords you choose for your ads play a huge role in forming the bigger picture. They are ones that take your content to the audience and if keywords are wrong themselves, your content will be reaching the wrong people. This aspect becomes even more important when you are dealing with a platform like Google AdWords.

So, how will you find the right keywords for your content? Firstly, brainstorm all those words that your audience might use in your niche to search some relevant content. Put yourself in the shoes of a buyer and think about what you would have used as a keyword to search for the content you are looking for. These keywords are more popularly known as the 'niche keywords', the reason being their direct relation to your niche. You also have to make sure that the keywords used are in line with the intent of your content theme.

The auto-complete search bar of Google is another amazing way of looking up relevant keywords to use in your campaigns. In this way, you can get different variations of the same thing. Moreover, you will get the keywords in the order of the ones that are more commonly searched for. Keep testing different keywords and keep tweaking them which brings us to the last tip of this topic...

Tip 3 – Keep testing and adjust accordingly

This point is so important that this definitely deserves a separate mention. So, don't stop experimentation until you get the results you were craving for because if you are not getting them, the problem lies in your strategies and not anything else. Optimization and constant improvement are the secrets behind a successful ad campaign and you should never forget that.

Well, apart from these tips, you should not stress about getting it all right at the first try because it is not going to be that way. There will be downfalls too but the key is to not stop trying.

But wait, you also have to decide the platform on which you want to run these ads. The platform should be the right one for the product(s) you are writing about and it should have the target audience you need. Testing and all is fine but in order to make sure that you take an informed decision, we have curated a list of the best paid traffic sources that are usually used by affiliate marketers and how they can be good for you.

1. **Google AdWords**

   This is nothing but the paid advertising platform of Google. Whenever you perform a search on Google, you are bound to get a couple of ads on top. Those are the advertised posts which appear at the top of the search results even before the organically listed webpages are ranked. Buy who is this type of advertising for? Well, you must know that out of all the online searches, 77% of it is occupied by Google. Thus, almost any content creator or entrepreneur can use and implement Google AdWords in their business. Such is the versatility of this amazing platform. Think about it this way – what do you do when you want to buy something? You search it on Google, right? Well, that is exactly something your readers are doing as well. People have their faith on Google for showing them the right results and thus, this also makes Google one of the best platforms for ad targeting as people will come to Google to get their queries about purchase decisions and certain products answered. And you need to keep your blog posts ready to answer all those questions.

2. Facebook Ads

Among all other social media platforms, Facebook currently stands to be the most famous one. Well, they also have the largest ads platform on social media. The different parameters used by Facebook for enhancing their ads targeting capabilities are amazing. Moreover, they keep updating their features from time to time to give you a better ad experience. The current number of active users on Facebook is 2.2 billion. Unbelievable but true. So, you will definitely be getting your target audience on Facebook. All you have to do is make the best use of all the advanced options that Facebook gives at your disposal and construct an ad campaign that yields you the right results. Another amazing feature that you can enjoy from Facebook ads is retargeting. The Facebook Pixel is a feature that can be put on your website and so this will help you attract those people's attention who have visited your website in the past. The idea behind this is that the effort required to convert a repeating visitor is much less than a new visitor.

3. Instagram Ads

Now that Instagram is owned by Facebook itself, the platform has undergone several major changes over the course of last few years, namely the Instagram Live and Instagram Stories. The main idea behind Instagram is to make it a platform for all the visually-appealing things. And the best part is that today there are over 600 million active users on this photo-sharing app where you can now share videos too especially with the help of IGTV, which has created a different world altogether. You can set your goals for advertisement according to your requirement. You can either run the ads to garner engagement or you can also do it with the aim of paid traffic. So, when should you actually use Instagram more than Facebook? The answer is not simple. But if the products on your affiliate marketing blog is about something that is visually appealing and the target audience is mostly young people, then Instagram can be the perfect platform to experiment your ad campaigns as a beginner.

But no matter which traffic source you choose, you should always their restrictions and regulations because they all have some. Not looking out for those restrictions and advertising just about anything would lead to warnings and permanent closure of your ad account and you definitely wouldn't want that. These restrictions usually circle around misleading banners which are constructed to attract visitors but don't really provide realistic promises. Moreover, you will not be able to promote all types of content on any mainstream ad network, for example, any adult or sensitive content.

You should also ensure proper quality of traffic. The biggest drawback plaguing every form of social media is the huge amount of bots. This is also termed as fraudulent traffic. But you must not fall into the clutches of such a sham and remind yourself that your business reputation is what matters the most. So, be careful of such activities and play with credible traffic only. Do plenty of research about everything that has been discussed in this chapter and don't leave any of the stones unturned. If you follow all these steps, success is not far away.

Chapter 6: Low Ticket Programs And High Ticket Programs

Now we come to the chapter that you were probably waiting for. Here we learn all about the low ticket and high ticket programs. The definition of a high ticket item is something that will give you a huge amount of time which you can probably use to sustain yourself for a week and in some cases, a month or even a year (yes!). This is the 'big fish' that every affiliate marketer wants to catch. Alternatively, the low ticket items mostly include things which will fetch you a small commission, for example, e-books.

Now to fully understand how these different programs can affect your sales, let's study an example. Let us say that you are currently making a revenue of $15 by selling one copy of a certain e-book. That might appear all exciting when the first sale comes in but is it enough for you to sustain yourself? No. So, in order to make, suppose $30,000 in a year, you will have to sell at least 2,000 copies of that same e-book. Now, that is something quite challenging to do.

The only way in which you can attempt to do this is by creating a website. Once you do that, you will have to devise strategies in order to direct more and more traffic to your affiliate links and maybe after a year, your website will finally be attracting 1,000 unique visitors each day. For the adverts that you place on your site, the clickthrough rate might be anywhere around 1-10% at an average and your conversion rate will also be something of the same value. This means, that in every 1-100 days, you will be making 1 sale. And you will be getting this by working day and night. So, if you now see the bigger picture, low ticket programs can surely give you sustainable revenues but only when your website has tons of different products, a huge zeal for excelling and invoking the marketing ninja inside of you and a great plan.

But on the other hand, if you sell high-ticket products that can fetch you $1,000 on per sale, then a total of 30 such products will be enough to give you $30,000 a year. And most importantly, you have 12 months to sell 30 products which definitely makes the picture a lot easier. You will not only have a sustainable income but also an extra amount of time in your hands that you can utilize in your own ways. So, do you see the world of difference between high-ticket and low-ticket programs? Having 30 happy customers is way lot easier than making each and every one of those 2000 customers happy.

There is another factor that comes into play in these low-ticket and high-ticket products. The customers buying low-ticket products are usually the ones that keep complaining about them and keep asking discounts. But the ones who are spending on the high-ticket products are easier to maintain. They are the ones that are serious enough to pay a huge amount of money on a product because they understand the value.

To steer clear of merchants that won't pay you enough commission, you should know about the features to look for in an affiliate marketing program before becoming a part of it. So, here are some of them.

High rates of conversion

The merchants perform that the best have a much higher ability to convert the traffic that they receive into potential sales. There is a term that is used in the world of affiliate marketing and it is called EPC or Earnings per Click. This term is used to denote the money that per click in an affiliate marketing program generates. But on the other hand, this term can also be used to signify the amount of money earned by the affiliate on the basis of per click. You must have understood by now how important the role of EPC is because without it, you literally cannot pin-point the performance of the merchant. Judging merchant performance is so important because of the fact that there are so many merchants on the web that claim a lot but do not actually have any proof to show that.

But on most affiliate networks, you will be able to view the EPC data and this will assist you in making a comparison between all the closely related merchants on the web. When you see that a merchant is having a relatively low EPC value, then either that merchant is new or their conversion rates are not that good.

Fixed commission that is generous or a percentage-based system

You will come across several advertisers who pay very low commission rates – either in the low double-digits or sometimes even in single digits. Just steer clear of such people as they are not worth your time. Any advertiser who is willing to pay you a sustainable rate of commission will definitely have the aim of building a relationship that is mutually beneficial and profitable. Hence, they usually know how they should be appreciative about the work put forward by the affiliates.

A low threshold for payout

Whenever the payout threshold is low, you will automatically have more enthusiasm and motivation to work towards that affiliate marketing program for the simple reason that you will get to access your payment faster. There are merchants that have no threshold value for payouts while some have the minimum value set to $100. But when most affiliate networks are considered, the standard threshold value for payout is $50. But anything above $100 is unjust.

A cookie length of minimum one month

When marketers are allowed only a few days to make their traffic convert, it is not fair because that timeframe is too low for anyone. For the prospects to finally become consumers, the marketers should be allowed a month so that they can reap the benefits of their promotional effort. The standard industry practice is giving a 30-day referral period but what should be made commonplace is a span of 90 days.

Deep linking capabilities

The capability possessed by an affiliate to create a link directing to a very specific webpage on the site of the merchant is called deep linking. An example will make this clear. Suppose, the affiliate can give a link to an article that will somehow connect to his post in place of giving any old-school generic affiliate link directing to a homepage. This entire system gives greater success when it comes to conversion of traffic for the sole reason that the potential audience is being sent to landing pages that already possess targeted content. The affiliate tracking apps that are available in the market often offer deep linking options but in some cases the option has to be enabled by the advertisers.

A high-performing affiliate tracking software

Every idea's success has a cornerstone and when it comes to affiliate marketing, the tracking software becomes a cornerstone. The software should not only have dashboards that are user-friendly but also a tracking system that is smooth and reliable. All of these together with a robust reporting mechanism make way for an excellent user-experience. Every piece of activity data like the number of conversions, impressions and clicks should all be readily available. This makes evaluation of performance a cakewalk.

Efficient program management

In order to scale and run the affiliate programs in an efficient way, the merchants should be having dedicated affiliate managers. The role of the managers includes welcoming everyone with open arms so that these people can promote their products. But this procedure can only be made faster when the screening and approval of the affiliates is done in a timely manner and the affiliate managers make sure of that.

So, these are some of the criteria that you should check and keep in mind while you are selecting your affiliate marketing program.

Now, if you are still baffled as to where you can find all those high ticket affiliate programs, this list might just help you out.

- **BigCommerce** – With over 60,000 merchants, BigCommerce is definitely one of the well-known high-ticket affiliate programs in the world of e-commerce. Because of the presence of some advanced functionalities and numerous built-in features, BigCommerce is a real hit among the growing brands. One of the special features of this platform is that there is a provision for bounty payment amounting to 200% on the total price of the plan. Thus, the equivalent of this is that, you can $60, $250 or even $1500 at times for each paying customer. Apart from that, the cookie policy spans over a period of 90 days and you will get access to a weekly newsletter for affiliates that contain some of the latest SEO advice for you to implement.

- **Shopify** – Known as one of the most popular and advanced ecommerce website builders in the world, Shopify also has a very good affiliate program. They have over 400,000 merchants on their platform. The most profitable thing is that your conversion rates will automatically become boosted with Shopify because of their high reputation. Whenever an user signs up by clicking on your unique referral link, you will have the potential of earning $58 for each of those users. Moreover, you can even get an amount of $2000 for every Plus referral and this sum is quite a good one.

- **3dcart** – This e-commerce platform is ever-growing and so is their affiliate program. Their generous commission structure is something every affiliate should check out because of their endless benefits. For every paid conversion, you can earn a commission of up to 300% and by joining their Partner program, you will have the potential to earn a separate 25% recurring commission too. Their affiliate managers are quite responsive and can help you out whenever you are stuck with something. To ensure access to a reliable third-party tracking, the website has teamed up with ShareaSale and Commission Junction. The platform has over 4000 affiliates working with them.

- **Volusion** – If you want to give a boost to your efforts in the e-commerce world, then Volusion can be your best friend. They are not only a highly advanced website builder but also have several responsive themes, payment gateways and inventory management. They also have tools that can help you with handling your client relationships, SEO marketing and email marketing campaigns. They use

CJ affiliate to offer their affiliate program. With them, you can earn a one-time commission payment of 200% which is calculated on the client's hosting plan.

- **ClickFunnels** – This platform assists its users in creating a landing page that can assist people in creating marketing funnels. One of the most crucial aspects of a sales funnel is the landing page but they are not the only aspects of the entire funnel. There are a series of pages involved which ultimately make the customer convert and take their buying decision. They offer a recurring commission of 40% for every user. Apart from that, you also get another scope of earning when there are sales referred by those users whom you had referred in the first place. This is called sub-affiliate commission and this is of 5%.

- **Leadpages** – This is also a landing page builder and is widely known for its amazing affiliate program. Their landing page builder is of a drag-and-drop type that is of high utility to both Instagram and Facebook ad creators. Another important feature of this platform is their split testing tool and their ability to get seamlessly integrated with other marketing tools and applications on the web. They also have a rare feature, that is, there is a scope to earn commissions by sharing free content. They have some free short courses on their site and when you share the link of these courses with others and a customer signs up following that link which ultimately leads to a subscription, then you stand a chance of earning a commission. The recurring commission rate is 30%. You will also be able to host webinars together with them.

- **ManyChat** – This is a bot platform that will help the users manage their businesses in a seamless manner because of their sales, marketing and support services that you can use on Facebook Messenger. Integrating a bot in a business can definitely give it momentum by instantly increasing lead generation and sales. They also have a 100% commission rate.

- **Bluehost** – Well anyone who is interested in web hosting must have heard of Bluehost because of such high functionality and popularity. They have a variety of services like WordPress hosting, shared hosting, dedicated hosting and VPS hosting. They offer a flat fee or commission for every referral and it is an amount of $65. But you must know about a small yet considerable detail – you have to accumulate a sum of $100 before you can withdraw the commissions you have made. But on the bright side, they offer a cookie policy that stays for 90 days. Their customer tracking system is also advanced and this makes sure that you get your share of money for every referral you make.

- **Kinsta** – This is another of the platforms that offer services of managed WordPress hosting. Businesses which fall in the medium to large range are their main target customers and they have devised a special started plan for all of them. Apart from this they will also give you access to an extensive resource material that contains utilitarian content which is all about affiliate marketing. Their commissions range anywhere between $50 and $500 for every sale made and they also have a provision for 10% recurring commissions. They also offer other additional benefits like a 60-days cookie policy and a dashboard which is extremely user-friendly.

- **Cloudways** – This is another of the hosting services that are hugely popular. They provide a 24/7 expert support whereby you can solve all the queries you have. Their entire base of knowledge is quite extensive and they also have some of the best dedicated affiliate managers. They will also provide you with resources with which you can boost your affiliate marketing techniques. Their commissions are in the range of $50 to $125 for every sale made. The only drawback is the payout threshold which is quite high at $250. The audience targeted by Cloudways is mostly individuals and medium range businesses.

- **Liquid Web** – Known for providing data center solutions and managed web hosting solutions, Liquid Web is a company that is known for possessing a variety of partner programs. For commissions, you can earn anywhere between $100 and $1000 depending on a few factors and they will also give you recurring commissions. They have a 90-days cookie policy and send out special newsletters to affiliates on a quarterly basis. They also have referral programs which are specially made for IT consultants. You can also join their reseller program and get access to a tiered set of program discounts.

- **StudioPress** – This company is known for coming up with some of the major themes in the world. The Genesis Framework is their brainchild. More than half a million sites on WordPress ue the Genesis Framework as their theme. If you are someone who surfs the internet quite often, then you are bound to come across a website that has been built using the Genesis Framework theme. Although StudioPress is no longer a separate entity and has merged with WPEngine, no change has come to their individual affiliate programs and they are still separate. But you do need an approval to become their affiliate. The commission rate is quite handsome at 35% per sale made. They also have sub-affiliate commission rates of 5% and a 60-day cookie policy.

- **Template Monster** – This website too is responsible for providing different types of plugins and themes for WordPress along with other content management systems as well. They have a highly dedicated affiliate management team along with a 365-days cookie policy! For any first purchase, you can gain a commission of 30% and for all further purchases, a commission rate of 10% is set.

- **Udemy** – Being one of the most popular eCourse libraries, Udemy hosts courses on a variety of topics and has more than a million students under its umbrella already. They also have thousands of tutors on their platform who are teaching different skills. The website also offers discounted rates on some of the smaller training courses and students literally wait for such opportunities to come. You can earn a flat 20% commission for every sale and also get access to thousands of promotional material. But the only catch is that they have a 7-day cookie policy.

- **Coursera** – With over thousands of courses available on their platform, Coursera may not be as vast and extensive as Udemy but they definitely have their own fan base and their affiliate program is better too. Firstly, their commission rates vary from 20-40% for every sale made and most importantly, they offer a 30-days cookie policy which is obviously better than Udemy. Their affiliate program runs through Rakuten LinkShare. Their courses are also top-notch having some advanced content like quizzes and lectures that are framed after considerable research so as to provide the users with maximum knowledge.

- **Amazon** – The Amazon affiliate program is definitely the biggest but they do not provide hefty commissions. But with a proper strategy, you can make some good amount of money from Amazon affiliate program too. Their commission rates vary from 4% to 8.5% and they mostly depend on the total number of sales you made in a month. So, in order to increase your income margin, you will have to sell a lot of products or you can promote the high-ticket items on Amazon. Promoting high-ticket items is way easier and all you have to do is find the right audience who are really willing to buy those products. 4-8.5% of a high-ticket item is also quite a handsome amount of money and the best part is that there is no end to the variety of products on Amazon and so you have the full freedom to choose your niche.

So, these were some of the affiliate programs that have a considerably higher rate of commission than others in the market.

Chapter 7: How To Scale Up And Expand Your Business?

Three things are of utmost important if you want to become an affiliate marketing ninja and make a sustainable income out of it. These three things are – persistence, time and patience. Whatever you have learnt up till this point in this book will only get you started because the next most important thing that you are yet to learn is how you can scale up your campaigns and thus expand your affiliate marketing business.

This chapter talks about some of the most effective affiliate marketing strategies that you can implement in your business.

Don't scale too soon

This is something you need to learn even before you start scaling. If you do not scale your affiliate marketing campaign at the right time, you will never be able to realize the benefits you have been looking for. The problem with most people is that they lose patience and scale their campaigns way early in their affiliate marketing journey. When people are not willing to walk the extra mile, they will not be able to reap the benefits as well. The golden rule of scaling is that – a campaign that has a 75% ROI is much easier to scale than the one which is still at 25% ROI on a daily basis. So, you need to wait until your campaign is solid.

We have already discussed methods in previous chapters which will help you increase your profits but here is a recap of some of the easiest methods you can implement –

- Improve the audience you are targeting
- Think about better angles, ads and landing pages
- Pause the websites that are not bringing you any money
- Test offers

Pre-Scaling

So, if your campaign is not yet ready, it needs to undergo a process of pre-scaling whereby you will have to optimize it. Scaling requires resources and if your campaign failed just because it was not ready to be scaled, it will be a loss. So, in order to ensure that nothing goes to waste, you need to properly set up your campaign. Now you must be wondering what the difference between optimization and scaling is. Well, this is something everyone gets confused about. The difference lies in the gravity and size of the changes you are making. Optimization is all about the smaller changes and specific alterations that are done. Scaling is done after optimization is completed as this is the step you should take after having built a strong foundation in the form of a greater number of conversions.

So, here are some of the techniques of optimization that you should practice in order to make your campaign ready –

- Ensure that the campaign that you have designed runs equally well on mobiles and tablets, in other words, mobile responsive
- Adjust the call-to-actions or headlines or ad copies if and when needed
- The social media ad images should be changed if they are not grabbing enough attention or are performing poorly
- Don't invest everything on a single landing page and instead split test different landing pages

If this pre-scaling stage is followed properly, your campaign will automatically get a boost to reach the next stage faster. Once your campaign is ready, start scaling.

Increase your existing budget

This is the simplest of all the strategies mentioned in this chapter and well, this is something you all must have thought about. Investing more in what you are already doing is the first step towards scaling up your campaign. This is also quite a flexible strategy as it does not depend on the type of traffic source you have. So, with this strategy, all you need to focus on is figuring out what works best for you. If you find that your existing campaigns are bringing you a considerably sustainable amount of money, they why not scale them up by investing more? This will expand the reach of those campaigns much more. If you find that increasing the budget did the trick, you can allocate more funds later on so as to increase the performance of the same campaign even more.

But proper utilization of that increased budget is essential so that none of the money goes wasted. Here are some tips that you can keep in mind –

- Start off by increasing the budget of your Facebook ads. Facebook is the social platform that has the maximum number of users and so increasing your ad budget there will benefit you by increasing the potential reach.
- In case you are using search traffic, then try bidding on keywords that are more expensive.
- You should also invest more money in placing the ads at strategically better positions that are more prominent.

As you read about the rest of the strategies, you will find that most of them require you to spend more money in some way or the other but they also speak about some other considerable changes.

Acquire traffic from a different source

If you have found a campaign which, according to you is performing well, or a promotion angle that is offering more conversions, then you can attempt a traffic source transition in order to scale your campaign up. In simpler words, what you are trying to do is simply to replicate the aspects of that same success which you have seen with the hope that the same thing happens with you. Thus, you will be acquiring traffic in a way that will be different from what you were doing before. It's true that there is no guarantee of this working out but there is no harm in trying.

For example, suppose one of your campaigns on Adwords is doing really good. What you can do is try and run native ads and see the influx of traffic then. Are your Facebook ads bringing you some big numbers? Why not try the same type of ad on Twitter or Instagram? Yes, it might seem daunting but at times, it can actually work.

Expand your audience globally

Once of the greatest scaling opportunities is to gain traffic from multiple countries and not just one. But in order to dive into this strategy, you need to first build your stronghold in one country. Moreover, this is one of those strategies which can be tested rather easily. All you need to do is make a few tweaks here and there and adjust the parameters in order to make the new campaign. But the selection of the new country is very important. You need to select a country that is similar in some way to the country that you were already promoting in, that is, the country that was generating the conversions up till now. For example, if your preliminary campaigns were based in US, you can launch your campaigns in a country like Canada which is a lot similar to US. Firstly, both the countries have a majority of English-speaking audience. Secondly, due to the similarity in cultural altitudes and geographical proximity, both the countries have quite similar buying behaviors.

But, on the other hand, if your preliminary campaign was in the US, you cannot base your next audience to be in Japan. Both are completely different from each other and you will not get conversions. With time, you will understand the concept better and you will know which country pairs well with exactly which other country when it comes to campaign promotion.

Obtain a cap increase

Advertisers are the ones who set caps on the campaigns and this is done mainly due to the following two reasons –

- The advertisers usually set a specific budget for the campaigns and they do not usually want to exceed that allocated amount of money.
- They want to attract a high-quality traffic and not be flooded by too many leads.

Now, if the campaign that you have designed is running well and has managed to reach the cap way before than anticipated, this means that the quality of traffic that you are generating is high. At such situations, you can request for that cap to be raised on grounds that your campaign has the potential to earn more. But the quality of traffic you generate will play a huge role in the approval of increase of that cap. The advertiser would not be willing to make a cap increase if you are not providing leads that will actually bring in some revenue to the advertisers.

But in case you think you fit this criterion perfectly, all you need to do is contact your affiliate manager regarding the issue and then see whether he is willing to grant you the request of raising your cap.

Try to get a rate increase

This is rare but if you put your best foot forward, who knows you might be actually able to get your commission rate increased! But again this is only possible when your campaign is working extremely well and generating a lot of conversions, in other words, more revenue for the advertiser. Only then will the advertiser consider getting your rate increased because even he will want to gather more traffic. This will boost your ROI instantly. You can also get it done by contacting the affiliate manager. Although, don't bother taking all the stress if you are not generating quality traffic.

Capture emails of potential customers

A capture page can be used to collect the emails of potential customers. This is actually a part of long-term scaling strategies. This is also one of the ways in which you can churn out the full potential of a promotion you did for an offer. There are several services online which you can use and this will make a way for you to collect the emails of the users. The users will give their emails through an opt-in page.

You might be wondering what the goal of the strategy is. Well, your ultimate aim is to collect as many email addresses as you can of those users who were already interested in a specific niche. This will also help you construct a stable relationship with the user as you are providing them with an ongoing service and targeting them those product campaigns that they might show interest in.

Maintain your campaigns properly

This is one of the crucial steps that every affiliate marketer tends to miss out leading to a variety of problems. You should not deviate from your other campaigns in order to scale up one campaign. This means, you should not become so engrossed in one campaign that you forget to maintain the others. So, you should constantly be alert and keep testing new angles. This is important because what if the scaling doesn't work out? Then you will be left with nothing but loss. Don't let that happen. Don't ever betray your home base just because you want to expand.

Ensure proper cash flow

A proper and stable cash flow is crucial for the running of scaling campaigns. There is nothing worse than the inability to run a campaign just because you cannot fund it. But you must also not spend on your credit cards just because you need funds. This can easily lead to the formation of huge credit card debts.

If you are still unsure about scaling your affiliate marketing business, then think about it in the way of any traditional business, for example, a shoe store. If you are the owner and you find that you have made huge sales in this quarter, what would you do? Would you let things remain stagnant or would you make use of this perfect opportunity and boost the growth further? I would probably go with the latter option.

The most important lesson about an affiliate marketing business is that you have to treat it like a business. If you form your mindset then the path will become easier. Take the business approach and then let your mind brainstorm ideas for campaigns. The strategies mentioned in this chapter are some of the best ones you can use to scale your campaigns.

Chapter 8: Mistakes To Avoid With Affiliate Marketing

Everyone makes mistakes and so can affiliate marketers. But this chapter lists some of the most common mistakes which can be avoided if you learn about them. Mistakes are more common when you are just a beginner because that is the stage when you perform all the trial and error experiments with your campaigns and strategies. And that is exactly how you become a pro gradually. It is true that a mistake is what makes you wise but at times, these mistakes can be a costly affair and so are better off avoided. So, here are some of the common mistakes that every budding affiliate marketer is bound to make and the chapter also speaks about what you can do to prevent them.

Mistake 1 – Wrong product choice

Affiliate marketing campaigns cover every possible product on this plant and the product need not always be something physical. It can be digital too. But with so many options also comes the need to make the right choice. But can making the wrong choice impact your affiliate marketing strategy? Yes, it can. And so you need to be careful while selecting the product as this is one of your basic steps as an affiliate marketer. This can be your defining moment towards success, so don't rush it.

Your niche should be something that will drive you and inspire you to make good content. You shouldn't be forcing yourself to sit in front of your laptop and do research on products to promote. It should be your passion. When you are inspired from your niche, you can easily devise several other marketing strategies and activities around it. Moreover, the passion might take you to such a level that your work becomes even more authentic and unique and that is exactly what will help you to stand out from the rest of the affiliate marketers. A simple search on Google about ideas on affiliate marketing niches will bring you thousands of results but picking something randomly never works.

One very common mistake that several budding affiliate marketers make is choosing a niche just because it brings more money. You need to understand one very simple thing. No matter how prominent or cool the niche is, you will never be able to make it big if you yourself are not interested in it. Believe it or not, nobody in the world is a natural when it comes to affiliate marketer. Every big affiliate marketer of today started out with something they love and then they spent days and nights researching and sharpening their skills. But if the product choice is wrong, you will just feel like a slave doing this just for the sake of money and not because you really want to.

Mistake 2 – Promoting too many products right from the beginning

This is another mistake which people make but don't really see the fault in it. When you are just starting out in this field, there will be a temptation to include as many products as you can and start promoting all of them. Don't do that. The default approach towards affiliate marketing for any new person in this field is being over-enthusiastic and over-ambitious. But this will ultimately lead to stress and demotivation when you have to figure out proper strategies for all these products. You will quickly become less and less enthusiastic and drop the entire strategy altogether. It is easy to get distracted when you have too much on your plate and you will not have any time for yourself or for your family.

The value you are putting in starts lowering down and this, ultimately, brings down the number of sales. So, if you want to be smart, then focus less on the quantity and more on the quality because that is how you climb the ladder of success. Pick a handful of products which you personally feel good about and would love to promote. Research extensively on them and focus all your energy onto those products. When you commit your brainstorming capacity and focus on a single product at a time, you will come up with better ideas and statistics show that you will also find it easier to convert your promotions into actual sales.

If you are thinking that approaching affiliate marketing in this manner will do you no good and will only shun your growth then think again. There is no harm in proceeding one product at a time. Why cause havoc by trying your hand out at many things when you can make each product a success and then proceed? Every campaign is different from all aspects and thus, they need individual attention. So, you need to provide the campaigns with what they need and success is not far.

Mistake 3 – Only trying to sell and not help

With affiliate marketing, people often develop a mindset that is all about selling and not actually helping the audience with any information. If this continues, you will gradually start losing the audience that you have. Don't let sales become your only priority. Yes, you will have the tendency to do it, but remind yourself about long-term profitability. The mindset of making profits only will not give you poor results but also generate mediocre content. Good-quality content is what you should focus on. When your content is good, audience will follow and so will the sales.

Your writing should be focused on how the readers can benefit from it. Every feature should be explained in detail and think about all the probable questions that might pop up in the minds of the readers. Once you have figured the questions out, make a separate FAQ section with every piece of content and answer those questions there so that your audience is not left with any confusion. Keep friction at bay. The placement of banner ads can be sometimes frustrating to the audience. So place them accordingly so that they do not drive your readers so angry that they have reached a point of no-return.

Whenever you implement some sort of outbound sales tactic, some consequence will come. It is up to you to decide which ones you really want and which ones are not worth the hassle.

Mistake 4 – Poor quality website

This is another mistake that affiliate marketers make. Your content is definitely important but your content is not all about what you write. It is also about the platform. When your website quality is low, you will notice your traffic decreasing which results in a low volume of sales. If you are not an experienced web designer, don't worry because you don't have to be. No one is telling you to be perfect from the beginning. But with the resources that are available in today's world, making a good website is way easier than ever before. WordPress is one of the best places to start because of their user-friendly approach.

User experience matters a lot if you want to retain your audience. If there are too many ads on your webpage or if the page is not responsive enough, then your audience might simply migrate to some other page providing the same information. A messy template is also one of the many reasons which can scare off your visitors because your website might appear to be too complex for them. When you lose audience because of these cases, there are very low chances of gaining them back because no matter how much improvement you make, those people will remember your website for the bad experience they had.

You can understand this well when you compare it with shopping. Shoppers always prefer those shops which are clean and tidy and have everything arranged in a proper manner. They are even likely to spend more in such shops. But they will not visit an overcrowded mall because they cannot figure out anything over there. So, some of the things that you should make sure while building the website are –

- The website should be easily navigated
- Every section should be properly categorized and easy to find
- The website should be responsive

- The calls to action should be prominent and clear
- Every page should have only one call to action
- The on-site elements should be properly highlighted on the webpages and the design should be chosen accordingly

It's true that building a website can be overwhelming but when done with patience, it is not something impossible.

Mistake 5 – Content that is regular and of high-quality

Have you every though about what your product is as an affiliate marketer? Well, the answer is quite simple – it is your content. Every affiliate marketer wants to get more sales but in order to make your audience, you will first need to have good content. If readers find your content to be credible and valuable, they will automatically want to rely on your advice when they want to buy a product. The common misconception that almost every affiliate marketer has is that if you have 10 mediocre posts then it is equivalent to one great post. But this is a lie. It never happens that way.

No matter what type of content you produce, whether they are posts on product comparisons or product reviews, your sales will be directly or indirectly affected by the quality of your content. If your content is not actionable or insightful, then there is no use of publishing content at all. Consider yourself as the buyer every time you compose a new post and then think about the fact whether the post would have been useful to you or not. The universal rule of getting any person hooked to your writing is to make your content interesting.

The first step to composing a new post is to decide the topic. Once that is done, you need to research keywords. Find keywords that are relevant to your topic and have less competition. This has to be done if you want to outrank the competition that is already present. You should also check the word count of the posts that are ranking high on the first-page results. Then, set that word count as a benchmark for your own posts. Don't forget to include images in your posts because it is normally seen that posts with images automatically rank higher than posts that do not have any images at all. Lastly, be regular with your posts and don't make your audience wait too long for the next post.

Mistake 6 – Not keeping an eye on the performance of your website

Not making use of a tracking tool is another of the common mistakes made by affiliate marketers. You cannot simply have a glance at your website and say whether it is performing good or bad. You need to have access to advanced tools with which you can study the metrics. If you do not track your data, you will not be able to optimize it and without these two things marketing is simply nothing. Whatever strategies you are implementing or whatever tweaks you are making to your strategies or campaigns will have an effect and these tracking tools will help you study that effect. You need to be able to recognize all the patterns that are working out in your favor. Google Analytics is the best tool to monitor all aspects of the website performance but if you want, you can use any such similar tool as well.

Does your website have a good speed? This is another important aspect that is highly overlooked. Studies have proved that whenever a websites takes longer than 2 seconds to load, the audience bounce rate automatically increases by a whopping 50%. You have to keep it in mind that everyone is impatient. Everyone wants to see the content now or never. If you keep your audience waiting, they will simply find another site that won't be delaying them. Mode of content delivery, large file size and response times of the servers are some of the usual reasons of a slow website.

If you are facing problems with your file size, then you can use any of the online tools to compress your image. But you should keep in mind that the quality of the image should not be compromised. Taking these small steps can help you towards reducing the load time of your website.

Mistake 7 – Neglecting content readability

As already mentioned, readers are impatient. So, you have to take every measure possible to make your content user-friendly and readable. Whenever your content is hard to understand or the sentences are confusing, the tolerance level of your readers will start decreasing. The font size you use also matters. You need to choose the size that is not too big or too small. Avoid anything that is below 16pt. But the font size is not the only determining factor acting here. Your font style will matter too. Avoid fonts that are not clear. Moreover, prefer a serif font when it comes to constructing paragraphs.

Don't make your sentences long. Keep them short and crisp. A sentence should contain approximately 25 words because according to research, anything more than that becomes confusing to several people. Paragraphs should follow the same rules. Don't make them too long.

If you don't know the meaning of a word, then don't include it. An average reader prefers a grade eight or seven level of readability. Even those readers who have high academic qualifications prefer the readability level to the one mentioned before.

Mistake 8 – Ignoring SEO

Ignoring the basic aspects of SEO can definitely cost you a lot. If you do not include the proper meta descriptions and title tags, it will be impossible for people to find your content. And the sole motive of publishing these posts is to drive traffic so you should not forget SEO. The title tag should be compelling so that readers are bound to click on your post. If you are using WordPress, then the Yoast SEO plugin is a very good option to optimize your content and make it SEO-friendly.To establish a proper hierarchy within your content, internal links are something you should implement.

Mistake 9 – Not making evergreen content

Something trendy comes up every other day on the internet and it can become difficult to keep up at times. But there will always be those topics which are evergreen and you should definitely include them on your website. Now, it is true that these topics have an immense amount of competition because everyone is writing on them. Moreover, they might also not be of much value to you as an affiliate.

But, when implemented correctly, these evergreen posts have high link building value. Sustainable content in the long-form layout can also be made more credible by adding phrases like '2019 updated edition' and your audience will automatically become interested in the updates.

If you think your content has any of the above-mentioned mistakes, then there is no harm in revising it again. Make the appropriate changes and then hit the Publish button.

Chapter 9: Strategies To Help Your Affiliate Links Outrun The Competition

The entire landscape of affiliate marketing has drastically changed over the past few years. Affiliates are now subjected to tighter legislations and thin content never does well with Google ranking. And top of all these things, the general competition has also increased by ten folds. So, if you truly want to get ahead of others in this game, you will have to play smart.

You need not be any expert to outrun others who are already established in this field. But what you need to do is push boundaries, give your best and follow the things mentioned in this chapter.

Strategy No. 1 – Stick to your niche

The number of niches that you can experiment with is plenty in number and the list is probably endless. But you need to focus on your own niche instead of trying to dominate over twenty. Yes, you will hear from others who maybe making millions from some niche which has just emerged. But does that mean you need to start doing that too? No. What you need to do is stick to your niche no matter what so that you can become an expert in that with time.

Moreover, when you juggle with so many niches at a time, you can never focus on any one of them. Deviating your focus to all the niches will only result in poor quality work. The result would be that you will have two dozens of niches and maybe each one has its own website but none of them will bring home a sustainable revenue.

This does not mean that you shouldn't experiment with the niches. Do as much experiment as you want but do not forego a niche just because you are not getting a quick success. Try your hand at a niche, do all that you can to make it boom and if even then you don't notice any growth, consider changing your niche.

Strategy No. 2 – Content is king

Your content will speak volumes about your work. If your content is solid, others will not be able to compete with it.

You, as an affiliate marketer, are the middleman in the picture and so you also need to prove your value. For doing that, you need to come up with content ideas that others probably cannot compete with. Being an affiliate marketer has several advantages over brands that are already established. The first thing is that you have the opportunity to be agile and if you want, you can act instantly with your new content marketing strategies.

Make your content so good that others fall short of resources to even think about competing with it. Everything should be on point starting from the content itself to SEO, site speed, and even social media share-ability.

In today's world, you will find tons of affiliate marketers but when it comes to really testing or interacting with the products they promote, there are only a handful of marketers who do that. But the key strategy of developing your own dedicated audience is to grab their attention and provide value through your content. You need to provide details and some insights that are impossible for the consumer to gather all of his own. One of the best ways to do that is creating hands-on product comparison and review videos. You can also narrate anecdotes stating how that particular product fits like a glove into your daily life. This will make the audience believe that you are really acquainted with the product and with time, they will be ready to take your word for it.

Strategy 3 – Give some special bonus of your own

This is another strategy that can make you different from the thousands of affiliates out there and drive your audience to click on your affiliate links. You can sweeten the pot by giving your audience something extra. For example, one of the easiest ways to do this is by giving a special Facebook group access to those people who actually bought the product with your link. This group should have only those affiliates who had purchased the same product through your link.

You can also try rewarding those customers who have referred their friends. Word of mouth is something that will help you in spreading your business. Just get a plugin related to a customer referral program and you are all good to go. Now, your audience will then be able to share their unique link with their friends which will bring them to your website. And then you will earn from that extra portion of audience. But don't forget to reward your audience who promote you through their own links.

Strategy 4 – Practice hedging your strategies of SEO

This strategy is all about distributing your eggs and not keeping all of them in one basket. It is very similar to what happens in an investment portfolio. All of the money is not invested in any single entity. Instead, it is divided among bonds, stocks and other commodities so that your money remains safe through the ups and downs of the economy. Just like that, the Google algorithm undergoes some swings from time to time. Your SEO strategy has to be full-proof in order to survive these swings. The best way to do that is hedging your strategy properly.

First is the white hat strategy which is mostly effective for the long term. This will require the maximum amount of effort, time and money. During this strategy planning session, you will be focusing on a diverse range of topics at a time. But this strategy should be implemented on the main domain of the brand only. When it comes to short-term results, this is not the strategy you should be looking forward to. But in long-term, this is the safest bet you have got.

Second is the grey hat strategy which is purely made for acquiring medium term results. This strategy is all about setting up micro sites or buying other sites which are your competitors. The basis of this strategy is that tactics like widget links and guest blogging can be scaled to yield good results for the next 6-12 months but they won't be working after a period of 2-3 years.

Third is the black hat strategy or which is commonly known as the short term strategy. This approach is quite aggressive.

The marketers buy hundreds of domains and then an extensive amount of link building is done which promotes these websites to higher ranks but that lasts only for a couple of weeks. To maintain that rank steadily, the entire process has to be repeated over and over again like a loop.

But if you want to make it big in your affiliate marketing business, then the best bet is to combine all the three strategies and form a multiple-layered diversification so that even if something fails, you always have a backup.

Strategy 5 – Practice out-branding, out-working and out-thinking

The competition is huge and so you have to give your best if you want to outrun that.

Out-branding. There are some underdog websites who have outrun the competition with a do or die attitude. This has been even more commonly seen in affiliate marketers who deal with credit cards and pay day loans. A simple search on Google would make it easier to understand for you. Use the keyword 'compare credit cards' and see which of the two sites rank 1st and 2nd. You will notice that both the companies listed are not any financial institution or bank. So, these companies have figures out a way to beat the competition they have with highly renowned banks and financial institutions that are focused on those same search terms as well.

Out-working. Every one of you must have heard about ProBlogger and Mashable. Yes, they are a success today but did you know that they were actually a one-man company when they just started. They out-hustled all the competitors they had. The same thing applies for those who are working in the field of affiliate marketing. It is not impossible to achieve that higher status or ranking in the Google search results but all you need is a more dedicated and solid strategy that can get you there. In case of Mashable, they used to publish as much as 7 blogs on a daily basis. That was way more than everyone else and fast forward a few years, Mashable ranks on the first page of Google whenever it is something in their niche. So, the endnote is that if you are into a niche that is over-competitive, you will have to possess the zeal that will make you work the extra hours.

Out-thinking. Last but not the least, you have to be smart. When you think smarter, you will always stay one step ahead of others working in the same niche.

Strategy 6 – Focus on building a recurring affiliate revenue

There is nothing that can be guaranteed when it comes to affiliate marketing. It is true that the market is extremely volatile and this is due to a variety of factors. The factors usually are case-sensitive and differ from one person to the other. For example, for Mr. X, it can be the Google algorithm that is not working in his favor while for Mr. Y, it can be because his main affiliate program is closing down.

But you need to be ready with a backup in order to face such unforeseen circumstances. What is the solution? You need to focus on recurring affiliate revenue generation. This will also keep you motivated while you are figuring out new ways to beat the competition. Of course, one-time payouts might seem good in an instance and there is no harm in them but with a recurring revenue, you are securing your own future.

Strategy 7 – Diversify

Many affiliates make the mistake of focusing all their energy and resources in one direction or one traffic source only. This mistake did cost a lot of affiliates their jobs back in 2011 when the initial Panda update of Google was released and thin or low-quality sites were pushed back in the search results.

Those who did not learn from their lesson faced a blow in their face again in 2012 when the Penguin update of Google was released. So, the safe lane to take is to build an audience that you own and build it by creating some high-quality content.

You can also diversify by focusing on different things. For example, maybe you were focusing only on one-word phrases as the keyword. Then it is time for you to concentrate on the long-tail keywords. According to research, these long-tail keywords are the ones that account for 70% of the searches on the web and are alone responsible for giving you a 36% conversion rate.

You can also try shifting your focus to a new demographic region or an audience that speaks a different language but only if it applies to the product you are promoting. You can also take into consideration the sales funnel and focus on different portions of it. For example, if you find that your competitors are more concentrated in building the top tier of the sales funnel, you can focus on strengthening the last tier which is located in close proximity to the call-to-action page.

With the market becoming ultra-competitive each passing day, these are only some of the strategies that can help you make it to the top. No one knows what will work best for you so you need to try your hand at everything. But don't make the mistake of trying out everything at once. Implement one strategy and then wait for the results. If it works then continue along that line and if it doesn't, start with something new. This list was meant to help you brainstorm your own ideas as well. Reaching the topmost rung in the ladder of success is not easy but it is not impossible if you are determined enough.

Chapter 10 (Bonus): An Action Plan To Kick-start Your Affiliate Marketing Business

If you have read all the previous chapters of this book, you must have formed quite a good idea about the various aspects of affiliate marketing and how everything works. So, this is a bonus chapter that lines out the exact steps you need to follow in order to kick-start your affiliate marketing business as a beginner. Everyone has to start somewhere but in order to get success, you need to do it the right way. Like any other undertaking, even affiliate marketing needs a plan and following that plan will bring you closer to your success.

Here is a step-by-step approach to affiliate marketing that will not only help you set up the business but also direct it towards the path of generating revenues.

Step 1 – Planning

The planning stage of setting up an affiliate marketing business is the most overwhelming but don't worry, you'll get past it. It is very normal to be tensed and feel like you are in the dark about everything. Relax! You are just starting out. But you need to do an extensive research to learn the basics and if you have read this book then you already know all that you need to know in order to start. The first thing that you should do is find the niche that you can work in. This is the first and foremost step because if you do not know what you are going to promote, you will not be able to figure out the audience let along build a website.

For starters, you can jot down all the things in life you are passionate about. You can become an affiliate of literally anything and everything. You should possess a certain interest in the field you want to start working with because when you love what you do, you will always stay motivated to work. Moreover, the niche you choose should not be shallow otherwise coming up with newer blog posts will become difficult for you as a beginner. You should also reconsider starting with a hugely popular niche for the simple reason that it is also going to have an immense competition to deal with.

Step 2 – Build your website

Once you are done with all that research, now it is time to put things into motion and build your own website. But wait! You also need to brainstorm a domain name. Every detail related to this has already been discussed in Chapter 3. But here I am going to discuss it in short. Well, unlike what most people think, building a website is not complicated especially with user-friendly platforms like WordPress, anyone can build a website. Once you have chosen a good domain name, buy it. The next step would be to choose a proper hosting plan. You can get quite affordable options in that too.

Now it is time for you to install WordPress. Choose a simple theme that is customizable and start creating content. Now, the content you put up on your website should not be anything random. It should be relatable to the audience and completely fall in your niche. Don't skip from one niche to the other every other month because your audience will then get confused. Master one niche and be an expert in that. Another important aspect of your content that you should keep in mind is that it should be engaging so that your readers don't lose their interest halfway through the post.

Step 3 – Choose your affiliate programs

Now it is time for you to choose the affiliate programs you want to work with and also select the products you will be promoting through your website. Now this is something you must have probably covered a bit when you were deciding your niche but now you have to dig deeper. Since this is something which will serve as the source of your income, you need to research extensively before you finally settle for a program. One of the most important things that you should definitely check while choosing the program is how much commission they are going to provide you per sale.

The affiliate program you choose should have products that you yourself would have personally used. If you don't believe in the products yourself, why promote them to others? If you continue such form of affiliate marketing you will never be able to gain credibility and trust of your audience. In order to become a success in this venture, you have to be as authentic as it can get. You should promote only those products which you think are trustworthy. You should also check how good the customer support of the affiliate program is and whether they have an affiliate manager or not. Suppose you have a problem regarding something, will they contact you instantly? You should choose a program that has prompt responses because you are bound to require support at some point of time.

Step 4 – Create high-quality content

As already said before, content is king. Creating good-quality content can be time-consuming indeed but it will also pay you off well in the future. So, you need to have patience and start building new posts in your niche regularly. One of the most common models of content is writing product reviews. When it comes to generating a sustainable amount of affiliate income, product reviews can go a long way to help you out. The best example of this type of content model is *The Wire Cutter*.

You can also try constructing blog posts that revolve around some common day-to-day problems that people face and what products they can use to overcome those problems. Research various forums on the web to know about the things people are now talking about. Pick the topics that are relevant to your niche, do some keyword research and then construct the blog post.

Another way of creating an information website is to put in some evergreen posts that literally serve as a knowledge hub. These posts are all about information that never ages. But before you plan an evergreen content, the most important part is to do proper keyword research.

Giving some type of informational product to your readers is another way of attracting traffic. This can be anything like an e-book or a webinar. The goal is to set up the base for email marketing. When your audience signs up for the free stuff, they provide you with their email address which you can then use for promoting your affiliate products.

Step 5 – Build your own audience

This is something that goes hand-in-hand with quality content production. When your content resonates with the audience, you will automatically find traffic flocking in. When an audience is literally interested in what you post, they will also be more inclined towards making a purchase. And this is what you need to make revenues.

Social media is one of the easiest ways in which you can build an audience for yourself. There are so many social media platforms to choose from – Facebook, Instagram, Twitter and Pinterest. There are other networks too which are often location-specific. If you are just a beginner, then you can also start by writing guest posts for other websites which have already gained a considerable amount of popularity and rank way higher in Google search results. This will give you exposure to the audience who might be willing to read posts in your niche.

Another important way that you should implement is by building an email list. Form a lead magnet by providing your audience with some informational product and then you can use that magnet to gather the email addresses. Don't push sleazy sales pitches but instead create some useful content that the audience might be actually interested in. Through those content pieces, you can direct the audience towards your website whereby they can click on your affiliate links to make the purchase.

And in between all these, don't forget the SEO strategies as they are the ones which will help your posts reach the right audience group.

Step 6 – Implement analytics

Analytics are an important part of achieving success in the scope of affiliate marketing. So, you need to set up your Google Analytics account. When you learn about the details of the traffic data, you will be able to point out exactly what type of ad copy is performing well when it comes to converting an audience. The data that Google Analytics provides the users is vast. Yes, it can seem a bit complicated at first but with time, you will find it easier. Every piece of information that you gain from the insights of Google Analytics can help you to increase audience conversion if proper tactics are used.

You can know literally everything about your audience. You can find out the geographic location they are coming from or even the device they are using to browse. You can also find out the times of the day when your website is attracting the maximum amount of traffic. Geolocation is one of the most useful strategic metric that you can implement to increase traffic and sales both. When you know the geolocation of your audience, you can customize your ad copies or emails accordingly. You can also think about other aligned locations to promote your data in because of the similarity in buying habits of the people belonging to the two locations.

Step 7 – Ensure profitability

You also need to ensure profitability if you want to continue on your affiliate marketing strategy. Well, you might not be able to see any income in the initial months but with time, you will see sales coming in. But with that gradual rise, there will also come a point where your income will become stagnant and there will be no further growth. But you should not allow that to happen. Keep maximizing your profits.

But for starters, if you do not want to spend more than you earn, start with a few products only. The more the number of products, the more overwhelming it can become for you. Test different campaign strategies and don't go all in with just one. With gradual testing, you will understand what is actually working out for you. There is another important factor that people often tend to overlook – demand. If you are trying to promote a product that doesn't have that much demand in the market, you will never see good results.

So, you need to listen to the market. The market will give you signs regarding what you should do and all you need to do is look out for them and respond accordingly. Being a highly competitive field, there are several new updates that keep cropping up and you need to watch out for everything new so as to stay in the loop.

Step 8 – Maximize your performance level

To churn out the full potential of your affiliate marketing campaign, at some point or the other, you will have to optimize it. You should also focus more on the landing pages that you are building. They are the ones to grab your audience's attention. Firstly, you will have to understand your audience, know exactly what they want and then construct the landing pages accordingly. Customize your pages from time to time so as to make them suitable for the audience you have.

You can also consider giving some extra incentives that will drive your audience into converting. These extra incentives can be anything from free trials and exclusive discount rates to freebies or anything that is free. Keep testing and you will find the perfect fit for your growth.

Step 9 – Scale up

When you scale up your affiliate marketing strategy or campaign, you do it to bring in more profits. But first you have to deal with the budget concern. You need to ensure that you have the right amount of cash flow before you start scaling up your campaign. Don't ever think about meeting the costs using your credit card. That is a bad practice and can easily line up debts.

One of the first steps that you can take in order to vertically scale your campaign is to increase your daily budget. But your ROI should be solid. You need to remember that every campaign in the world of affiliate marketing has the potential to be scaled but every campaign has its own time. If you do not scale your campaign at the right time, you won't be able to see the results you were expecting. This means, you should not scale your campaign too early or too late.

Another important strategy of scaling that you can use is by expanding your global reach. Research which countries align in culture and buying habits with the country you are currently promoting in. Then, include that other country (with similar metrics) under your target umbrella. This way you can bring in a completely new set of traffic to your website.

Every detail related to scaling has been discussed in Chapter 7 in case you want more information.

Step 10 – Automate

All the strategies and steps that you have learnt so far are definitely strenuous and involve a lot of work on your part. And you definitely need to perform all of this manually so that you can learn it all. But later on, when your business booms and reaches a certain success level, you will have too much on your plate and you will have to implement automation for most processes.

The first thing that you should automate is email-marketing. This strategy has the potential to generate a lot of sales when implemented in the right manner. The next thing that you need to handle is segregating your leads. This can also be automated with the help of different platforms that you can find through a simple Google search.

One of the strategies to grow your affiliate marketing business is to be active on social media and then promote your posts there. But this need not be done manually as you can easily automate them.

When you create so much content for your website, it also means you have to do that much amount of proofreading. But with technology becoming advanced day-by-day, you don't really have to do that. One of the best tools that you can use for proofreading is Grammarly. It is very easy to use and it can check all the grammar errors and spelling mistakes that are present in your post.

Over the past few years, automation technology has taken a completely new face and thanks to that, affiliate marketers can now go on expanding their business without having to worry about hiring any more personnel. Now you need to adjust your budget and ROI accordingly because all these automation processes won't come for free.

So, if you are someone who is willing to dive into the world of affiliate marketing, this 10-step action plan is just custom made for you. Follow it step-by-step and you are sure to reach your goals soon enough.

Conclusion

When you have read the complete book, you will develop a total grasp on the concept of affiliate marketing. By now, you should be all ready and geared up to start your own business. If you keep thinking and rethinking, you will never be able to start and *now* will always be the best time to start.

With affiliate marketing, you will be in charge of all the decisions as you will be working for yourself and not anyone else. The main effort is to set up your strategies and content. The phases that come later on are mostly about reaping the benefits and some tweaks here and there. The key benefit of being an affiliate marketer is that you are not actually making any of the products, you are only selling them.

But even affiliate marketing is all about the audience and so you have to do everything you can to keep your audience satisfied and provide some actual value through your content. If you create something that is already present on the internet, why will the audience come to you? The goal is to be unique and authentic. Your posts should have your personal touch that no one can replicate.

You can also try creating videos to make the content even more enticing and immersive. Who doesn't love the idea of making money while you are enjoying your vacation or sipping your coffee? With affiliate marketing, you can make that dream come true.

Lastly, if you find this book helpful in any way, don't forget to leave a review on Amazon.com!

Instagram Marketing

The Best Tips & Tricks to Grow Your Business: a Step by Step Guide for Beginners with the Best Strategies to Maximize Your Small Business' Profit Using Advertising!

Michael Robert Fortunate

Table of Contents

Introduction

Thank you so much for purchasing the book Instagram Marketing: The Best Tips & Tricks to Grow Your Business: a Step by Step Guide for Beginners with the Best Strategies to Maximize Your Small Business' Profit Using Advertising! In this book, we will talk about Instagram marketing and how it can help you to grow your business and achieve financial success. Believe it or not, Instagram is one of the best social media platforms to grow your business on, and it can also help you to create a plan that will help you make a lot of money and live a healthy, well-rounded life.

If your goal is to build up your Instagram profile page and to get a lot of followers, then the information provided to you in this book will help you tremendously. More specifically, we will help you get there by using some secret Instagram marketing strategies that only successful Instagram marketers know. If you are ready to grow your page into millions of followers, then make sure that you get started on this information provided to you. As always, make sure that you read this book until the end and not just skim through it.

It is essential that you read this book throughout, as a will help you build the right knowledge base to grow your Instagram page. There is a lot that goes into it, and we will break it down for you step by step, so you do not feel left out when building up your Instagram profile. You can use this knowledge to build up your Instagram page or to grow your business.

Chapter 1: Instagram Marketing 101

In social media marketing, Instagram is one of the newer tools that will help you grow your brand recognition. If your goal is to get recognized as a brand or become an online celebrity, then there is no way that you will be ignoring Instagram. Instagram will help you, as it has billions of monthly visitors. Instagram will give you the platform you need to grow and be successful, but do not take our word for it. There are many resources that can show you how many people have become celebrities. That is all thanks to Instagram, and you can genuinely grow it to a multimillion-dollar brand. There are many things Instagram can help you with; let us talk about the basics and go from there.

One of the first things Instagram can help you with is building a great SEO. If you do not know what SEO is, it means search engine optimization. If you want free, unpaid traffic, the best way to go about it is to rank high on Google. Google appreciates it when a website has a bunch of social media platforms they are connected to, more specifically, Instagram. If you have Instagram, and you promote it, the chances are your site is going to rank extremely high on

Google. Instagram will not only give you the platform to grow, but it will also give you the free and paid traffic that you have been searching for. Secondly, Instagram will help you tremendously to network with many successful businesses and people. In 2019, many people are resorting to Instagram to connect and network with people. The reason behind that is you can reach many people online; most of them will only connect with you on Instagram. If you are looking at the accounts you follow, you would know that something as big as Nike puts an effort on Instagram, and promotes their products there.

This is the reason that you must use Instagram not only to build a portfolio but also to connect with people and go from there. Many people call Instagram as an entity's online resume, so treat it as such. Another thing Instagram can help you with is to get invited to events and travel opportunities. Building upon the networking part of Instagram, many people who are active on Instagram will get invited to events where they can talk and meet with people. It will help you not only to travel the world but also to grow your business as a brand. Finally, one thing that Instagram can help you with is advertising. Be visible to your target market online so that they can buy your products. If you are in the market of growing your business, there is no better way to reach your market than by using Instagram marketing.

You are essentially paying Instagram to target specific people, which will help you to get more sales. Primarily, every single brand on this earth uses an Instagram advertisement to get more sales. This is one of the essential things you can do to grow your business. Instagram does it all for you. It helps you connect with people. It enables you to build your brand, and finally, it helps you to be the person you want to be. There is no excuse for you not to use Instagram, whether it is for personal use or to grow a brand.

Will Instagram Work for You?

As you might know, Instagram has over billions of people visiting online. Recently bought by Facebook, Instagram has indeed grown in the past year. When it came out, it was mostly a place for people, primarily photographers, to upload their photos. Now, it is a place where you can connect and grow your brand. Many of you might be wondering, is Instagram easy to use, and can it be used by an average person who does not know how to take photos? The truth is that Instagram can be used by anyone who has a smartphone and can take a picture. This means that you do not have to be a professional photographer, which is what makes Instagram one of the best tools to follow when it comes to growing your brand and getting more recognition.

All you have to do is take a photo of your product or yourself and post it on Instagram. Your goal in posting on Instagram is to establish a call to action. Whatever you post must have a call to action. For instance, if you are posting a product that you are looking to sell, include a "Buy It Now" tagline. Or if you are trying to get more engaged followers, write down on the comments, asking what they think about this post. It is effortless to get involved followers and to get people to buy your products by simply following the rule of a call to action. All you need is an iPhone or android that can take photos for you to post on Instagram. Thanks to Instagram, you can edit it and make it even look more professional.

Your main goal should be to post relevant content two to three times a day. Think about the material that you are about to post on your Instagram. Make sure that whatever you post relates to your brand and the people you want you to follow. Do not post about cars if your page is about to makeup. Posting twice or thrice a day and keeping the content relevant will help you to keep your audience engaged. That is one of the most important things to remember when starting your Instagram and growing exponentially. The only thing you need is a smartphone that you can use to take photos. Sometimes, you can even repost other people's photos by simply tagging them in the post. This will help you to grow that brand. Also, make sure to post content about your brand. Doing so will help you grow your page even further. The truth is many people use Instagram stories to increase their engagement rates. Make sure that you leave no stone unturned and that you are genuinely engaging your audience. With your products, you need to grow it into a big brand.

Convey Your Message

One thing to remember is always to convey your message. This would mean having a call to action, as mentioned earlier. For instance, let us say that you have finally completed your video or post. Make sure to ask your viewers to like it or leave a comment. This will allow you to convey your message without sounding spammy. It also makes sure that they do so at the end of your post/video.

It Has to Be Both Ways

You have to realize that social media has to be both ways; it is a relationship between the brand and the customer. Hence, having a great engagement rate is very important when it comes to building up your social media platform and brand. One thing to remember when increasing your engagement rate would be to stay connected with your fan base. Always reply to them, and be positive toward whatever they have to say. Even if they are negative, always respond in a positive manner.

One of the best ways to practice 2-way communications on your social media accounts is by acknowledging the positive comments coming from your audience or followers. You can do this by commenting back with a simple "Thank you." Another way is by affirming their comments on your posts by writing things like, "We know, right?" or "Spot on!"

The most crucial two-way communication can happen when somebody posts something critical or negative about your brand on its social media account. Never react to it with the same spirit, emotion, and tone of writing in which the negative comment had been posted. Instead, take the high road by, first, acknowledging their concern, e.g., saying something like, "I am sorry to hear that" or "I can imagine why you feel that way." By responding that way, you will not be validating their critical or negative comments about your brand or post. You will just be telling them that you are not dismissing the way they feel, or you are saying that their comments are as logical as eating soil on a hot summer day.

In many cases, bashers are disarmed when they hear (or read) that their comments were not easily dismissed or when they see that their opinions were validated, even though they were not necessarily accepted to be exact or accurate. Doing so also shows your audience that your brand is classy and professional.

A basic definition of marketing is that it is an activity where products and services are promoted to prospects or potential buyers to maximize sales. So the apparent goal of marketing is to sell as many of a product or service as possible.

The 4 Ps

Marketing activities are composed of four essential elements, which are collectively known as the 4 Ps. These are the product, price, place, and promotion. To effectively sell your products and services through social media, you will first need to get a basic grasp of these four elements or 4 Ps.

Product

In the marketing industry, product refers to the process of knowing, choosing, and creating a product or service to sell. To create a product or service that will sell well, you must learn to look at your products or services from the perspective of a buyer. To be more specific, you must learn to look at three critical things: your target market's needs or wants, your products' or services' ability to meet those needs or wants, and your competitors' products and services.

Price

Price refers to the consideration you are willing to receive in exchange for your products or services. How much money you are eager to collect from your customers? This is possibly the most competitive aspect of any product or service. Competitors try to bring their prices as far down as possible in an attempt to get more customers to patronize them.

And while lowering prices is often considered an excellent competitive strategy, there will be times when raising prices may be the wise thing to do. When? The best situation where you can raise your product rates is when the competition is limited or even non-existent, and the demand for the product is very high. Another consideration is when your products or services are considered a luxury, like Rolex, Porsche, or Apple. If you are in the luxury niche, the relatively high price can even make your products and services more desirable because it will establish your customers as belonging to an exclusive or elite group who can afford such luxuries.

Oh, pricing is not just about the amount paid for your products and services. It may also include payment terms and complementary items that can increase your products' and services' perceived values. For example, a relatively high-priced item can sell many units if customers are allowed to pay for it on an installment basis.

Place

Place refers to how you will bring your products and services to where your customers are or how your buyers or clients can access them. Being an entrepreneur, it is essential for you to regularly review how your business can get your products or services to your customers. Even the cheapest of products and services will not sell much if customers can't access them.

If you are dealing with a physical product or service, location is a significant consideration. You may have to relocate your business to where your customers are. However, if you are wise enough to take advantage of social media marketing, in terms of promoting or selling your product, you can use the Internet to deliver it to your customers. Then the location will not be a limiting factor for your business.

Promotion

Promotion refers to your marketing strategies and tactics and how you implement these to make as many people aware of your products and services as possible and, more importantly, buy them. The more people are aware, the bigger your market is. The bigger your market, the higher your sales can be.

Promotion involves practically all means by which you can bring your products or services to your prospects' attention. And more than just doing that, the development also includes how to position your products and services in their minds, i.e., how they will perceive them in the best possible way. An excellent example of this is Apple's iPhones. While arguably the most expensive smartphone on the market today, it still sells a whole lot of units every time a new model comes out. People are willing to camp outside retail stores several nights ahead of the release of the latest models to make sure they are among the very first people to get them. Why?

Apple, Inc. was able to position the iPhone in the minds of millions of consumers as the Mt. Everest of smartphones with a sense of exclusivity and sophistication. For instance, some claim that the Chinese smartphone Xiao Mi churns out some of the best performing, top-quality smartphones in the world for a fraction of the price of even the lowest model iPhone. But why do people still pay more than they should get practically the same performance from an iPhone? A sense of exclusivity and sophistication would be the answer. For example, Xiao Mi's phones are highly unlikely to give the same touch of class, elegance, and exclusivity as the iPhone does, even if it comes to the point when the former might outperform the latter. But the iPhone is better positioned than any other phone in terms of quality. That is the power of positioning.

Promotion is the primary topic of this book and, in particular, social media promotion. Now, let us get into the meat of social media marketing, shall we?

As mentioned earlier, Instagram is a social media platform where not only you can upload your pictures and short videos but also edit them with various filters and borders, among others. You can post on Instagram and share the same posts on four other social media platforms, including Facebook and Twitter. Many businesses have started to shift to Instagram marketing for selling their products and services simply because our minds tend to process information better through sight (visuals) and sounds. Some of the biggest names in the business that are actively marketing their brands on Instagram include Red Bull, Virgin America, Adidas, and Intel. And they do so in different ways.

Virgin America takes a less creative but practical approach to market on Instagram. An example of this is how they promoted their first-class flights. They took photos of the immensely popular Pomeranian puppy named Boo on their trips and posted them on the Virgin America Instagram account.

Others like Intel take a relatively more creative approach to Instagram marketing. They market their latest computer processors but not by showing pictures of the chips or processors themselves, which are very dull and boring to look at. Instead, they post well-edited photos of the top computers that use those processors. By showing off the sexy machines that used the boring-looking chips, Intel can engage its audiences and promote their products more effectively. They can do this by showing its audience which of the top and visually stimulating computer models their chips are being used.

The credit card company American Express also takes a creative and indirect approach to promote its credit card services through Instagram. In particular, they do not post pictures of their credit cards; that is also boring and limiting. Rather, they post pictures of the activities and events that the company sponsors. They also make use of hashtags on their Instagram posts to position their financial services as a necessary part of fulfilling and living the modern lifestyle.

While you can upload short videos on Instagram, they need to be short (maximum of 30 seconds only) in order to be meaningful. If you'd like to upload videos, better do so on YouTube instead. Instagram, for social media marketing purposes, is best suited for posting and editing great pictures.

And speaking of focusing on pictures, social media marketing on this platform is not as simple as pointing, shooting, and uploading. It is a bit more complicated than that, but not so complicated that you will not be able to do it yourself. It begins by planning your content, which we will focus on in the final chapter. You have to think about your content and choose the kinds of images that you will strategically share on your brand's Instagram account.

After taking the pictures or images that you determined will be best for your social media marketing campaign, you will need to edit them to give them the "oomph" or "wow" factor. You can edit them using the app itself right before you post them. Instagram features several cool preset filters, or you can customize them yourself using the app if you are familiar with photo editing. Doing this can turn "ok" into "great" and "ho-hum" into "wow"!

Lastly, you can optimize your image's contribution to your brand's overall social media campaign by coming up with perfect hashtags. Doing so can help the leading search engines easily categorize your pictures into specific keyword categories and make them even easier to be discovered by others.

Other Instagram Best Practices

One specific way to do this on Instagram is to post images or pictures of the people who make up your brand or products and services. And that includes posting pictures of you! Doing so will give your brand a "human" face and something to personally connect to. And when people see the faces behind the brand or product, they are more likely to trust it, engage with it, and patronize it.

Another way to help your prospects and existing customers connect with your brand on a deeper level is to post images and pictures of the behind-the-scenes stuff, such as how your products are made and packaged or how it looks like when you render the service you are marketing. Posting pics and images of things like these can help people trust your brand better due to a better sense of familiarity. They know what goes into your products, who the people rendering your services are, etc. Just be careful not to show too much information on the posts so that your competitors will not be able to copy you.

Chapter 2: How to Set It Up

Getting Started on Instagram

Creating your Instagram account is best done on a mobile device, as Instagram has been optimized for mobile usage. While you can still create your account on the desktop version of the platform, it may not be as easy as it can be, and sometimes, it can be more challenging to navigate, and there are fewer features available on the desktop version of Instagram. So, to get started, you will want to go to the application feature on your cell phone and download Instagram from your app store. Once the app has been downloaded, you can launch it and follow the on-screen process for creating your account, which will include inputting either your email or phone number and then choosing a password. Once you have done that, the next page will require you to choose a username for your account.

Choosing Your Handle

The Instagram handle that you choose needs to be clear and easy to remember; otherwise, your audience may not be able to find you again once they leave your account. Also, you want to make sure that the moment people see your username, they can make some form of a clear connection between who you are and what your company does; otherwise, they may not be tempted to click onto your profile page. In general, most brands will use their company names for their handles, as this makes it easy for you to be found on Instagram. For example, Nike, Adidas, Walmart, and Nordstrom all use their brand names for their usernames on social media platforms, as this makes it straightforward for them to be located. If you are a personal brand, you may need to change the way you approach your social media to ensure that you can be located and recognized by social media users. Generally, personal brands will continue to follow the same rule of thumb as other brands, which is using their names as their usernames.

For example, Kendall Jenner's username is simply @kendalljenner, making it easier for her to be discovered online. There are, however, some exceptions to this rule of thumb when you are creating a personal brand online. For example, if you are someone who has a long, challenging name or one that has multiple spelling, using it for your username will likely result in not being located online. In this case, you can use a nickname as your username and then use the same nickname everywhere online, or you can use an easier spelling of your name. For example, Nicki Minaj's real name is Onika Tanya Maraj, but this would be difficult to remember and spell; therefore, she branded herself as Nicki Minaj. This makes it easier for her fans to locate her online or anywhere they may seek her out, which makes her brand both memorable and simple. When you create your username, refrain from using odd spelling, usernames that are similar to what has already been used online, or special characters or numbers.

Unless your character or number is a part of your brand name, attempting to make your username unique by adding these characters will instead make it more challenging for you to be located by the users you wish to connect to. Remember, this is how people are going to look you up, and this is the name that people are going to remember you by. If you want people to recall you and locate you easily, you need to create both a username and a brand that people will remember. After you have created your username, you will be taken to the main screen where you can begin navigating the application. Here, you continue to fill out a few more parts of your profile before you begin interacting with anyone on the platform. You do not want to be putting in work to connect with your target audience if your profile is still not developed enough for people to identify you. This ensures that no connection is a missed connection.

Crafting the Perfect Bio

Once you have created your username, the next thing that you are going to need to write is your bio. On Instagram, your bio can be up to 150 characters in length and can include links to other profiles and hashtags that may be relevant to your brand. Your bio allows people to know who you are and what you are about, though you can also use it to leverage sales and market your business through your profile.

Using your bio wisely is the best way to ensure that you can use it to increase your memorability, as well as the amount of interaction that people will have in following you and supporting your brand. When it comes to writing a bio that will help you make sales, there are three things that you need to focus on: catchy content, being informative, and promotions. You want your bio to be catchy enough that people are interested in actually reading it. It also has to be informative so that people can get a feel of who you are and what your company is about, and it can be promotional so that people are more likely to click on the link that you can provide for them. Typically, complete sentences are frowned upon in bios unless you are using a single short sentence, so refrain from using anything too excessive or wordy. In most bios, rather than using sentences, people share lists of their interests or what their brand is all about. Writing your bio properly is essential, so be sure to take the time to identify what is going to work for you and your brand.

The best way to get a good feel for what will work for your unique brand is to go to the pages of other brands in your niche and read through their bios so that you can see what works and what does not. Take a look at the bios of those who are successful versus the bios of those who have not yet accumulated a large following, and try to see any trends or differences that seem to set the two apart. You want to be emulating successful brands, of course, so attempt to recreate trends that they are using in their bios through your bio but more authentically so that it resonates with your brand and your unique target audience. In addition to writing your bio, you will also want to share the link to your website so that people can see more about who you are and have the opportunity to shop online if you have an online storefront.

If you have many links that you would like to share with people, consider using a service, such as the Link Tree, which allows you to create a professional, personally branded landing page that has buttons to the various websites you want to direct your audience to. If you are marketing multiple things on your accounts, such as a freebie offer, your signature offer, and the opportunity to follow you elsewhere online, these different links can make it easier for you to direct your audience around to your services or other accounts. Regardless of how you choose to structure your link, make sure that you do provide one so that people can click it and get a deeper feel of who you are and what you have to offer. The following are great bios that can be used for your brand. Of course, you will need to adapt your bio to suit your unique brand or niche, but these will give you a great starting point to get a feel of what works and what sells when it comes to bios.

- A gourmet cheese company, "Gourmet Cheese:" The Right Wine. A Great Party. Need We Say More? #linkinthebio"

- A fashion blogger: "23 // Fashion // NYC // Lattes and Lipstick. Shop my outfits at the link below!"

- A life coach: "Chasing goals, living big, enjoying life. Live your best life – check out the link below!"

- A jewelry company: "Diamonds for every occasion. #Linkinthebio"

- A local limo company: "Ride in style for less – Vancouver/Calgary/Toronto. Book at the link below."

Uploading Your Profile Picture

Your profile is going to require a picture as well, which will provide your audience with the opportunity to visually see who you are and begin to make the connection between your name and your image. When it comes to making branded accounts, you have two options with your profile picture: upload an image of your logo or upload an image of yourself. Whatever you choose will depend on what type of company you are running and which image you want people to remember. For most companies, the logo will suffice as this is the easiest way to begin building brand recognition through your business. As people come to associate your logo and username with each other, they will also come to recognize your logo and identify it anywhere else where they may spot it. This can be huge for brand recognition, which is why if you are running a company, your logo is the only thing that your profile picture should be. Make sure that you upload a high-resolution image and that it fits perfectly in the profile image circle so that your logo can be seen. If it is blurry or hard to understand, people may skip over it because they are unsure as to what is that.

If you are branding yourself, you may prefer to use an image of your face rather than an image of your logo as personal brands typically seek to inspire brand recognition through facial recognition. Make sure that you use a clear photo that accurately reflects your brand so that it makes sense with the overall image that you are attempting to create. For example, if you are a travel blogger, use a picture of you with a great outdoor backdrop that will help people make the connection.

If you are a real estate agent, have an image of you smiling in front of a home or a blank wall so that you have the emphasis on yourself and your influence as a salesperson. Do not use selfies, poor quality images, or images that seem out of place in this space as this can result in people feeling confused around your brand, which can lead to fewer followers and, therefore, fewer sales. You should be leveraging every single aspect of your page to create one uniform image that accurately reflects your brand image. Make sure that you never leave your profile image empty, as people will not trust or interact with companies that have not yet uploaded profile images. Refrain from communicating with anyone until this has been done, as most people who see profiles without images will assume that these profiles are either scammers or not yet interesting enough to pay attention. The profiles with attractive, clean, and high-quality profile images that look enticing are the ones that end up getting followers, so wait until you have filled this in before engaging with people's content or following anyone's profile.

Important Instagram Settings

Instagram is optimal for businesses, which is why so many micro-brands are using it to connect with their audiences. On Instagram, there are a variety of necessary settings that you should adjust to ensure that your profile is ready to support a growing brand. This way, you can get the most out of the platform. There are four things that you need to do when you launch a branded account that should be done right away. These are switching to a business account (so that you can run paid advertisements), adjusting your privacy settings, turning on two-factor authentication, and changing your story sharing settings.

Switching to a Business Account

Switching your account to a business account is simple. You do so by going to the settings for your account, which can be located at the top right corner of the homepage. See those three lines? Just click that. From there, go to the "Account" option and tap "Switch to Business Account." If you do not already have one, Instagram will help you quickly set up a Facebook page that your Instagram business account will be linked to. This step is necessary, even if you do not plan on using a Facebook page, as it will allow you to engage in certain exclusive business activities on Instagram. Among these include tagging products in your photographs, running paid promotions, and setting an address or location for your business on Instagram if you have one. Once you have switched to having a business account, Instagram will also give you access to crucial analytical information. This information will ensure that you can track your success through monitoring the progress of posts, watching your follower growth, and even get a clear outline as to who your demographic is and whether or not you are effectively reaching the right people through the platform.

This makes the business features on Instagram even more valuable. While a business account is not necessary for running a business on Instagram, if you desire to get any traction and build your business account on Instagram, you will want to have access to all of the exclusive business features that they offer.

Adjusting the Privacy Settings

On Instagram, specific privacy settings can be used to limit who can see your account and what can be seen or done on your account. You are going to want to go in and make sure that any privacy settings which may be turned "on" are turned "off" to ensure that your privacy settings are not hiding any part of your account. Make sure that people can comment on your photos and share your posts, follow you, and message you back through your stories so that people can engage with your profile in as many different ways as possible. Keeping your account private in any way can lead to people not being able to engage with you, which can reduce people's desire to follow you. Remember that one of the main reasons that people are on social media is to build relationships with others. You need to be available for the relationship-building process!

Two-Factor Authentication

Having a two-factor authentication is necessary for anyone who wants to run a business online, as it ensures that people cannot hack your account, steal your followers, and block you from it. Getting your account stolen can also create havoc on your brand image if the hacker's intentions include just that.

Two-Factor authentication will require you to approve of all new logins, either through your phone number or email address. This means that if anyone attempts to log into your account remotely so that they can hack you, they will not be able to get in without your code. You can enable two-factor authentication by going back to your settings menu, tapping "Privacy and Security," and then tapping "two-factor authentication." There, you will be walked through the process of verifying either your phone number or an email address that can be used to make your account more secure. If you do ever receive a request to log in, but you have not attempted to log in on a new browser, it is essential that you immediately change your password on Instagram. If you have received the code, this is proof that someone has identified what your password is and has successfully logged into your account. Of course, they will be stuck in the login process since they do not have your verification code to complete the two-factor authentication login, but this still means that your account has been compromised. By changing your password, you can ensure that no one can somehow hack into your account and begin compromising your business through Instagram.

Chapter 3: Strategy With Instagram

Instagram, like many of today's social media platforms, offers businesses, big and small, the incredible opportunities to reach both massive audiences, as well as a targeted audience to connect with them, engage them, and ultimately convert them into customers. However, the more brands that join Instagram, the bigger the competition, and the harder it is to stand out in a person's feed. Instagram opened up its new ad feature in 2015, utilizing the Facebook advertising system. With this, marketers can now reach a niche segment of the population, which is currently at 800 million users and growing. Instagram ads have become an avenue for brands looking to increase their engagement and, by extension, their profits, to the 500 million active users who use Instagram every day. In this chapter, you will learn the basics of Instagram ads. We will go through the "what" and the "whys" of Instagram ads, so you have a firm foundation to get you started on creating ads, measuring performance, and improving your ad results.

Why Use Instagram Ads?

Since launching its ad platform in 2015, Instagram has driven more than one billion user actions to date. Just last year alone, advertising dollars have doubled, and its advertiser base, which began at only a few thousand, is now at 500,000 advertisers.

In 2016, a survey by Strata found that 63 % of U.S.-based ad agencies included Instagram advertising into their marketing budget for both their own companies and that of their clients, as well. This is a significant jump from the year before, which showed that only 34 % of advertisers chose to include Instagram advertising into their marketing arsenal. This makes Instagram the most popular choice for advertising. It's not only that. About 60 % of Instagram users are under 30. By 2019, agencies estimate that Instagram will make close to 7 billion in profits through worldwide cellphone ad revenue, thus increasing the profit share of their parent company, which is Facebook's global ad revenues.

Five Reasons to Use Instagram Ads

If you have not started exploring Instagram ads and you think it is worth it, here are a few reasons to help you understand its benefits:

1. Instagram has a vast audience growth. 26,965 brands were looked at by TrackMaven across all industries, and they found that brands witnessed a 100 percent median follower growth from 2016 to 2017. This shows that Instagram is among the fastest-growing social media platform to date.

2. Instagram receives a lot of attention from its users. On a daily average basis, users spend a total of 50 minutes on Facebook, Facebook Messenger, and Instagram. In North America alone, an average of one in 5 minutes is spent on browsing Instagram or Facebook.

3. Instagram can generate intent from its users for the ads they run. In 2016, Instagram conducted a study and found that 60 percent of users mentioned that they have learned about a product or service via Instagram. At least 75 percent said they took part in an action, whether it was telling a friend, purchasing a product, visiting a site, or searching for information after they saw something on Instagram.

4. Instagram can target specific audiences for their ads. Instagram and Facebook share the same advertising system, although their algorithms may be slightly different. Both Facebook and Instagram have the most potent targeting ability, which means that

marketers can specify their target audience based on demographics, location, behavior, interests, and search data. You can also target users based on their interactions with other sites and profiles.

5. Instagram can produce desirable results for its corporate and business users. There was another survey conducted by Instagram that looked at over 400 campaigns worldwide in ad recall. The study found that Instagram's ad recall was 2.8 times higher than that of other online advertising channels. The types of ads that Instagram offers are around five in terms of ad formats. These are Photo ads, Video ads, Carousel ads, and Canvas Story ads, among others. All these ads are available for you to use toward your target audience's feeds and stories, enabling a smooth user experience while you browse and explore Instagram. These are also available in your Facebook Ad manager, so marketers can utilize Facebook's user data that enable targeting at a precise level. Let us explore the various ads in the next section of this chapter.

The Different Types of Ads to Use in Instagram

Photo ads can be one of the best ways to tell your story, whether it be your business or your brand. It is, in fact, top-notch visual content with even more people. When it comes to using photos, there is no room for bad, low-resolution images. If you want to stand out and be seen, you need to have a distinctive look and feel for your photos that mirror your brand. You also need it to display your product beautifully and authentically, and these photos need to be consistent with your branding guidelines and look and feel. Photo ads also enable marketers to target a particular age group. With the latest updates on Instagram ads, marketers can also include call-to-action buttons, such as "Apply Now," "Book Now," "Call Now," "Contact Us," "Get Directions," "Learn More," "Get Showtimes," and "Download Video."

Video Ads

These come equally in terms of the most favored content on Instagram. According to data by Instagram, the time spent watching videos is more than 80 %, and videos were posted more than four times in 2017 compared to 2016. The year 2019 is now even a great time for brands to gain on this fantastic way to capture the user's attention. When making videos, you need to make sure that you feature your brand first thing in the video, as it is the best way to get recognized.

Why do this? The answer is so your audience will recall your brand once the video is over. Your video on Instagram should not be longer than 1 minute or 60 seconds simply because the user's attention is not that long to begin with. People want to get to the point fast, and you need to give them an idea of this, at least in the first 5 seconds of the video. A reliable video does not need to be long; 15 seconds will usually be enough. Just like photo ads, there are call-to-action buttons that can be included, as well. These are: Apply Now, Book Now, Call Now, Contact Us, and Download Stories.

Carousel Ads

The unique thing about carousel ads is that it allows users to swipe through a series of videos or images. And there is a call-to-action button that connects them directly to your website or blog. Carousel ads offer brands the uniqueness to tell a story that is longer to their audience, and this will allow them to get into multiple products, share different perspectives, or dive into a single service in a combination of videos or images. Carousel ads work great for exercise and fitness profiles, recipe and food profiles, and even makeup and travel.

Like the other ads, carousel ads can also be targeted to a specific segment if you want to show the versatility of your content or to show various creative assets, such as fashion, food, and design. The call-to-actions that carousel ads support are Apply Now, Book Now, Contact Us, Call Now, and Download Stories.

Stories

These bring a whole new dimension to Instagram ads. Instagram users view Instagram Stories daily; this represents a massive amount of audience that you can reach with it. The only difference with Stories is that it expires after 24 hours. But you can keep them as your profile Highlight if you want to. This is an ideal format to use when you have limited-time offers, promotions, and seasonal discounts you wish to promote. Another great thing about Instagram Stories is that if your account has at least 10K subscribers, you can also add a link to your Stories, so your audience can swipe up when they want to find out more from your website, blog, or YouTube channel. Stories enable brands to go a little crazy by adding face filters, texts, gifs, and effects to create fun and creative promotions. The call-to-action that can be used with your Stories using the swipe-up feature include

Apply Now, Book Now, Contact Us, Call Now (video only), and Download Story.

Facebook Canvas

Facebook Canvas is another immersive video format ad for Instagram Stories specifically optimized for mobile use. It loads quickly for a smoother viewing experience. On Facebook, there are plenty of Canvas templates that make it easy for you to build a Canvas ad that suits your needs for Instagram. Companies can choose one of these ad templates or create their custom Canvas for a unique ad experience. These templates enable you to use a combination of videos and photos to showcase variety. These templates are great if you want to show a range of products and include a campaign video. The supported call-to-action buttons that can be added in canvas ads are Apply Now, Book Now, and Contact Us.

Now that you know the different kinds of ads on Instagram that you can use, you are now ready to explore more about Instagram ads and put these ads into practice.

How to Advertise on Instagram

This is a brief to give you an idea of how advertising on Instagram works. We will explore, at a deeper level, how you can create, build, and publish your ads so that they become successful and worth the money you invest in. Essentially, to create ads on Instagram, all you need to do is connect your Instagram account to your Facebook Business Page manager. This allows you to use the Facebook Ad Manager, where you can create ads that run on both Instagram and Facebook or just one of the accounts. The choice is yours.

What if I do not have a Facebook account? While it is possible to open an Instagram account with a Facebook account (you can easily create your Instagram profile with your email address), you can't create ads without a Facebook account. This is because, to create an ad on Instagram, you would need to connect your Instagram account to your Facebook Business Page to use Facebook's Ad Manager. Besides, it is much easier if you had a Facebook account because you would be able to grow and build your audience on both platforms. But because Facebook and Instagram are connected and if you want to push your brand to your target audience, then having both accounts would make sense for your business.

The Ad Manager lets you build and create ads to run on both Instagram and Facebook, or you can choose to run it on either platform. You can also customize your target audience, make payments, monitor the ad's progress, as well as work on other features on the manager. If you already have a

Facebook Page, here is how you can connect it to your Facebook Ad Manager. First, visit business.facebook.com. Click on Create Account. Enter a name for your business, select the primary Page, and enter your name and work email address. Enter all the necessary details requested on the onboarding flow. Once you are done setting up, you can then link your Instagram account to your Business profile.

Here is how you can do it: Go to your Business Manager. Look on the left side of the Page for Business Settings. Click on it and click again on Instagram Accounts.

- Click Create New Instagram Account.

- Add your username and password, then click Next.

- To authorize one or more of your ad accounts to use the Instagram Account, check the box next to each ad account and click Save Changes.

If you are unsure whether Instagram ads would benefit your business, the best thing you can do at the end of this book is to give it a try anyway and see how your customers respond to your ads. Having an online account and social media platform for your business means that you have customers looking at you on the Internet. Furthermore, this means that they are already interacting with other brands and ads on social media. So, whether you are a B2C or a B2B business,

Instagram advertising will benefit your brand, as long as you have customers online. Getting started with Instagram marketing and advertising is secure, and this book will help you make it a smooth-sailing process. All you have to do right now is link your Facebook Business Manager. And you are already on the right path.

With an impressive 95 million daily posts (according to Hootsuite) and 25 million registered business profiles (also from Hootsuite) and counting, Instagram advertising is poised to take over the world. This photo-sharing and video-sharing social media platform has dramatically changed the marketing game for businesses, opening up a world of possibilities and new ways for businesses to connect with their clientele. Companies have been able to dramatically connect with their audiences, engage with their target demographics, and drive sales like never before. This is all thanks to the power of social media. About 80 % of Instagrammers (according to Hootsuite) on the platform are actively following at least one business profile.

Define Your Goals

This social media platform is highly competitive, but this also provides a unique opportunity for businesses to engage with their followers. How does a brand stand out successfully? The answer is by doing more than publishing just pretty pictures and the occasional video. For a brand to call its advertising efforts successful, it must develop a well-defined, creative, and detailed advertising strategy. This can only be done if a brand has a clearly defined set of advertising goals that can produce measurable results. Let us start by defining your goals. A lot of businesses, especially the new ones, sometimes struggle with this aspect. Defining goals is not as easy as it may seem. It is not just about saying our goal is to have as many followers as possible because a goal needs to be specific. The more detail you are, the better your marketing and advertising strategy will be. If you are struggling to figure out how to get started in defining your advertising goals, try starting with these questions:

- Why did you decide to use Instagram for your business?

- How do you believe this platform will help with achieving your overall marketing and business goals?

- What is the specific advertising budget you will be able to commit to this platform?

- How much time can you commit to advertising on this platform daily?

- In what way is Instagram different compared to your other social media platforms?

- What does success mean to you?

What are you primarily using this platform for? Do you want to connect with your target demographic better? Or do you aim to build greater brand awareness? To develop higher brand loyalty, perhaps? Is this platform a way in which you offer customer service?

What sort of content do you intend to advertise? Is that content focused on educating your target audience about your business? There could be a long list of reasons and rationales for using Instagram and why you think this method of advertising is going to best help your business meet its goals. As long as you are able to define each reason in detail clearly, you are off to a good start. The advertising goals that you set will have a massive influence on the kind of metrics that you will use to track the success of your efforts, so that is something you might want to keep in mind. Confused? Let us clear that up for you real quick. Let us say you were using Instagram as a platform to engage with your audience as one of your advertising goals, then the metrics you would be using to track that success would be engagement metrics. Engagement metrics involves analyzing the number of comments, likes, and shares that a post receives.

So, how do you start defining your goals? Once you have sorted out your reasons (specific reasons) for choosing this platform, you are now ready to move onto phase two of the goal-setting process.

To start setting active advertising goals, here are the things that you would need to do:

- Define your target audience. Who are you aiming to target through this platform? If you have already got a good idea of the demographic you are going after, an excellent strategy to employ would be to start customer profiling. This will give you a better sense of what kind of content your target is after, the sort of hashtags they use, and even what communities they belong to on Instagram. Think of this stage as your due diligence. The more information and details you can gather to create your customer persona, the more definitive your advertising strategy will be.

- Define your objectives. The first question you should ask is, "What does your business hope to achieve by advertising on Instagram?" What can you do on Instagram that you cannot compete with other social media platforms? How does this platform integrate with your other social media platforms and marketing strategy? Ideally, your objectives should try to increase brand awareness among your target audience, showcase your brand and company culture, shine the spotlight on your products and services (and why they are different), increase audience engagement, and inspire brand loyalty. Your objectives should also seek to build a more engaged community, connect your brand with both audiences and influencers, increase sales by driving traffic to your site, and more. Your objectives will be the ones to help you navigate and decide on the next course of action.

- Have clear guidelines for your team. If there is a team of people involved in helping you run your Instagram advertising efforts, it will help if everyone was clear on what they are responsible for. Guidelines help to ensure that everyone is working in the right direction toward achieving your advertising goals.

- Conduct an Instagram audit. This step helps you constructively observe your profile. It is time to take a good, hard, critical look at it. An audit must be done to see if your profile is meeting your business needs, and if it is not, you should know what can be done about it. This step gives you a sense of where you should be focusing your advertising efforts on. Your audit needs to tie in tightly with your goals because every measure that you take should be leading you one step toward achieving the goals that you have set for your brand.

Examples of Advertising Goals and Objectives

Throughout your time on Instagram, your business goals will shift and change according to your business needs. As you accomplish one goal, a new purpose could come in its place, and the key to successful advertising on Instagram is learning how to identify which goals will be complemented by the right kind of advertising objectives. Here are some examples to give you an idea of how to get started.

- Building Brand Awareness (Goal): To achieve this goal, the accompanying advertising increases your reach and engagement by boosting your posts. For example, you could create a business ad that is aimed at the people closest to your business vicinity and try to reach as many people as possible. Creating ads that help your audience understand the value of your brand is an excellent way to start increasing brand awareness, especially among new customers.

- Target Potential Customers (Goal): Suitable advertising objectives to help you achieve this goal could include increasing website conversion and lead generation by collecting relevant information from individuals (newsletters, new signups, etc.). Objectives could also include how to raise engagement by creating the right kind of ads to help market your events and how to communicate those ads effectively to your target audience group.

- Increasing Sales (Goal). Advertising goals that can help you achieve this include creating ads with coupons, one-time offers, or special discounts to increase engagement. Encourage existing Instagrammers to get in touch with you through your app (to encourage more app downloads and participation), creating ads that spark conversation and help your brand better communicate with your audience.

Tips to Run Your Own Successful Instagram Audit

Conducting an audit is so important because it helps you consistently check that your strategy and goals are on track the way that they should be. Take the review as an opportunity to help you reassess your business and your advertising goals. After all, you want to make sure that all that blood, sweat, tears, and countless hours that you are spending on your branding is all worth it in the end and helps your business's bottom line.

Here's how you can run an audit of your Instagram.

- Are your KPIs and goals on track? How are you going with your advertising and marketing goals so far? Do your current business goals line up with your advertising goals? Are they working to complement each other? The purposes do not necessarily have to be the same, but they do need to work together to support your overall business goals directly.

- What are your business voice and branding like? Does your Instagram have a look, sound, and feel to it that is consistent? Is your branding showing clearly on your profile? Does your Instagram look and feel like the rest of your social media channels? What you are aiming for is for an Instagrammer to be able to come to your profile, take a quick look, and almost instantly be able to get a feel of what your brand is like and what you offer.

- How are your aesthetics and content shaping up? Content must be consistent. Consistency of your brand's story is the key to advertising success on Instagram. Your audience must know that you are still active and that your business is still active. If your profile is only updated once a week or once every other week, your followers are going to quickly lose interest because nothing is exciting or interesting enough to remind them that your business is here, that it still exists.

Content and Hashtags

Curate and plan your profile's content carefully, and you will see how quickly it can transform from ordinary to incredible. How well are you engaging with your followers? Are you having the right amount of two-way conversation with your audience the way that you should be? Do your followers feel like your brand genuinely cares for its customers? Do you respond within a reasonable amount of time to the direct messages or comments that you receive on your profile? If you are not doing any of this, your advertising efforts might as well be a waste. It is never going to be as effective as you want it to be without the right kind of audience engagement. No comment should be left unanswered, and no direct message should be left without answering it. Every time someone on Instagram takes the time or effort to either mention or contact you, reciprocate it. No exceptions.

Are you using hashtags? Love them or hate them, hashtags are here to stay. A post with a hashtag included gets an average of 12.6 % more engagement than a position that comes without a hashtag. Which one do you want to be? The answer is the former. The questions you need to ask yourself are whether your business is using the relevant hashtags (are they related to your audience). Are you using a hashtag that is unique to your brand and used consistently, or are your hashtags too generic, which is causing your business to get lost in a sea of thousands of other posts with similar hashtags?

Chapter 4: Organic Traffic and Growing Your Page

Perhaps the essential part of being on Instagram is growing your following so that you can have an audience to market to. You have contributed to your ability to grow your following and increase your outreach. There are still several things that you can do to improve your Instagram account. Start seeing higher engagement rates. In this chapter, you are going to discover what it takes to grow your following and start generating success through your Instagram account.

Encouraging Engagement on Your Page

The first thing that you can do to start increasing your audience is to encourage people to engage with you on your page. Remember, the Instagram algorithm favors it when people engage on other users' pages, which means that if you can get your followers to start engaging with you, then that would be good. You can feel confident that they are going to start seeing more of your content, too. You can encourage engagement in two different ways: engaging with others and asking for engagement from your followers.

When you engage with the people who follow you regularly, they feel more inclined to engage with your posts because they begin to feel the development of a relationship. The back-and-forth support between you and your audience becomes a regular part of your relationship. When you go out of your way to go through your follower list and start engaging with people, you actually "break the ice" between yourself and them. This makes them feel more comfortable and engaged with you and your brand. You can do this by regularly going through your list of followers and tapping on random accounts and engaging with their content. Leaving a few heartfelt comments and liking some of their recent posts is an excellent opportunity to start engaging with people. This also inspires them to like back your content the next time they see your content. As you post, you can also ask for engagement by saying things like, "We love summer! Do you?" This encourages people to speak up. You can also increase engagement by writing captions that say things, like, "Comment with your favorite _____!" or "Tag a friend who would love this, too!"

Asking your followers to engage with your content in this way helps them break their thought process from mindless scrolling. Instead, you help them choose to participate in your content. Another great way to encourage engagement is to run giveaways on your page. This allows you to set rules that require individuals to engage with your post to enter the giveaway. Often, companies will decide on what they want to give away. Then they will set the requirements for individuals. For example, "Follow us, tag a friend, and share this post to your stories to enter in the giveaway!" Then, they will leave the giveaway for a certain period, allowing them to experience plenty of engagement from their followers. This type of behavior drives up engagement on that one post, but it will also support you in driving up engagement on the rest of your posts as well. You do not want to be engaging in too many giveaways, however. Two to four giveaways per year are plenty, and this is a great way to get involved with more followers.

Regularly Updating Your Following List

The people and the hashtags whom you follow are the ones that populate your main home screen, which allows you to see images that everyone you are following shares posts regularly. You want to ensure that you are regularly updating your following list so that you are only seeing people who reflect those that are actually associated with your branding or positioning. You might feel inspired to follow personal interests on Instagram, but this is typically best reserved for private personal accounts instead of business accounts. You want to ensure that your time spent scrolling through your followed accounts is spent investing in the growth of your business so that this becomes productive in the long run.

You can update your following list by going through the people you follow and unfollowing anyone who does not make sense to your brand. This way, you are not seeing content that is entirely irrelevant to you or following accounts that are unlikely to provide you with any return on your engagement. You can only support or unfollow up to 60 accounts in an hour, so take your time with this, and do it regularly so that you do not have many changes to make to your account. It would help if you were doing this every week so that you are staying relevant in your industry and seeing the latest trends and people who are coming up. Once you have unfollowed everyone who is not connected to you, you can start going to your most popular hashtags. See if there are any new hashtags or followers for you to pay attention to through the top posts in these searches. This way, you can start following new users who may support you in bringing more attention to your account each time you engage with their content or interact with them.

In addition, when you follow new hashtags that are trending in your niche, you can keep tabs on what's hot. You can also go ahead and start using those hashtags on your photographs so that you can stay relevant, as well. This type of research creates two powerful opportunities for growth in one move, so it is worthy of your regular attention and time!

Saying the Right Thing at the Right Time

On Instagram, you need to make sure that you are answering the right thing at the right time. By posting the right content at the right time, you can ensure that you stay relevant and that your content relates to what your audience is going through or thinking about. Your audience will be likely paying attention to and engaging with your content. The easiest way to say the right thing at the right time on Instagram is by following your audience.

Paying Attention to the Trends

Pay attention to the latest trends, concerns, and issues. That may be arising that people are paying attention to. For example, if you are in the blogging industry and you blog about current events concerning famous people, you would want to stay up-to-date on all of the latest trends and gossip. You would also want to blog about them as soon as they reach your eyes. The same would go for any industry that you are in. The moment you see a trend or topic waving through your industry, you need to be prepared to get on board with it, customize how you share it according to your unique brand,

and offer it as soon as possible. In addition to following unexpected trends that arise in your industry, you also need to be following expected trends like holidays or scheduled events that are relevant to your audience. For example, if you are in the fashion industry, you should be paying attention to popular fashion events like Fashion Week and the Victoria Secret Fashion Show. If you are in the tech industry, you should be paying attention to the latest device launches and information regarding events that are big in the tech industry, like the annual E3 event.

These types of events occur consistently, and they are extremely helpful in allowing you to stay relevant in your industry. Pay attention to the information being released by those who drive the industry like influencers and developers. It is important that you avoid talking about things out of season or out of turn, as sharing information too long after the event occurred can result in coming across as irrelevant or outdated. Typically, people who see companies sharing outdated information will believe that this company is not paying attention and does not care enough to stay in the loop with what is going on in their industry. As a result, people will not follow you. Remember, we live in the digital age where information can become available fast, and trends can rise and fall even more quickly. It would help if you were ready to get into these trends and start creating your brand's name in the heat of the moment, not after the trend or information has already started declining in popularity.

If you find that staying with the trends is harder than it looks, try finding three to four people or blogs. Follow those who are always quick to jump into new trends, and pay attention to these individuals or resources. This way, you are not overwhelming yourself by trying to follow too many people at once, becoming lost in what is relevant, what is a trend, and what is entirely irrelevant to you and your audience.

Targeting Your Audience Through Your Words

You now know that Instagram's biggest way to target audiences is through hashtags. This is how you can reach new audience members and start growing your audience fast. However, there is another verbal element that comes into play when it comes to creating an impact through your captions and writing. This is by having words in your captions that resonate with your audience.

You do not want to be using words that do not make sense to your audience or that sound completely irrelevant or outdated. This will lead to your audience becoming disinterested in reading what you have to say and struggling to actually "follow" what you are trying to tell them.

The best way to speak like your audience is to pay attention to what they care about by following them back and listening to how they are speaking. Regularly scroll through your feed and read what the people you follow are saying so that you can get a feel for what their language is like, how they tone their messages, and if there are any unique slang words, phrases, or acronyms that they are using to connect with their audiences. The more you read your niche's captions and comments, the more you are going to become familiar with how they are speaking, what they are saying, and what they are reading. This way, you can begin emulating their language through your posts and saying things in a way that makes sense to your audience.

When you do start emulating your audience, there are a few things that you will need to refrain from doing to avoid having your audience tune out from what you are saying. One thing to remember is that you need to prevent emulating your audience to the point that you lose your authenticity because you sound like you are identical to those whom they are already reading. Make sure that you pay attention to your brand's voice and your mission statement and adapt the industry's language to meet your tone and not the other way around. If your mood seems too off-base for your industry, you can consider casually adjusting it slightly to fit the industry's needs more. But do not begin changing your approach too frequently, or you will come across as fake and untrustworthy. The second thing that you need to avoid doing is creating messages that are filled with industry jargon that your general following is unlikely to understand.

If you attempt to use industry jargon that is commonly used between those who sell products and services in the industry, but that is unlikely to be recognizable by those who purchase in or follow the industry, you may lose your following solely because they do not understand you. You do not want to be creating gaps and confusion in your marketing by using language that your audience does not know because this can make it unnecessarily challenging for people to follow you and support your business. Keep it simple, speak in a way that your audience will understand, and adapt the industry language to suit your brand's message and purpose.

Leveraging Instagram Stories

Instagram Stories are a powerful tool that can be used not only to nurture your existing following but also to attract new followers for your business. When you use your Instagram stories correctly, you can create a significant influx of engagement from your followers and add a personal opportunity to connect with your brand. It also allows you to create a more interactive page overall. On Instagram, people love interacting with the brands that they love and consuming as much of their content as they can, and Instagram offers plenty of ways for followers to do just that. As you upload stories throughout the day, you create the opportunity for your followers to feel like you are genuinely thinking about them throughout the day, which establishes a connection of care and compassion between you and your followers. Not only will this help you maintain your existing followers, but it will also help new or potential followers see how interactive and intimate you are with your following, which leads to them wanting to be a part of your audience as well!

The reason that stories work is simple. People are nosy, and they like to know the insider's information. This is not a bad thing either, but rather just a simple human experience where we all desire to be a part of something bigger than ourselves. And we want to connect with those around us to become a part of that "something bigger." You can position yourself as the facilitator of that "something bigger" by turning your brand into an experience that people can enjoy and an entity that they can share an intimate and compassionate relationship with. Stories give you a great option to do that because every picture or short clip you share reflects a part of your personal behind-the-scenes experiences. You can also curate your story feed to offer an even more exclusive and intimate feel by purposefully sharing things that will allow others to feel like they are genuinely connected with you through your feed.

The key to making your stories intimate and leveraging them to attract new followers and maintain your existing ones is to make sure that the content you share in your stories is exclusive and unlike anything that you are sharing anywhere else. Be very intentional in sharing things that are more personal and "private" than what you would share on IGTV or on your feed itself because this way, people feel like they truly are getting that private insight into your brand. Instagram stories are already somewhat exclusive because, after 24 hours, they are gone and cannot be viewed again. You can play up that exclusivity thing by sharing the right content, mentioning things that you shared previously that new followers can no longer see, and even by suggesting outright that your story feed is exclusive. Say things like, "Keep your eyes on my stories because I will be announcing an exclusive offer here first... Get it three days earlier just by watching the story!" or something similar to this. Another way that you can leverage Instagram Stories is by making story highlights which can enable your new followers to see exclusive tidbits of your previous stories.

So, if you are someone who regularly travels, and you often share intimate travel experiences with people, such as the restaurants you dine at or the people you meet, you might consider sharing these in your stories. Then, you can create highlights of certain moments from your travels that were most exciting or interesting so that your new audience can glance back through your stories and start feeling more intimately connected with you right away. Leveraging your highlight reels in this way is a great opportunity to show your new followers what to expect, give them that feeling of having known you and your brand for a long time already, and increase their interest in you right from the start.

Using IGTV to Increase Your Following

IGTV is a great way to increase your following. These videos stay in place for as long as you leave them up, which means that followers can look back through your IGTV channel and watch stuff that you put up days, weeks, months, or even years ago once it has been around long enough. You can leverage IGTV to create new followers by creating excellent IGTV videos and then promoting them elsewhere on the net so that people are more likely to click over to your channel and watch. Once they see your video and the quality of the content you create, they can choose to follow your page to get more if they decide that they like you. The big opportunity with IGTV is that you can promote your IGTV channel just like you would a YouTube channel or any other free video content on the net.

By creating great content and then sharing it around the net, you can encourage individuals to go over to your Instagram to be able actually to see the video. This means that you can funnel people from Facebook, Twitter, Snapchat, email, and any other social media platform to Instagram so that they can catch your free content and learn from it. To make your content accessible, you need to make sure that the IGTV videos you make are worthy of receiving views. In other words, you need to create high-quality and engaging content. Your audience wants to pay attention so that when you share it with other platforms. They are more likely to click through your channel and watch the content that you created. The best way to create valuable content is to offer entertainment, insight, or guidance concerning your industry so that your audience is more likely to pay attention to it and watch it. For example, if you are an astrologer, you can create daily videos offering the astrological forecast for the day. If you are a sports announcer, you can create a daily video that highlights the most memorable sports moment of the week or the latest stats of famous players or teams based on the sport that you announce. If you are an educator of sorts, you can create a simple ten-minute or less tutorial on how your audience can do something for themselves that ties with your industry or your area of expertise.

By creating valuable content like this, you make it easier for your audience to understand why and how they are gaining value from your IGTV, which means that you will have an easier time promoting it and getting traction from that offer. Once you have created fantastic content, make sure that you leverage it in every way that you possibly can. Share it across all of your other social media platforms, talk about it in your stories, write about it in your latest post, and make sure that you save it for a future date. If you create timeless content, you can always use it as a reference to older videos when a few weeks or months have passed so that you can use them as a marketing opportunity all over again. For example, if you are a make-up artist and you did a specific tutorial, you can promote the video as soon as you make it, and then refer back to it if you notice someone famous wore a similar look in a recent event. This is an excellent opportunity to create one piece of content that has maximum impact, meaning that you can gain even more followers just from one excellent time investment. When it comes to marketing, that is really what it is all about!

Leveraging Influencers the Right Way

Brands and influencers go hand-in-hand, as they are both responsible for helping to generate success for the other. If you are not yet aware, influencers are individuals who build a trusted following in a particular industry and then advertise for industry-specific brands to their existing audience.

A great example of an influencer, or a family of influencers rather, would be the Kardashian-Jenner-West family, who is known for becoming and staying famous for the reason that most people cannot understand. This is because this particular family blew up around the same time that influencers were becoming a thing, and they leveraged their star power to begin making brand deals and endorsing companies. At this point, most individuals in the family have their businesses, although they still make money by supporting other products and marketing these products to their respective audiences. Influencers are solely focused on generating a massive following of people who like and trust them in a specific industry that interests them the most and then marketing to their audience for the products and companies that they want. As a brand, you can leverage influencers from your industry by having them test out your products or services and market them to their audience. Since their audience is already established and trusting in the influencer, you can trust that once the influencer has tried and endorsed your products, your recognition and sales will increase as well. The key here is making sure that you are working with influencers correctly. On Instagram, there is an unfortunate trend of companies that are attempting to work together with influencers and who are going about it in the wrong way, which results in losing a lot of money in this area of potential growth.

These companies, not knowing that they are making such drastic mistakes, find themselves attempting to work together with low-quality influencers or individuals who are not yet authentic influencers, which means they are not making a massive impact. Rather than having their products in the hands of people who can make a difference, they are attempting to get their products into the hands of people who do not, indeed, have an impact on their target audience. Typically, they will do so by encouraging potential "influencers" to buy their products and then make money anytime they purchase the products. In the end, the most significant way that the company is making money is by having the would-be influencers buying products and not by marketing the products to their target audience. When companies use this method, they end up looking spammy and careless, which results in them being seen as low-rate companies that are not worthy of being trusted or invested in. In the long run, this leads to an unsustainable practice, which can also lead to the premature demise of a company that could have otherwise succeeded in the online space. If you want to leverage influencers, you need to make sure that you are getting your products or services into the hands of people who can have an impact on your growth because they are already so connected with your target audience. Although you may lose some money by giving products away for free to these influencers, you will ultimately end up gaining cash because they will drive a lot of traffic to your page and your website. To create this positive and sufficient momentum in your business, you need to ensure that you are plugging into deals with the right influencers. Be very intentional and cautious about whom you offer your products or services to, and make sure that every single influencer you work together with can genuinely make a positive impact on your business.

Also, approach them professionally through their messages or email if they provide one and not through their comment's section on their photographs as this also comes across as unprofessional and spammy. If you want your company to look poised, respectful, and worthy of trusting and investing in, you need to make these long-term investments properly.

Increasing Your Posting Visibility

When you are posting on Instagram, you want to make sure that your posts are getting seen so that you can maximize your visibility, engagement, and traction overall. Instagram's algorithm favors individuals who get a lot of traction on their posts quickly and will ensure that even more people see these posts by placing it in more favorable viewing spots. If you want to gain these more favorable viewing spots, there are a few things that you can do to maximize your posting visibility and earn more followers overall. As you already know, a posting schedule is a valuable way to start increasing your posting visibility. It enables you to be put at the top of search feeds around the same time that your audience would be looking for your types of posts.

You can also ensure that you are engaging with other people before you post so that you appear higher in their newsfeed with your new posts as well. Another way that you can increase your posting visibility is by choosing hashtags that are only used 300,000 times or less overall, as these make it easier for you to be posted in the "top posts" section of the hashtag. Most people will browse these posts first, so being seen in this section ensures that you are going to be seen more frequently by people in your target audience. Another way that you can increase visibility is by creating high-quality posts and posting them consistently between one and three times per day. The more you post, the more you will be seen, and if your content quality is high, people are going to continue following you and paying attention to your page. When you post content, follow all of the strategies to ensure that you are creating content that people want to pay attention to and engage with. Never post a photograph that is too low in quality, as this will result in you having fewer followers or people unfollowing you because they may think that your standards are going down. You may notice that more significant influencers and brands do occasionally post lower quality photographs, and the reason is that they can get away with this easily. They have a huge following already, and they are unlikely to be impacted by one image. You, however, can be affected early on in a massive way. You want to avoid having people think that you are, in any way, posting low-quality content as this can lead to the loss of credibility and, eventually, followers. Lastly, if you want to maximize your visibility, make sure that you are engaging specifically with the people who are following you. These are the individuals who already see you in their newsfeeds, which means that they are the ones who will be most likely to engage with you quickly when you post new content. If you can get your real following to join soon, it will be easier for new followers to find you in their discover pages or on the top post tabs, which makes it more likely for you to be identified and followed by your target audience.

Engaging With Your Followers

This is a great way to maintain your existing following, but it is also a great way to discover new people who will want to follow you. Think of it this way. Your current following is already a part of your target audience, which means that they likely connect with people who are a part of your target audience by going to your followers' pages and connecting with them through their content. You establish a greater connection with your following, which is also increasing your ability to be found by their followers and friends. When their audience sees you commenting on their posts, if they are interested in what your brand has to offer, they may then click through your page and locate you. So, not only will this improve the way the algorithm works in your favor, but it will also add another avenue for people to discover you on Instagram. Another way that you can leverage your existing following to gain more followers is to go to your followers' pages and click onto pictures that are relevant to your industry. For example, if you sell bikes and your followers post an image of the mountain biking on a cross-country trail, this would be relevant to your industry. You can then look at the list of everyone who has liked this picture and begin engaging with these individuals by going to their pages, liking their content, commenting on a couple of images of theirs, and then following that individual.

This shows genuine interest, helps you stand out to that individual, and increases their chances of following you back. Of course, Instagram only allows 60 new follows or unfollows per hour, so make sure that you leverage this tool carefully to avoid being seen as spammy or overwhelming to the algorithm or your audience. Once these new individuals follow you, your process of going through your followers and engaging with their content will further support you in maintaining and building your following because it makes it clear that you care. If you engage with someone to earn their following and then never engage with them again, people will start to see your brand as superficial, which can lead them to unfollow you or no longer engage with your content. Keep yourself genuine and connected as much as you reasonably can so that you are always building better relationships with your existing audience and new relationships with your potential audience. Lastly, anytime your audience connects with you by commenting on your pictures, replying to your stories, or messaging you, make sure that you engage with that individual. This shows that you genuinely care about them and what they have to say, and it creates a positive relationship between you and that individual. Take some time out of your day each day to respond to all of these forms of engagement to make sure that you are investing in building a meaningful audience. On Instagram, which revolves around its social experience, a little bit of returned engagement can go a long way when it comes to building lifetime fans and relationships with your audience.

Analyzing Your Results to Increase Your Growth

Finally, you need to make sure that you are analyzing your results on Instagram to encourage higher growth on the platform! You can analyze your results either through the in-app analytics provided through Instagram itself or through a third-party application if you choose to use one of those. You can do this; however, you feel most confident, as long as you are regularly checking in to see how your content is performing. By periodically checking in, you can ensure that you can track trends in what your audience likes the most, what content gets the best engagement, and what earns the most likes on your page. As you monitor these trends, it becomes easier for you to understand what types of pictures, content, and offerings your audience likes the most, which means all you need to do is start creating more of that type of content for your page. Your analytics are not only going to support you in discovering what kind of content you need to be creating for your page, but it will also help you determine what you should be creating and offering more for your audience. These numbers will tell you exactly what products or services your audience enjoys the most and what they are buying the most, which allows you to begin offering the same types of products or services. If your business is solely on Instagram, you can create offerings that are specific to your Instagram audience and focus on expanding in the area that your Instagram audience seems to support. If your business exists on several platforms, then you can pay attention to your analytics across all platforms and incorporate this into all of your future offers.

If you find that the analytics vary from platform to platform, consider creating a variety of offers and then selling the offers that sell best on each platform exclusively on that platform. So, if you are a computer technician, and you find that Instagram users seem to be more interested in purchasing tech products and accessories from you and Facebook, individuals seem to be more interested in buying your actual services. You can market, respectively. Any time you have a new product available, emphasize your marketing around that product on Instagram and market only slightly on Facebook. Then, whenever you have a service to offer, place emphasis on your marketing for that new service on Facebook, and only refer to it a few times on Instagram. This way, both audiences know that there is more to your business than what you are sharing exclusively on that platform. Still, you are not bombarding either audience with content that they do not typically pay attention to.

The last part of your analytics that you need to pay attention to ensure efficient growth is how your audience on Instagram is relating to your actual target audience. On Instagram, a few accidental mistakes can lead to your audience being entirely off the target, which can lead to you having a tremendous following that is filled with people who are not interested in purchasing anything from you or your company. If you notice that your target audience and your Instagram audience are wholly misaligned or that your Instagram audience seems to engage with your content but never actually purchases anything, you need to start addressing your strategy. You want to make sure that you are putting your emphasis on the parts of your audience that are going to support your conversion ratios by becoming paying clients; otherwise, your time spent on Instagram will be pointless. If you do find that you do not have the impact that you desire, go back to the beginning of this book and start reviewing the chapters where we discuss carving out your niche and finding your audience on Instagram. Refreshing yourself on this information and moving forward with a renewed perspective can support you and connect with the people that you mean to communicate with.

Chapter 5: How to Sell on Your Page

Selling on Instagram takes place over three simple steps: creating sales funnels, marketing to the people who are most likely to pay you, and using display ads to reach those people effectively. In this chapter, we are going to explore these three selling opportunities and how you can leverage them to maximize your conversions through the Instagram platform. While there are many ways to word your sales copy and many areas to post to on Instagram, there are generally three ways that will allow you to find followers who want to pay for your products. Sales funnels are the first one, and they are used to drive people around your profile in a systematic way that ultimately results in them clicking on your link and purchasing products. These are the easiest ones to create, but they do take some practice, as it can be challenging to know how to smoothly drive people around your profile through your stories, posts, and IGTV videos. The second way that you can sell on Instagram is by drawing people into your actual storefront if you have one through local marketing.

The rest of this book has been dedicated to locating global clients, so we are going to put emphasis solely on attracting local clients if you are running a brick and mortar business in your city. Finally, displaying ads is another great way to sell since ads make it clear that there is something for sale in the first place. You can use display ads as either posts or stories, depending on what your budget is and where you feel you are going to get the most traction from your ads.

Creating Sales Funnels on Instagram

Since Instagram offers plenty of opportunities to connect with your followers, it is easy for you to build Instagram into your sales funnel and start creating a higher conversion ratio through your account. Making your Instagram sales funnel will take some planning because you need to ensure that every channel on the platform is driving people through a "funnel" until they ultimately land on your website and find your products so that they can begin shopping with you. There are two different ways where you can drive people into your website: directly or indirectly. Directly driving people to your site means that you make one post, and it immediately sends people through to your website so that they can start shopping with your brand.

You do this anytime you make a post that encourages people to go to the link in your bio. Start shopping for the product or service that you were talking about in your post. You can also have the same impact by sending people to your link through your stories or your IGTV channel. As long as you are directly asking someone to go to your link, you are directly channeling them through your funnel. This means that indirect conduits will have a direct element since, at some point, you are going to need to bounce people from your Instagram profile to your website. Indirect sales funnels are a great way to provide your audience with plenty of information before they leave your page to check out your site as you have directed them to. Since you are driving them through two or three posts, you can provide plenty of diverse insight and information on your product, service, or brand before they ultimately land on your website. There are many different ways that you can drive people around your Instagram profile, depending on what it is that you are trying to accomplish and what type of content you have to offer. For example, you can encourage someone watching your story to go check out your post, and then, when they check out the post, you can have a piece written that helps them to check out your latest IGTV video, and then that video can lead people to your website. You can also have one post that directs people to your site and then use your stories, IGTV, and live video feed to drive everyone over to that story first, where they read your content before then clicking over to your website.

How you choose to funnel people through your page and to your website is up to you, though you should always be doing this or working toward building a funnel to ensure that you are directing people over to where they can pay for your products or services. That being said, refrain from making every single post, story, and video according to your marketing needs or funneling people around because people will quickly catch what you are doing, and they will stop following you. Some of your posts should be solely based on attracting new audience members to your profile through valuable content, interesting information, high-quality images, and relationship-building strategies like those outlined previously in this book. Of course, if you are building a sales funnel on your Instagram profile, it is only natural that you include that sales funnel on your website, too. When people land on your website, they should be very clearly drawn through your site to learn more about who you are and what you have to offer before landing on a page where they can look at your products or services. This way, they already know that they like your brand, and they want to shop with you before they even land on your sales page.

You should also have an e-mail capture popup appear on your website so that you can start capturing people's emails and building an email newsletter into your funnel. Remember that some people will need to land on your website several times before they pay for your products or services. You are going to need to continually funnel people over to your website and make your offers known so that people can continually land on your website and then make the decision to go ahead and purchase from you. Believe it or not, the more people land on your site, the more connected they feel to you, so even if they do not buy right away, they will remember their previous visits to your website and will begin to feel encouraged to shop with you the more they visit.

Local Marketing Strategies

Most of the strategies that we have been using to achieve new prospect clients are relatively broad and work great if you are running a global or remote business where the location of your clients is not entirely necessary. However, if you are running a local business, you are going to want to approach your marketing slightly differently so that you can reach your target audience in your local area. The way that you target your local market is simple, though it will require some intention and practice on your behalf to make sure that you are reaching the people that you are meant to achieve. The first thing that you should be doing is looking up local hashtags, especially ones that are explicitly related to your industry. For example, if you are a candle maker, you can use hashtags like "#newyorkcandles" or "#calgarycandles," which are unique to your local area. You can also start using hashtags that are specific to entrepreneurs or certain relevant hobbies in your local area. So when you take pictures, you can use these hashtags and connect with other people in your area who would also be interested in what you have to offer.

By using local hashtags in this way, you can ensure that you are reaching people who are close to you and accessing the local market, which will likely be more relevant to your target audience. Another way that you can market to your local audience is in person using strategies to get the people you meet in person on your Instagram account since you are likely using other in-person outreach methods to connect with your local audience. You can use this as an opportunity to have people follow you on Instagram.

They are then using Instagram to keep them up-to-date on your latest offers, sales, and new products or services. Many brands will do this by informing people about their

Instagram by word of mouth, including their Instagram handle on their business cards, and by putting their Instagram handle somewhere in their physical shop so that people can find it and see it. A particularly unique way that people are marketing in-person is by offering a photo op in their store where people can take pictures. In the photo op, they will generally include their store name and a unique hashtag that people can use to tag the store and their unique hashtag in their photograph, which not only connects the local audience with the brand but also creates free marketing.

Another similar practice that has been used in coffee shops and cafés is having the Instagram logo drawn on the coffee board with the company's handle written next to it and a live tracker of how many followers the company has. Every time someone new follows them, they increase the number on the board so that they can share their growth with their audience right there in the store. Ideally, you should be using as many different strategies as you can to drive your online audience to your in-person store, and your in-person store to your online platforms. The more you can connect with people both online and offline, the more relevant you stay in their lives, and therefore, the more likely you are to gain sales through your Instagram marketing strategies.

Designing Display Ads

Another way that you can drive up sales from Instagram is by using display ads, which can be featured either in newsfeeds or story feeds, depending on what type of ad you choose to pay for. You can use one or the other, or ideally, you can use both on your platform so that you are reaching as many people as you can, based on their preferred method of consuming content on Instagram. Should you have followers that prefer to consume content both through their feeds and their stories, they will come across your ads twice as often, which means that they will be twice as likely to click through and see what you have to offer. There are three different types of display ads that you can provide on Instagram: videos, static images, and carousel images. Carousel images will not work on Instagram story ads, so you will need to choose a different method of advertising if you are going to be advertising through Instagram stories. Each ad has its unique benefits, though the theme is that the more you get your brand in front of your audience, the more likely they are to click through and check out your website or follow you.

Additionally, your display ads will target more than just your existing audience, which means that you have an additional channel working for you to help you bring in new followers and customers through Instagram. You can set up your

Instagram advertisements by going to your Facebook account and opening up an ads management account. Then, you can go ahead and tap "Create Ad" on the left side of the screen and follow the prompts provided to you. Facebook's ads manager will ask you what your goals are with your advertisement, what you want the people who see your ad to do, and how you want to design the ad. You can then create it and choose which platforms you want it to run on, how, for how long, and with what budget. You will also determine who you want to see the ad based on their demographics, interests, and whether or not they are already following you. Once you have set in these parameters, all you have to do is publish the ad, and it will begin showing up on all the areas where you said it would.

When it comes to displaying advertisements, you must use high-quality images. This is very important for what you are advertising so that your audience immediately knows what you are sharing with them. You also need to use a caption that is direct, engaging, and interesting. Make sure that you give these posts your all so that you are creating something worthy of people stopping and paying attention to what it is that you are advertising for them. If you are not tech-savvy, or you find yourself struggling to make compelling images for advertisements, you might consider hiring a professional social media advertising agency to support you in creating high-quality publications. Many individuals are in the business of creating posters and putting them to work on social media so that you can start seeing better results from your paid ads. While this will cost you more money since you are paying someone else to design your ads, they will also be more likely to gain traction, making them worth your investment.

Chapter 6: Influencers

When it comes to Instagram marketing, one of the biggest markets is the influencer market. Making sure that you use Instagram influencers for marketing your product or for growing your page can help you tremendously when it comes to building your brand or making you more recognized. That being said, there are specific ground rules to look at when it comes to finding the right Instagram marketing for your needs. So in this chapter, we will talk about what to look out for when hiring Instagram influencers and how to get the best return from it. With that being said, let us talk about how to find the right influencer for your niche and how to go about advertising with them.

How to Find the Right Influencer?

One of the things to look out for when looking for influencers is if they have a following. Not many people realize this, but having a massive following does not equal a good return. For instance, as you know, many people can buy Instagram followers who are not engaged and will not react to any post, which is why when you look out for Instagram influencers, do you look for accounts that have a big following and get a ton of engagement? You can check the engagement by going online and looking at the engagement calculator. There are many calculators online that will tell you what the engagement rate is for a specific account. If you are looking to get a good deal and a good return on your investment, then make sure that you look for accounts that have at least a 2 % engagement rate. The 2 % engagement rate is for accounts that have at least fifty thousand followers to a million followers.

Once you have checked if the account has the right number of following, and the engagement rate is reasonable, then you can proceed with the negotiation and figuring out the right price for your shoutout. Keep in mind that the average rate for a shoutout is around $40 with a story swipe up. If an account below a million is asking for more than $40 for a story shoutout, chances are, they do not know what they are talking about, and you should look for other accounts. This is true for most of the niches; however, if you are in the makeup niche, then the prices will be a little bit higher.

To find out the right price for your niche, asked many influencers what their rates are, and they will give you the cost. Once you've got the price, average out all the influencers' rates and go from there. Make sure that when you are looking for influencers, you are looking for influencers in your niche. One of the worst things you can do is for you to start looking for influencers who are not in your niche. The truth is they will gladly take your money, but you will not get any return from it. Overall, make sure that you are looking for people who are in your niche.

Finally, the last thing to remember when looking for Instagram influencers is how open they are with you. If they are in it to grab your money and are not willing to negotiate the price, then there is a chance that they will not be the type of person you will want to work with. Most of the time, influencers will level with you and come out with a better price, which is why it is so crucial that you negotiate when looking for influencers and getting the best bang for your buck. If you are not negotiating the price, then you are leaving money on the table. Let us avoid that. These are the basic rules for finding the right influencers. Make sure that you use all the advice provided to you in this section, as it will help you to save a lot of money but, more specifically, get a better return on your investment.

Why Should You Use Influencers?

Many people might be wondering why is it so crucial for them to hire an influencer and promote their product or their page. The truth is that Instagram influencers can be a fantastic tool when it comes to growing your page or your business. The great thing about Instagram influencers is that they have a broad engaged audience that will be ready to buy your products or start following you. This is something you can't rule out in regards to growing your business. Make sure that you use Instagram influencers, especially in the beginning, as they are very crucial for your growth. More often than not, you will not have an idea of how to market your page using Instagram ads. Granted, we have given you the tools for it, but that does not mean that you will be successful from the get-go. What Instagram influencers can do is give you the warm traffic that is ready to follow you or buy from you. Once you have gotten enough sales or enough followers, you will have a better chance of being successful with Instagram ads. The more deals you have in your pixel, the better the chances of being successful in your Instagram ads. Influencer marketing can facilitate that for you.

Moreover, in the beginning, you will have a better return on investment if you use Instagram influencers. Instagram influencers are straightforward to use and can be very reliable, which is why you should not ignore this and utilize it in the beginning, and even when you are more successful. To this day, many businesses like Nike use Instagram influencers to grow their page and business, so do not rule out the possibility of Instagram influencers. The reason that they work is that they have a warm audience ready to buy, an audience that trusts their word. Also, they have spent years and years growing their page, so they know what they are talking about.

Shoutout for a Shoutout

If you are not aware of this method, then let me clarify it for you. This method requires you to give a person shoutout, and in return, they give you a shoutout. This is a great way to grow your page or to get more sales without spending a lot of money. This method has been used by many people to get a ton of deals on their page and to grow their page without spending a lot of money. If you do not have a lot of money to start with, then this method can work significantly for you when it comes to influencer marketing. The great thing about influencer marketing is that you do not need a lot of capital to get started. You can have no money and still see great results, which is why you must use Instagram marketing to work toward your advantage. In this instance, you can see that having no money makes no difference when it comes to Instagram influencer marketing, as he or she can do something called a shoutout for a shoutout. However, there are specific rules to this method, so let us talk about it. The first thing you need to make sure when doing a shoutout for a shoutout is that you both need to have a similar following.

Do not expect a page with a million followers to give you a shoutout when you only have a thousand followers. If you only have a thousand followers, then make sure that you partner up with someone who has two thousand followers or at least close to it. Now, if you are wondering how the returns will come from someone who only has a thousand followers, then let me tell you that it will be pretty good. This method, although it will not work as well as someone who has a million followers, will slowly yield you a good return, and you are a free investment.

You will indeed get some followers and some sales. This is for people who do not have any money and yet want to grow their Instagram page. If you are in that bucket, then make sure they use this method by messaging a lot of people, with the same following, to give you a shoutout. One thing you need to make sure is that the person you were going to do a shoutout for does not have any fake followers. The best way to check that out is to ask them their "top countries by follows." If most of them are from India or China, then chances are, they have bought the followers. You do not want someone who has a lot of bot followers.

Chapter 7: Tracking

In this chapter, we will talk about ways to save money when operating your business. Keep in mind that although this chapter is not Instagram-specific, it will still teach you how to save money when running a company. We have given you every tool required to get you in the best position to start your Instagram business, and now, we will provide you with one of the best tools out there to budget your spending and overall income. As you know, it is one thing to have a budget, and it is another thing to have a proper plan. Sure, you can sit down and say, "I am going to spend an x amount of money on this x amount of money on that" and so on, but without a proper plan and smart budgeting, you are not going to get to the goals what you are looking for, which is why I present to you, the 50/30/20 rule. But before you get started, make sure that you were able to review your spending, and you have created an idea of what your budget is going to look like. This rule will not work if you do not know where you are starting, so make sure you get that sorted. Also, make sure you have a pretty strong emergency fund before you begin this 50/30/20 rule.

The 50/30/20 Budget Rule

This budgeting rule is one of the best out there, and if you do not believe me, then you should know that Harvard graduate and bankruptcy expert Elizabeth Warren created this rule. This plan is also used by many influential people out there, so there is no denying that this plan works. We always recommend that you follow the 50/30/20 rule for budgeting goals, but if you find something which works better for you, then, by all means, you can use that as well. With that being said, let us get into the meat and potatoes of the rule 50/30/20. Before you start budgeting anything, the first step would be to calculate your after-tax income. Your after-tax income is your paycheck after you get it in your account. Essentially, what after-tax income means is the amount of money you end up getting in your bank account.

This is for people who are employed; figuring out your after-tax income would be effortless since it will be shown to you in your pay stub. On the other hand, if you are self-employed or you have your own business, then your after-tax income would be your net income. This would include your income after paying taxes, paying off your employees, and your profit margin. Mostly, whatever profession you are in, your after-tax income means all the money in your pocket. Once you have managed to figure out your after-tax income, the second step would be to limit all your needs down to 50 % of your after-tax income. Your needs could be your housing, car payments, car insurance, gas, and anything that helps you live your current lifestyle. Your lifestyle needs to fit within the 50 % margin of what is your net income, so if you make $3,000 a month, you should not be spending more than $1,500 a month in keeping your lifestyle afloat.

Now, to further understand this, you must differentiate between needs and wants. Your wants include anything that you can pay later or purchase later on. There is no need to have it every month or to pay for it every month necessarily. An example would be your cable bill. You can live without a cable, and if you can't, then it is not among your needs. Another example of a want would be a monthly subscription to Spotify. Do you need Spotify? Or is it just a want? That is for you to figure out.

On the other hand, a need could be your rent, and you can't live without a home, which is why it makes it a need. Another example would be your credit card, and you can't live without your credit card since you needed to build up a credit, which makes it a need. Everybody's wants and needs are entirely different, so you need to sit down and figure out all your wants and needs.

Also, remember, your needs should not exceed more than 50 % off your after-tax income. If it does, then you are living way above your lifestyle means if you have to cut down on certain things which are causing you to go over budget in your needs. Once you have figured out your needs, and you have put it in 50 % of your after-tax income, we will not talk about your wants. Yes, while budgeting and still enjoying your life and having all the desires that you are looking for, however, it should only be 30 % of your after-tax income. Now on the surface level, this sounds great. You can buy anything you want with 30 % of your income. For you, this could be a new car or new shoes. But wait for a second, there is something you need to find out before you start spending all your money on extravagant things.

Your wants do not include all those wild things which you might be thinking of, and these include your other urgent necessity, such as Netflix subscription or your phone bill. This 30 % of your income will go toward things that make your life convenient and enjoyable, but it is not necessarily something you cannot live without. For clarification, we will give you some examples. Your wants include your gym membership, car repairs, cable bills, and phone bills.

Most people will spend more on their wants than other things, especially in buying the latest clothes or brand new iPhone. We understand you need clothes and communication tools, but you do not need to make it extravagant unless it fits within your budget. Anything like regular clothing fits in your needs, and anything you want needs to be something. We know it is tricky to understand, but if you are having problems understanding it, then please read through it over and over until you do. The best way to understand it would be to ask yourself: do you want it, or do you need it?

Since you have covered up all 50 % and 30 % of income, we now cover the last 20 %. Your previous 20 % will go to all your savings and debt repayments. As we told you before, if you need something to be paid off, then that goes into your needs section. On the other hand, if you have a credit card payment which is just a minimum payment, then that goes into the 20 %. This will not necessarily be a need but more so to pay off and to build credit. The best way to describe 20 % is to know that 20 % will be used to pay off any debts and or to pay your minimum credit card payments, for instance. You should spend that 20 % of your income to pay off your debts, build the emergency funds, and also to build up your retirement funds.

Anything extra or additional debt will go into 20 % of your income when it comes to paying off your debt. Do not be confused with 50 % and 20 %, and 50 %. What you will be paying is an absolute necessity; it is something you can't live without. On the other hand, 20 % will be covering things that you want to pay off eventually or to build a certain amount of wealth, and hence, 20 % of your income will go toward your minimum credit card payments or to pay off a small loan. Anyway, before you set up your 50/30/20 budget, find out what your wants are and what your needs are, and then base it off accordingly. Everybody's 50-30-20 budget rule will be a lot different from the other person's budget, which is why it is so unique and works a lot better than any other budgeting rule out there. Sit down and write out all of your wants and needs. Then once you have a great idea of where your money will be going in regards to the 50/30/20 rule, it would be easier for you to start building a vast financial portfolio.

We will now give you an example of a 50/30/20 rule, and hopefully, in this way, you can understand how this would work in a real-life scenario. In this scenario, you make 42,000 a year after-tax or $3,500 a month. You live in a decent-sized home, and you are living by yourself. You drive a fully paid off car, and you are a firm believer in the minimalist lifestyle approach, which means you do not have the habit of spending money on extravagant things in life. However, you like to spend money on traveling, and you also want to watch documentaries on Netflix.

Since you just adopted the minimalist lifestyle, you still have some debt to pay off, one of them being your student loan, which is $10,000 and your credit card, which is $2,000. With this as your living situation, let us break down how you would be able to budget your income accordingly. Since you make $3,500 a month, you can't spend more than $1,750 on your needs, and if you are, then you need to lower your lifestyle needs. Your house costs you $1,000 a month, which is under your needs, and your grocery is $400 a month, which is under your needs, and your minimum credit card payment is also a type of need, which is around $50 a month. Finally, your average spending per month on clothes is $100 a month, summing up your needs to $1,550 a month, which means you have $200 left to spend.

The second thing we need to cover would be the 30 % allocation, and your wants include your phone bill, which is $50, and your Netflix subscription, which is $7 a month. Your internet is $50 a month, and your utilities, such as gas, electricity, water, etc., all average out to be $400 a month. Your 30 % is $1,050, and you spend $507 a month, leaving you with $543 to spare. Finally, we get to the last 20 %. This means you have $700 to spend on your remaining 20 %. You can distribute it how you want to when it comes to debt payment and future planning. Since you have the credit card to pay off, you can pay it off within ten months, save $200 every month, so the other $200 can go into your retirement funds, and the final $200 will go into your emergency funds.

The last $100 is for your student loans, and now, if we include the previous 10 % of your income, you can spend it on whatever you want, such as traveling or buying things, whatever you want. If you remember, we had a surplus of $743 a month. Since you now have $743 to spare, what should you do with it? Well, to answer this question, we need to figure out what your overall goals are in life. For example, your main goal this year is to travel to Alaska and to redo your kitchen. Your trip will cost you $500, and your kitchen will cost you around $5,000. What you can do is save $500 of that $743 a month to have the money saved up for the kitchen and also keep the remaining for your trip.

You will have excellently utilized the money, therefore causing you to enjoy your payment and to be smart about it. When you are doing your budget, make sure you are utilizing all these tools to get the best results possible, and to figure out what is important to you. If you have a surplus of money, you can either save it, or you can figure out if there is a more prominent use of that surplus. Some people even donate money to a great cause. So, if that is something you enjoy or would like to take part in, by all means, do that. Overall, do not let the surplus go to waste. Use it for things that have high value to you.

We have pretty much covered up how to use the 50/30/20 rule, so let us give you more reasons as to why you should budget. Look, it does not matter which budget you use, as long as it works for you. If you do not have a budget, you will end up realizing that there are a lot of things that will go wrong, so let us talk about them. The first one does not have a budget. Having a budget is the single most excellent tool that you have to capture everything in your finances. To reach your financial goal, you need a budget; it is easy to get started with it by using the 50/30/20 method or any other method, and it will be useful for your entire life. If you do not have a budget, you need to start one immediately.

If you do not have a budget, it does not mean that you are missing out on being able to use a budget to reach your goal. It is hard, if not impossible, to get a handle on what you are spending your money on or how you are supposed to be saving. If you are on the right track for saving, all of those things can be boiled down to you living a financially free life, so get your budget as soon as possible. Also, estimate your expenses on your budget. The reason that this is so crucial is that most people tend to be bad at remembering how much things cost and what their overall expenses are. Chances are, you do not know your numbers either, which is why it is essential to have your names written.

It is going to be an inadequate budget in the end, and you want your budget to be as accurate as possible. There could be one month where you put less gas, and on the other months, you put more gas, which is why you need to update that number. Also, you need to have something, like supporting documentation. For example, if you forget your numbers, the next month will become a haze for you because of unusual expenses.

This gets us to the point of preparing for the things that pop up, maybe every quarter or every year. These are things that you are not always thinking about; they also add up. Some bills appear quite randomly. Think about things like your car insurance if you are paying that every six months or maybe your car registration, which is happening every year. Even if you are spending your homeowner's insurance every year, you do not have a mortgage, so you are just writing a check for that. These things add up. Also, Christmas and birthdays are kinds of things that are easy to overlook, and some of them can be quite expensive, so you want to incorporate saving for these one-time expenses spread out over a year if it is costly.

Another tip would be that every single budget should have some amount of savings. If you are starting with income at the top, subtracting your expenses, do not wait for savings to be at the end with whatever's left. Make savings a priority.

But if you leave it in the end, then you are clearly not prioritizing your savings. One organized tip would be to take the money out of your paycheck and put it directly in a savings account without it even touching your regular checking account. Hopefully, your employer can allow you to send that money instantly to that savings account so that it is done, and it is prioritized. You are less likely to use it accidentally or something like that.

Another no-no is not having an emergency fund budget. Having an emergency fund is a fantastic tool that will allow you to monitor and manage your income for unexpected expenses that are crucial. It is the best way to combat problems in the future, and planning to have an emergency fund in your budget would be fantastic.

If you do not incur any emergency, you can put that money into your savings account. Otherwise, remember that injuries or illness can sometimes take months to recover from; a job can be lost. Make sure that your budget is funding that goal if you do not already have that much today. Another thing you should not do is forgetting to budget for entertainment or fun money. We have always included some amount of fun money or entertainment in our budget. Now, depending on where we were in our financial position, it has very much helped us keep up with our savings budget. We have had a lot of room, and we had a lot of fun sometimes. Also, sometimes, we do not have as much room.

It would help if you had some leg room to have more fun. The truth is that you want to like your budget, and let us be serious who hates having entertainment or fun money. Everybody has an interest or has things that they want to do, and if they are free, then that is fantastic. You can do them a lot. Still, if they are not free, which is okay and pretty standard, then you are going to want to have some money in your account to be able to pay for them, and not having them is going to create a budget that you do not want to stick with.

Finally, you should always be realistic about your spending habits. If this is your first budget or you are updating your budget, then you probably have some big goals, you want to pay off a bunch of debt, or you want to fill that retirement fund. You are prioritizing your emergency and retirement, for example. But you do not want to prioritize them so much that you are unrealistic with how much you are going to spend on your other needs, such as groceries or gas for your car or your car insurance. You will give up on your budgeting if you are too strict with it, which can happen if you try to be too aggressive with cutting your budget. If your budget is aggressively done, it is going to lead to the kind of budget that you will be breaking continually.

With that being said, we conclude this topic. You have to realize that budgeting takes time and effort, and therefore, you need to figure out everything about it before you start working on it. The common misconception is that the 50/30/20 rule is the way to go. But in reality, any budgeting works, as long as it works for you.

This is why we broke down all the mistakes you might be making when you are budgeting. This will give you a better idea of how to budget on your own. Like we mentioned previously if you do not want to follow the 50/30/20 method, that is fine. You can follow any other way that you want.

Trends to Watch Out For

Before we end, here is a quick read about the trends on Instagram that you need to watch out for you to use to your advantage. As Instagram is now going into its ninth year in business, it has evolved throughout the years as new features are continually made available, and people begin incorporating those new features into their user experiences. In the coming years, it is expected that the evolution will continue as we learn how to use these features in new ways to offer unique brand experiences for our audience. Naturally, you do not want to enter a new year using outdated strategies to attempt to target your audience. So, before we begin looking into specific strategies and approaches, we are going to dig into some specific marketing trends and strategies that you will need to look out for. Of course, it is challenging to predict exactly what will come in the new year. We cannot guarantee as to what new features may become available and how updates to the app may change the way we use it when it comes to interacting with your audience.

However, it is pretty clear that specific trends are already growing in popularity, and it is not incredibly challenging to keep track of upcoming trends as long as you learn how to stay engaged. Like any platform, Instagram is filled with patterns that you can quickly identify as long as you are paying attention and engaging with the app regularly. While trends can be hard to predict, there are five trends that we suspect will rise on the Instagram platform in the coming years. The first trend is IGTV, which was launched in June of 2018, but we expect to see it take off and grow even more significant in the next two years. This platform is dedicated to those who use Instagram on their mobile devices and allow individuals to follow YouTube-like channels through the Instagram platform. Unlike other video services, however, IGTV is dedicated to vertical video formatting, which makes it perfect for use on mobile devices, as it offers the ability to watch the videos maximized on your screen. Individuals who are seeking to expand among their mobile audience and start creating more content for their followers to pay attention to can leverage IGTV for a variety of different uses. This includes sharing pieces of wisdom or knowledge in your niche, as well as sharing how-to videos and tutorials.

There are many ways that IGTV can be used to generate sales, but the best way is to ultimately get in front of your audience and start talking about your brand and the ways that you can support your audience through either your products or services. The key here, however, is to refrain from making it all sound too *salesy*. Instead of talking for five minutes about your service, for example, spend that time building knowledge and offering tips that relate to your audience's problems or challenges and then propose your product or service as a solution. This way, your audience has a valid reason to stay around and listen, rather than making it feel as if you have provided them with a prolonged advertisement for them to watch.

Another trend to keep track of will be the rise of micro-brands, or small businesses, who are sharing their content to followers and getting connected with their audiences. In the past, Instagram has continued to evolve to shine spotlights on small business owners, entrepreneurs, and local brands. It is believed that in the following years, this trend will continue to rise and will make it even easier for micro-brands to connect with their audiences and create an extra income stream through Instagram marketing. The biggest reason that this is likely expanding in trends is that Instagram offers many different ways to share your brand with your audience intimately, and people like sharing that personal connection with the brands they support. Most larger brands do not have the time or the means to offer that intimate relationship with their audience, which is the reason that people are increasingly leaning toward following micro-brands. As a small business owner or a personal brand yourself, having the spotlight being shined primarily on brands just like yours means that now is the perfect time to get on Instagram and start building relationships with customers who are looking for exactly what you offer!

Another trend to continue on Instagram is the use of story advertisements. If you are already on Instagram, you may see sponsored ads rising between the stories that you are watching. These paid advertisements are an opportunity to share screen time with your audience so that they can find your brand and begin following you in the online space. However, you do not have to use paid advertisements to get your advertising in the story feature! The number of templates for story layouts is increasing, which means that you can use the story feature to generate advertisements and share them with your regular story. While these will not go as far and can only be seen by your existing audience or those who locate you and choose to watch your stories, they can still be an excellent opportunity to leverage your stories for advertisement purposes.

Another trend that will continue is one for the e-commerce shops. Here, businesses have the opportunity to begin integrating e-commerce-related features into your page, which makes it easier for customers to locate you and to shop through you.

The most noteworthy feature that offers this right now would be shoppable posts, which allow you to post static images with products in them and then tag the products so that customers can be taken directly to a checkout link. That way, you can post something and encourage people to shop with you through the product tags on your posts. A great example of people doing this would be those who sell clothing or accessories, sharing images featuring their products, and then saying "shop the look!" so that people pause and look at the image. If they like it, they can easily tap the tags on the post and start shopping for the products that they desire. These posts do require a Facebook page integration feature to work, but once you set it up, this feature is incredible, and it is expected that it will evolve to be even more interactive in the coming months.

The fifth trend is one that happens every year in social media and is expected to continue this year: Instagram will be looking for ways to increase engagement with their audience so that their audience spends more time on Instagram. For Instagram, the more popular their platform is, the more people are likely to use it to build their brands and sell their products, which means that Instagram stands to have more paid advertisements going through its platform.

This means that they want to drive as much traffic to the platform as possible, making it even more enjoyable for everyone on the platform. It also means that they keep brands and customers connecting on the platform so that they can continue making money. In other words, Instagram wins when they help small businesses succeed, too, which means that Instagram will continue creating features to help out brands just like yours so that they can continue to grow also.

Conclusion

Thank you so much for purchasing the book, *Instagram Marketing: The Best Tips & Tricks to Grow Your Business: a Step by Step Guide for Beginners with the Best Strategies to Maximize Your Small Business' Profit Using Advertising!*

As you can tell, we learned a lot in this book. Not only did we teach you a lot of techniques that many Instagram influencers used to grow their page, but we also showed you how to do it the right way. Although this book has been entertaining, make sure you implement all the information provided to you for you to be successful. The book is not going to do the job for you, so make sure that you read the chapters correctly, and once you understand a specific topic and you feel confident about it, act on the tools given to you.

The sooner you work on your goals, the higher the chances of you seeing results. In addition, make sure that you take notes when you are reading this book. It might help that you take notes, as it helps you learn quicker.

If you enjoyed this book, make sure that you start by recommending this to all your friends and family, especially if their goal is to grow their own business using social media. Instagram truly is the way to go about growing your business or to start making a top side income. You can use Instagram to become the next multi-millionaire, or you can use it to make some side income. Either way, you will not be disappointed with the results after reading this book.

Lastly, I hope with all my heart that you have enjoyed this guide, and that it has been useful to you! And if you have come to this point of the book, thank you also for the time you have devoted to reading! I'm sure you've understood that it took a lot of effort to write it, and I'd be extremely grateful if you'd leave me with a 5-star review!

I wish you every success with all my heart!

Michael Robert

Fortunate

Facebook Advertising

The Beginner's Guide for Facebook Marketing: How to Turn Your Facebook Audience into Real-time Sales, the Best Strategies Used to Make Effective and Efficient Facebook Ads.

Michael Robert Fortunate

Table of Contents

Introduction

Congratulations on purchasing *Facebook Advertising: The Beginner's Guide for Facebook Marketing*. We live in a digital era where social media influence in our daily lives cannot be underestimated. Several billion people are present on digital platforms on a daily basis. Facebook makes one of the most popular social media platforms in this era. New and established businesses are moving in the digital direction and growing significantly from being on social media platforms. Facebook has audiences from all over the world to satisfy different businesses in various industries.

Serious entrepreneurs understand how crucial it is to advertise their businesses and products on Facebook. An estimated 80% of all the users of the internet are on Facebook. Over 60% of adults around the world use Facebook. This translates to billions of audiences that will be exposed to an advert when posted.

Facebook advertising suits businesses in all levels of entrepreneurship, whether you are a startup or an established business or brand; a Facebook platform will ultimately increase your sales significantly. The costs of Facebook advertising are seemingly low compared to conventional methods of advertising. In addition, you can be guaranteed to reap handsomely from Facebook advertising. There is no much time wastage with Facebook advertising as it is fast and efficient.

From the information above, you can already tell that there is indeed a great need to advertise on Facebook. The questions that may linger on your minds are:

1. How to start Facebook advertising?

2. How to make Facebook advertising work for your business?

3. How to attract the kind of audience you need on Facebook?

These and other specifics of social media marketing on Facebook are detailed here. The book will open your eyes to the world of digital marketing, specifically on Facebook and how to use it to your advantage. There are plenty of books on this subject on the market, thanks again for choosing this one! Every effort was made to ensure it is full of as much useful information as possible; please enjoy!

Chapter 1: Converting Facebook Ads To Real-Time Sales

Facebook has a relatively higher number of users than any other social media platforms. It, therefore, allows every business to interact with many potential clients. When many people see your products, it increases the chance of getting many buyers. However, traffic is not everything any seller wants for the business. It is more fulfilling when a business person achieves sales from Facebook traffic. The dream of every business person is to get a good number of sales after they put up an advertisement. Sadly, this is not always the case. Some Ads do not even get noticed, and if they do, they do not get any clicks. When a seller realizes that even with the traffic, they don't get clicks, it sends a signal that probably something is not right with the Ad. It's human nature to want to know more about anything attractive that comes their way.

To have more people notice and get eager to know more about your product, let us look at some tips and tricks to consider when creating your Ads.

Get Catchy Images to Use for The Ads

The first image has to stand out more than anything else to ensure everybody will see it as they scroll down their Facebook account. High-quality images are most suitable for this purpose. Images should be bright and full of color to make them easily noticeable. When they include photos of people, they should show happy people to win the Ad more clicks. The images will do even better if they feature the people using your products. At the same time, it's essential to consider the target population. A photo of a happy attractive lady will cause more men to click on the Ad and vice versa. For general products where the community gender doesn't matter, photos of beautiful ladies will do well in catching the attention of both genders.

It's advisable to use personal images so that the actual product corresponds with the Ad. Professional photography is on the rise has made it easier for sellers to get quality photographs of their products. However, a few sellers might not afford professional photos due to the attached cost. In this case, an excellent mobile phone or camera comes in handy and can be used to get outstanding images. Here are some tips to get beautiful photos without professional help;

- Keep the background clear so that the product stands out well;

370

- Ensure the product is clean and in its best state;
- Ensure you have good lighting so that the photos will give a view of the real product. Poor lighting also affects the color which may cause problems with some customers;
- Get several pictures from different angles to capture all the essential product details. For instance, someone selling a car will capture the outside and the interior, considering the most crucial information.

Include Important Product Details

Every product has featured that customers want to know. If it's a new product in the market, indicating details will make people understand it and probably get interested in having it. Ensure that you give details that are of interest before they ask. Some may not even ask because they don't get to think about it. Do your research to know what features most people will most likely get interested in knowing. Use those details for your product description. For instance, if you are selling shoes, most people will want a seller to indicate the material used, sizes, and colors available as well as the gender they suit. Therefore, a description of a shoe would look like;

'Unisex canvas shoes with a rubber sole,

Available in blue, black and white colors

Sizes 38 – 44

Delivery is done within 12 hours after confirming the order.'

Some viewers will get interested in the product after they have seen its details. Like any young person will get interested in a mobile phone that features an excellent camera. The person does not just view the Ad because he needs a mobile phone but because the features indicated are attractive to him. Other people will look for an Ad that gives the details on the spot because they don't want to contact many sellers. For example, someone will search, *'white canvas shoes'* because they want to narrow down their search to just what they want. A list of Ads with the three words will show at the top of the list. If a seller with the same shoes only indicated *'shoes for sale,'* the advert might come at the end of the list, and the client may not scroll to the bottom. Details will also make it easier for the seller to reduce the number of similar questions he receives. Some people are not patient enough to wait for a response if it's not instant. By giving all the necessary details, you can keep serious buyers in your 'shop' and get time to respond to them effectively.

Indicate Product Price Clearly

Once someone gets interested in a product, the next thing they want to know is the price. If the seller considers indicating the last amount on his Ad, it is good for him to specify that his price is fixed. This detail will help to avoid many messages of people who want to negotiate. However, it's advisable that you price your products higher, to give an allowance for negotiation. It's in many people's likings to negotiate for discounts, therefore, having a provision for the 'make offer' button adds to the number of people who contact you. Once a potential buyer contacts a seller, it's evident that they have considered buying the product and it's easier to convince them to buy at that point. Do enough research and know your competitors' prices. This knowledge will help you ensure that you don't set your prices too low or too high, lest you put off potential buyers.

Make the Company Policies Clear

Every company, big or small, should have well-laid policies. These will help the people who view their profile understand the company operations even before they engage. It also gives the buyers confidence because they feel that they are dealing with a serious seller who is well established. It makes it easier to convince such clients to buy since they know that the company is respectable. After the first successful purchase, most of the buyers will want to come back or refer their loved ones due to the trust they already have in you.

Company policies also help handle the expectations of potential buyers. This is because when they engage the seller, they already have an idea of what they expect and won't expect otherwise.

Create Separate Ads for Different Products

A seller can be tempted to put all his items in one ad, but it's not advisable to have them all together. It's good to have different Ads for different things. This way, all items will have equal chances, as different people may want to view different products. The best strategy to capture potential clients is through images, and people will rarely scroll through Ads to look for what they want if it's not in the displayed image.

In case you have a general sale, you can indicate it at the bottom of the Ad, and interested people will scroll through your wall to view the other products. You can also attach a link that directs buyers to your wall. This way, clients who may get interested in seeing what you have on the sale will click on the link.

Check the Available Categories to Know Which Is Best for Your Products

Groups are organized, so that related items end up together. Things like tables, beds, cupboards, and shoe racks end up in one category as furniture, and hence, one looking for a bed will go straight to that category. Each item on sale should fall in the group it fits best depending on what or where it is used. Some things can fall in more than one category and still meet buyers. If yours is like this, it's good to post them in all the categories they fit in so that more searches can direct clients to them. For example, sunglasses can be used for medical purposes as well as for beauty. Someone in need of sunglasses for beauty might search in the 'beauty' category. Another who may have been advised by a doctor might most probably search in the 'health' category. If as a seller you have yours posted in both categories, you will most likely have the two people view your Ad. However, be careful that your products don't fall in the wrong category. If this happens, no search will direct potential buyers to your product, and you don't want that. It can also risk your account of being blacklisted or even blocked.

Offer Free Gifts

It's in the nature of people to like free things. Depending on your product, get something you can give for free. Something related to the product will attract more buyers to view your advert, and it becomes easier to sell to them if they reach out to you. For example;

- Someone who sells ladies' clothes can consider giving free branded beauty accessories;
- A hairdresser can consider free hair clips as an after service;
- A shoe seller might consider a free pair of slippers or socks;
- Someone who sells machines can offer free assembling of the same.

It's wise to ensure that the word 'FREE' comes out legibly in the advert. If possible, the font should be more significant and color different to catch more attention. For example,

*Buy a pair of shoes and get a pair of socks for **free***

You can also have a message like;

*'hey there. Thank you for contacting us, visit our shop to get your **free** pair of socks'*,

for clients who contact you.

This is necessary because, after the attractive pictures/ videos, it will be the next thing that attracts more people to click on the Ad. The cost of the item you set up for free should be covered in the profit margin gained by selling the product. Nobody wants to run their business at a loss; otherwise, the efforts won't be worth a thing. When the gift is branded with your brand name, it's a way of making your advertisement go beyond Facebook. It causes awareness to people who might not have heard of your brand or product before. It's also a way of attracting the customer to return and send more interested friends and family your way.

Use as Many Keywords in Your Advert as Possible

When looking for a particular item to buy online, different people usually search in various engines using different words. It's good to know the keywords generally used by people searching for the product you want to sell. Make maximum use of them in your title and description. This will ensure that many relevant searches will land potential clients on your product. For instance, people who want to buy tables may use words like;

- Wooden table;
- Office table;
- Rectangle table;
- Second-hand table.

A seller with a description that captures, *'a second-hand rectangle table suitable for office use'* is most likely to be reached by all the above searches.

When more people see the Ad, one objective will have been met. It will cause traffic to your product, which is good enough. Since most people are searching the item with intentions of buying, the chances that you will make sales once they get in touch with you are high.

Offer Shipping Services Where Possible

Before a client concludes on the purchase, he /she will most probably consider how the product will reach them. Many online shoppers either don't have the time or don't want the struggle of having to transport things after buying. Most of them will buy from a seller who has delivery services, either free or at a fee. It is, therefore, a good idea to indicate availability or possibility of delivery services to maintain more clients on your wall. For clients who are from different cities, it's good that you know the courier companies available for their locations. Make sure you understand their charges so that you give instant delivery details when they ask. It is also good to be flexible to accommodate the customer's preference if they have a courier company in mind. Once the sale has been confirmed, it is again necessary to ensure you deliver in good time to avoid disappointments. Timely delivery will give you more return customers as well as referrals since it helps build confidence.

Get Ways to Make People Refer Customers to You

As a seller, you alone cannot send enough awareness to everybody. You need your Facebook friends and previous buyers to link you to their friends. You can make people refer others to you by using the following tactics;

1. Copy your link and send to your friends requesting them to share with their friends;
2. Appreciate those who refer people to you by giving them small gifts;
3. Ask people who have already bought from you to like your page and share with their friends;
4. Give a considerable discount to return customers and to those that prefer their loved ones to you. This way, you will create chains of different customers;
5. Give exceptionally good services to all your customers to keep them coming back. Happy customers will also preach it to their friends.

People who have been referred to you have more confidence in your product. For this reason, the more referrals you get, the better for your business.

Give Promo Codes to Be Redeemed at Your Shop

A promo code is given randomly with attractive discounts to lure customers. People who have a promo code will most probably show up at the shop to redeem it, and that's a sale. You can give codes redeemable within specified periods to keep clients coming. The codes also make more people visit your wall regularly to see when you have new promos. Some will refer their friends to your wall any time they see the promo running. We already know most of the referred customers will end up buying. When there are more views on your products, it's likely to translate to more sales, which is our primary objective.

Most people go through their Facebook wall for fun or looking to pass time. This is what causes traffic on Facebook throughout day and night. You can take advantage of this fact as a seller and make them notice your product. Using the above tips, any business advertising on Facebook will get easily noticed. When Ads attract clients to your wall, it's your duty as the seller to make sales. Convince most of the people that contact you to either buy instantly or come back later. Ensure that most of them also refer others to you by giving excellent customer service. This will keep your chain growing and ensure an increase in the number of sales as time goes by.

Chapter 2: Proven Case Studies On The Effectiveness of Facebook Ads

Before you start implementing anything in your business, it is always important to validate the quality of the tool that you wish to implement. This way, you can feel confident that you are going to gain the value that you desire out of the tool that you plan on implementing.

To help you feel more confident in the power of Facebook advertising, as well as to show you just how valuable this tool can really be, let's take a look at four different case studies that prove the effectiveness of Facebook ads. This way, you can see exactly what Facebook ads can do for you and how you can use them to improve your online revenue.

Case Study #1: Facebook Ad Retargeting Creates $5,800 Monthly Recurring Revenue

This particular case study was incredible as it offered the company a whopping $5,800 per month in recurring revenue from their Facebook advertisements. Design Pickle is a company that designs unlimited graphics for companies using a monthly retainer fee. This particular company found it to be somewhat challenging to promote their business using standard practices, so they decided to try Facebook advertisements.

Through Facebook advertisements the company offered the equivalent of a free trial, with no credit card required in order for customers to get started. The free product that customers could get was a single graphic designed for their business. They began to use leads to retarget advertisements, which enables them to market specifically to people who had already landed on their page. Through this, more than 50% of their new customers signed on from Facebook advertisements alone. This lead to $5,800 recurring monthly revenue from their advertisements.

Case Study #2: $14,114 Revenue From Facebook Advertisements

In this case, a company was able to generate massive amounts of leads which lead to $14,114 in revenue from their advertisements. The company SamCart used Facebook ads to sell their courses. In these Facebook advertisements the company spent $8240 on advertisements and made $14,114 in revenue. That's a whopping $5,874 in revenue from courses through Facebook advertisements alone.

Case Study #3: 122 Subscriptions Sold with $2.5k Ad Budget in 2 Weeks

Veeroll is a B2B company that was using Facebook advertisements to share video advertisements with their target audience. Veeroll launched a webinar and enrolled people from Facebook into the webinar through a landing page which was used to convert followers. The company ended up spending $2,500 in 2 weeks and sold 122 subscriptions out of the webinar conversion model. This resulted in $11,000 of monthly revenue, or $8,500 in profit after just two weeks.

Case Study #4: $163,969 Revenue in Just 34 Days

This particular case study was a remarkable one that lead to the company earning a massive $163,969 in revenue in just 34 days with a mere $5,989 investment. That's a $157,980 profit after just 34 days, and using a tiny fraction of the overall cost to get there.

This case was run by an advertising tech, Paul Romando, who acted on behalf of an unnamed company which was kept private for confidentiality reasons. With that being said, he returned more than 1,150 checkouts for his customer which lead to the massive income from the investment. This experience lad to a 2737.80% return on the investment in just over a month.

To create this particular ad format, Paul used a Facebook funnel which first lead customers to a lead magnet, or an opt in project that customers could check out. After that, there would be a different ad set shown to those who signed up for the opt in that was designed to take the individuals directly to a sales page. From there, they would advance through even higher ranks of products until they reached the "top tier" of products available through that company. This particular funnel is what helped Paul create such a massive return for the company he was working with.

Chapter 3: How Brands Can Use Customer Testimonials to Create Efficient Facebook Ad Funnel

O ver time, there has been a rapid increase in the cost and demand for Facebook advertising. This increase is after the realization that Facebook is the best platform to meet all types of potential buyers since most people use the app. However, Facebook Ads have increasingly lost their initial influence on buyers. This loss is due to an increased number of marketers leading to high competition. Among the audience on Facebook are some that are cold, some warm, and others hot. A sales-based Ad may not lure the cold audience into buying. A cold audience needs to be natured through awareness from being a stranger to becoming a buyer. An already warm audience that is familiar with your products requires a different approach altogether. To balance the audience, any marketer will need to build an Ad funnel.

An ad funnel is a series of campaigns that allow the marketer to deliver results from across all types of audience. A proper funnel has the following stages;

- Awareness stage;

- Consideration stage where the audience begins to build interest;

- Decision-making stage where they decide they want to buy;

- Buying stage.

At the awareness stage, the main aim is to catch the attention of the audience and earn your brand recognition. The audience at this stage can most probably be lured by the use of a video that is interesting and educative. The main aim is to catch the attention of more viewers who do not know about the product. Once the audience gets the awareness, a cold audience warms up and somehow appreciates the need for your product. At this point, some will research more about the product and even contact you for details. Some will want to buy it immediately while others will take time to think about it and may need further convincing. When building an Ad funnel, testimonials from previous customers are an essential ingredient. Here are some of the benefits of customer testimonials:

Testimonials Help in Building Trust in Potential Buyers

If a company employee tells a client how good their product is, the client will most likely not consider it seriously. This attitude is because they assume, he/she is just doing his/her job. However, if another buyer tells the same customer of how good the same product is, he/she will most likely consider purchasing it. This change of attitude is because customer testimonials are considered neutral and unbiased, in that a customer and not a business owner talks about the product. When the audience have already known about the existence of your product, some might be reluctant to buy. The reasons for being reluctant may vary. Some won't buy the product immediately because they don't know you, or they don't understand the product. Even so, some won't buy it because they don't trust you. Most people are not so fast in trusting strangers or products sold by strangers. In this case, a testimonial from someone who has interacted with you and used your product may work well in making viewers trust you. Even though the two are strangers, a person looking forward to buying your products is easily convinced by other customers. They tend to believe other customers will be honest and therefore trust what they say. With a good number of people having trust in your products, you are sure you will make a considerable number of sales.

They Work Well as A Selling Technique

Since they are not written in the seller's opinion, anyone who sees the testimonials will get interested in knowing more about you and your product. By using testimonials in the form of text, audios, and video forms on your website, people who might have never known about your product may learn about it then. The good thing is that they will hear about it from someone who has used the merchandise and not the seller. They will, therefore, get the idea of how useful the product is and might consider trying it out. Other buyers have heard about the product before but are reluctant to get it. They also get the feeling that the product is meant to help them in certain areas of their life. By this, you will save on advertisement cost. The testimonial will do enough advertisement. Needless to say, a testimonial is likely to be more convincing for decision making compared to an ordinary ad. This is because of the confidence built through the fact that the product has been helpful to other people.

They Help Viewers with A Better Understanding of The Product

Some people will see a product tagged for sale but not understand what it is or how helpful it can be. The reason behind this is most people going through Facebook will not take time to read long posts about a product. For such a client, a brief testimonial highlighting how helpful the product was gives them an idea of what it is. For example, if an image shows two photos of the same person, it will get her interested. At a closer look, she will realize the person has pimples in one image and has smooth skin on the other. She will at that point most probably conclude that the product helped clear the pimples. Having done that, they have viewed and started building interest in the product. In the instance that they have the same problems or know someone who has the same problem, they will start weighing on whether to buy or not. [Decision-making stage].

In the instance that your product had more than one benefits, different testimonials will highlight various benefits. By that, people that view them might gain interest in respect to either of the benefits. People who would have otherwise feared to try the product will get more reason to want to try it and refer friends who might benefit from the product too. Potential buyers get most of the product details and familiarize themselves with the product through the testimonials, making it easy for them to make a decision. When such customers get in touch with the seller, they usually come to buy rather than to enquire.

They Work Well in Maintaining Previous Buyers

Buyers feel more confident when they see other people recommend products they are already using. It makes them feel they made the right choice by purchasing it and will most likely become routine customers. When customers see their testimonials feature in the business ads, they feel appreciated and get the feeling of brand ownership. These people become your brand ambassadors, even beyond Facebook. The clients become loyal to your business and increase their emotional bond with it. Loyal clients also refer to other potential buyers by word of mouth.

On the other hand, some buyers who probably had tried the product but did not see results can feel very disappointed. If they don't get reasons convincing enough, they may not want to come back to your shop. However, such customers can be maintained through testimonials. For instance, some products, such as beauty products do not show results instantly and might require constant use to show tangible results. In such a case, already disappointed customers might be hard to convince that the product is good. They can only understand how it works when they see testimonials of people who had used the same and gotten results. These testimonials give them the confidence to want to try the same again, this time with a more positive attitude.

Testimonials Can Overcome Negative Incites

When it comes to social media, sellers cannot control the views of different buyers. Some people will write nasty comments on particular ads, probably because the product did not meet their expectations. Some will comment badly out of malice, while some competitors will want to paint a bad picture of you. When it comes to the audience, most people will scroll to see what other people think about the product. Several good testimonials can help repair damages caused by the negative comments on the post. In this case, it is wise to select an outstanding testimonial that refers to the product in question. In this case, a good testimonial must;

- Highlight the product's benefits;

- Tally with what you have indicated in your advert;

- Come from someone who can be identified;

- Prove that your product is the best.

They Play A Big Role in The Conversion Rate

Through the ads funnel, the audience is converted from a total stranger to a buyer. Most Facebook users who come across the ads are not on Facebook to search for products on sale. They will most probably not buy immediately they see an advertisement. Catchy videos that display testimonials are a good way of making them notice your Ads and click on them. Once they click on the video and watch to the end, they are able to get some crucial information about the product. The presence of good testimonials is what will lead them to consider visiting your website. At the site, their main agenda will be to see the product being referred to in the testimonials. This category of clients goes through the funnel stages and get convinced faster through the testimonials than through what they would have seen in an ordinary advert. Credit goes to the testimonies, first for introducing the product with confidence that it surely is good, and for proving that it has been tested. Studies have shown that most online buyers decided to buy after going through several customer testimonials.

It Creates A Positive Reputation for Your Product and Business

Keenly selected testimonials from your customers create a good image of your product, more strongly than what you state in your ads. Consequently, this gives more customers a vivid good picture of your product and business. As an end product, they erase any doubt about the product being of good help to them. Testimonials also help in giving a clear difference between your product and your business from that of your competitors. Besides, once a good reputation is created to the society about your product, the chances of attracting new customers and maintaining the current ones rise. When many customers like your products and give testimonials, chances of the product brand going viral increase. When a product goes viral for a good reason, positive returns are recorded, which is the main aim at the end of the day. The beauty of a good reputation is that it gets more people to want the association with the product. It also makes it easy to post your Ad on different sites and increase the product's awareness.

When your product has a good reputation, fans share about it on their social media platforms. Their friends, family, and colleagues will learn about you through them and most likely want to know more about the product. They will be marketing your product as they take pride in it.

They Help to Increase the Credibility of Your Brand

While big brands are already known to clients in the whole region, sellers with unknown brands have the task of making them known for them to be competitive. Most buyers are skeptical about the credibility of a product when they first see it in an advert. Testimonials from customers help with this by creating social proof. When people see testimonials of your customers on your website, they relax at the fact that other people know about you. Many people feel that since someone else has used a particular brand and says it is good, then it must be good. Most customers rate the credibility of a product or business, depending on the number of people who talk about it. They use this measure of credibility to determine whether they buy from marketer A or B. A company that has products of lesser quality but has many people talking about it will seem more credible. This is in comparison to one with excellent quality but few people talking about it. It's therefore evident that people trust what other people think about a brand than what they know about it. With this fact in mind, well-selected testimonials should feature on your website, citing beautiful photos of happy customers and good reviews. The more the testimonials featuring a brand or item, the better for the business. By doing this, you increase the credibility of your product, build a chain of customers, and make your brand competitive in the market.

Testimonials, When Used Properly, Are Very Persuasive

Most of the testimonials have stories in them which capture the attention of the audience. Because the stories are personified, they tend to create intense emotions, therefore, connecting the reader to the advert. When you connect emotionally with the audience, you can easily convince them to buy your product. Mostly they don't buy because of how they see the product but because of how they feel about the same. The language used is also persuasive because it is universal and in the voice of another buyer and not the seller. Visual aspects in the testimonials bring out more emotions, and they come out in a way more convincing than any other part of an advert. All a business person needs to know is how best they can use testimonials given by their satisfied customers to persuade possible buyers to become real buyers.

The above-mentioned points prove that business people should use customer testimonials to create efficient Facebook Ads. This is based on the fact that testimonials have proven to be a very strong convincing factor. They have also proven to help businesses increase traffic on their sites. With the need for every business to stand out, sellers cannot afford to ignore an essential detail as such. It is, therefore, advisable for every business person who has exceeded the expectations of his clients to request them to write testimonials. From the various testimonials, you are able to get, you incorporate specific ones for particular adverts. When choosing testimonials for a Facebook ad, it's recommended that you use an affirmative testimony that is likely to catch the attention of any random Facebook user. Many people get attracted more to videos and images as compared to texts. Testimonials in terms of videos and pictures will, therefore, be a better option for use in any Facebook ad. The reason they are mostly preferred is because they can show real emotions, body language, and audios at the same time. This tactic works well in making the emotional connection possible. Video Testimonials also help brands reach through masses of people who are of different language groups. Even though some cannot understand the language used in the advert, they can view images and watch videos to get the context. With the clients' testimonials acting as advertisement Medias, they help in cutting costs on commercial adverts. This use of testimonials reduces the expenditure of the business but rises the income through sales.

Chapter 4: Optimizing Facebook Ads

F acebook is an online social media networking platform that allows people all over the world to communicate and interact with one another. It is one of the leading platforms in the world that has enabled people around the world to feel closer to different parts of the globe.

With this in mind, Facebook, the social media giant has optimized its operations by creating promotion options such as Facebook ads. These options allow business owners to sponsor their preferred posts and cover a broad market. The ads can either feature Business posts, motivational posts, religious posts, and sports. With an efficient ad, there is no doubt that any company can reach the target market with little resources.

Nowadays, business firms can use different categories or types of ads given to promote their products on Facebook. These can be categorized into four groups, namely:

1. Traffic Improvement Ads;
2. Consumers Appreciation Ads;

3. New products ads;
4. Lead ads.

a. Traffic improvements ads

Aim at improving the number of customers that can see a product that has been advertised. Every business must strive always to acquire more customers.

b. Consumer Appreciation Ads

Most firms and organizations, in general, always focus only on getting a customer and stopping on that once they have convinced the customer to buy their products. However, any firm should strive to make a onetime customer a regular customer. That's why Facebook offers this ad to enable a company to appreciate their customers.

c. New Product Ads

This category of ads allows a firm to sponsor and advertise a new product to its targeted audience or consumers.

d. Leads Ad

This type of ads enables a customer to optimize his or her contacts with the company to receive ads at any time. It allows business owners to reach out to the right market without having to dig deep into their pockets.

Optimizing Facebook ads means that a sponsored post on Facebook gives the most successful output from the targeted audience. This book looks at some of the techniques an organization can use to get the most successful result from a Facebook sponsored post.

Here's how business owners can Optimize Facebook ads;

1. **Being Distinct**

    A firm targeting to run an ad should always focus on being specific on what they are about to advertise. First, they should be specific on a product they are about to advertise, be distinct on the consumers they are targeting and also specify the target age bracket of the consumer they are focusing on. For instance, when it comes to a product to do with small babies, the company's focus should be on females aged between 16-35 since, at this age bracket, many ladies have babies. When a product is mostly targeting the youths, then it would be advisable for a firm to select a certain age group so as to reach the optimum target market. This is even easy because Facebook gives you all the options that you need.

2. **Investing in Video Ads**

Video ads and animations also play a big role in attracting more customers and keeping those that already exist. Just like cartoons, video ads are attractive and will always make your target consumers more likely to follow the ads. These videos should not be necessarily expensive but should be of high quality and well-produced to avoid embarrassments that may create loopholes in the overall marketing campaign. With video ads on Facebook, one is assured of good and optimum results that will be of big benefit to the business.

3. Maximizing on Potential Customers Who Visit Your Website

Most competitive firms are always able to know those who visit their sites either by following their IP addresses or by even offering pop up for the visitors to subscribe. A firm may use this advantage by making these people their target market when doing an ad on Facebook. These people are normally the first people to see the sponsored post when it is posted on Facebook. This might help in convincing a customer who had visited the site and not made his or her mind on purchasing a particular product or service. This tactic is always useful as a back up to convince a customer and finalize a deal.

4. Understanding the Target Group

This means that a marketer should be able to understand those who'll access the advertisement. For instance, a marketer should know the target group that is already aware of the product so that he/she should not waste resources in re-advertising to them. More energy should be focused on new potential customers.

5. Getting Detailed Information About Your Target Group

A good Facebook ad marketer should know the age and gender of the target audience. Not all audience performs the same, and hence, an ad should not ignore the important fact that even their financial power is not the same. Thanks to Facebook, business owners can easily get more information about their audience from a simple button click. Knowing the age and gender of your audience is essential, as it gives you the knowledge of what needs to be done to meet the requirements of such an audience. For instance, it would be of no use to advertise ladies' clothing to all the audiences without categorically focusing on the ladies. By taking specific audiences, this can allow one to get the optimum result that he or she requires.

6. Pick Out an Audience Depending on Their Level of Income

Facebook ads platform offers business persons a chance to pick their audience or target market in accordance with their levels of income. Given that the audiences might have different levels of income, some people prefer to buy things that are highly priced while others would prefer to buy cheaper stuff. With this in mind, a marketer can maximize on by picking a specific audience in regards to their financial income. Getting the audience that prefers goods that are highly-priced would be a gold mine to the marketer or a firm because they will end up making a good profit.

7. Demographic and Climatic Conditions

Facebook ads allow business owners to choose an audience from specific demographic areas. Climatic conditions would also be considered by a marketer when advertising his or her products. For instance, it will be poor for a marketer who sells jackets and sweaters to target an audience that is in arid and dry areas. But it will be of great profitability for a marketer to target audiences in cold areas with the same products they will highly sell. Given that Facebook is almost all over the world, the marketer can easily divide his/her audiences in accordance with their demographic surroundings.

8. Scheduling Your Ads

Facebook allows a person to schedule his or her advertisements to a time of his or her convenience. With this, a firm will be able to schedule their product advertisement to a specific time that is profitable. Most businesses target to advertise when they are on their peak so that they can sell well.

9. Having a Clear Objective of The Ad

All successful businesses must always have an objective for them to thrive through the daily growing competition. Just like in a football game, every team must have an objective in every season that they play. Therefore, for one to have the best results, a marketer must always have specific or several objectives before running an advertisement on Facebook. A person must well know what he or she would love to achieve after running an advertisement. With that in mind, one is sure of getting the best result he or she expected.

10. Designing Your Facebook Ads

Given that audiences will tend to use different gadgets when accessing their Facebook account, it is prudent for a marketer to design his or her ad for both the phone layout and personal computer layout. This will help in maintaining the attractiveness of the advertisement in both gadgets. One should also make sure that the advertisement is in the right place where it can easily be seen by the target audience. Also, consider the Facebook marketers budget that he or she is willing to use for the advertisement process. One should not choose a budget that he or she is cannot manage. With the practice of the above-mentioned points, businesses can use the ideas to have optimum final results after running an ads Facebook ad. Facebook is a great platform, and every marketer should utilize it to reach the target audience with much ease. It saves on the amount of money that would be spent if the marketing is done physically.

Facebook Ads Techniques

1. Objectives

This is the most important aspect before even running an ad on your Facebook. One must at least have clear objectives or goals that he or she is considering to achieve after running the advertisement. In normal life, for one to succeed in doing anything he/she must first what he/she wants to gain from it. Objectives basically are the basis of every successful task that one might have. Having these objectives helps one understand what action the audience will take once they see the advertisement at first glance.

The first objective that a successful advertisement should have is creating awareness. Your audience must at least familiarize yourself with the products or services that you offer.

Another important objective is having conversions. For instance, most marketers would wish to make their audience to go to their website. To do this, your ad would probably have an incentive such as a discount to your customers. To make them go to your website, you should not give out a discount code to your customers before they go to your website. You should put a structure that takes them to step by step to your website where they, for instance, insert their emails before getting the discount code. With this, you will have the upper hand in that at least you will have the customer's contacts, and you can communicate with them from time to time.

2. Setting Up Your Audience

The second step of having a successful Facebook ad campaign is by setting up the ideal customized audience that you prefer.

Focusing is essential in your campaign and how you focus can either make your ad perform perfectly or fail terribly.

Some of the things to look at when choosing your audience will include;

a. Location

First, you must have a location where your audience to be that is in accordance with what your product line is. For instance, if you are from Africa and your products are arts and crafts and African indigenous crafts that attracts tourists it would be prudent for you to set a location where most tourists come from, and that is basically the west of Europe. With that, you are more likely to get more audience in Europe compared to Africa where the audience will not be so much. Basically, setting up the most suitable audience would be a great step in making the advertisement very successful.

b. Age

This is another essential step in getting the right audience with Facebook ads; one is able to choose his most appropriate audience age in line with the product that he deals in. For instance, if the product you are dealing with is mostly fashion, it will be prudent for one to focus on the young generation that is the youths between let's say 15-35. It will be of no use to focus your advertisement of the latest clothing fashion and swag to the older age for they are prone to ignore the advertisement.

c. Gender

Gender should also be considered when running advertisements on Facebook. Different genders prefer different products hence the gender that you target should go in line with the product that you sell.

Facebook ads offer a marketer the choice to choose the gender that they would prefer to reach. For example, it will be of importance to choose the female gender when dealing with ladies such as earrings, lipsticks, etc.

d. Language

This is another important perspective to consider. The language that you use during advertisements should go well with the target audience that you will pick. Given that we have different languages in the world, a good marketer should choose a language that is well understood by his/her target audience with ease.

Other factors to consider would be; interest, the behavior of your audience. For instance, if your business deals with events organizing such as weddings, you should as well choose the audience who have an interest in weddings or birthday parties.

Finance is another factor that should be factored a good market must choose the budget that he or she is well convenient with.

Testing Your Ad

This is the final step for one to have a very successful Facebook ad campaign. One should at least first test his or her ad before it goes live on air. Thanks to Facebook, one has an opportunity to test his ad before it starts showing live. This helps a promoter or marketer to see how the ad will appear in phones, personal computers, and other gadgets that the audience might use.

This is where the marketer customizes his or her ad by choosing the themes, pictures, videos, or music that he or she would prefer to use to run the advert. Most importantly, the success of a Facebook advertisement will depend on marketer's strategy and the most important objectives. The most effective strategy that is always preferred is by creating multiple ads that categorically explain your products and services. For instance, you can create an ad that contains multiple images, videos, and a fine-tune audio sound.

The success of your advertisement will depend deeply on the strategies that a firm or individual use to advertise their products, choosing the right audience, gender, location and interest of your target market can be of great help and can easily make a Facebook ad campaign successful and productive and achieve optimum results.

In general, Facebook has proven to be a great platform where businesses can be promoted and even sales made. Most firms have used it, and the platform is growing day by day as a profitable platform to do business. It is a platform that if well utilized, it can lead to successful business growth and an increase in sales.

Apart from influential business people, celebrities, celebrated artists use it to promote their ideas, songs, and concept. From this, it's clearly evident that Facebook ads have the main objective of promoting market areas and audiences around the globe as a whole.

Chapter 5: A Step by Step Guide on Creating Facebook Ads that are Efficient and Revenue Saving

With the emergence of several marketing strategies today, Facebook is one of the platforms used in creating enticing advertisements. The chapter highlights a step by step guide on building productive and efficient Facebook Ads essential for your business management plans.

Subsequently, there are different methods used to create Facebook Ads in plenty of books, but this one encompasses the most efficient and revenue saving. Facebook Ads may take various forms depending on the type of advertisement displayed. Each step discussed in the book entails descriptive details of the necessities to ensure the creation of Ads suitable for the vast market. More so, the book provides additional information for the benefit of creating productive outcomes.

The first step is always crucial as such; the chapter introduces the most critical information to ensure the following steps become successful. The concept adopted to generate the guide on creating Facebook Ads that are efficient and revenue saving is dependable and can be put into action immediately. The following steps primarily follow the previous ones precisely to avoid confusion. The last step, therefore, gives you the go-ahead to implement the best Facebook Ads for your audience.

Step 1: Creating Your Facebook Business Manager Account

Facebook account is another thing, and Facebook business manager account is another one is used for your business while another is just for socializing. Setting up a Facebook business manager account is the initial step to ensure the creation of a more sophisticated campaign. Unlike many e-commerce platforms, Facebook business manager houses all your details, including ads, customizing tools, and business pages for ease maneuver within your Facebook Ads strategy. You may also download Facebook pixels to manage your ads, which some users find it very essential to monitor ads' progress.

Creation of a Facebook business manager account provides the first step to the nature of Facebook Ads that are efficient and revenue saving. Visit business.facebook.com and click on Create Account. You will then submit your business name, Facebook business page, title, and email address. Fill then spaces and add advertising account through clicking Business Manager Menu and selecting Business Settings. Click Account and Ad Account and create or add an advertising account.

Step 2: Select the Right Objective

Facebook comprises of more than two billion monthly users henceforth attracting several brands to Facebook Ads as a means of marketing their products and services. The first thing to conduct before engaging in creating Facebook Ads is to choose a specific objective to fit into a given category of your campaign. Facebook initially asks you to select your purpose during the first step of developing your Facebook Ads manager. Choosing the right objective also enables you to focus on Facebook marketing techniques while yielding well-tailored results.

There are three types of objectives which include awareness, consideration, and conversion, guiding you correctly to your needs. Awareness focuses solely on brand recognition and reaches your audiences both on products and content. Objectives under considerations create traffic, product engagement, and provision of messages, therefore, generating interest for your audience to search for your brand. Conversions are objectives that enable your audience to get an urge to purchase your products through catalog sales, store sales, and conversions.

As such, awareness objectives are essential for campaigns and promotion of new businesses and you readily reach new potential customers. Conversion and store visits are crucial for increasing physical sales while narrowing down to more specific objectives, for instance, video views and mobile app installs. After selecting your preferred target and understand your goals, you are now aware of what you want to achieve in your Facebook advertisement.

Step 3: Select the Right Audience

Facebook has more than two billion active users of different ages, demography, varying interests, and distributed globally. It is therefore essential to narrow down to those relevant to the content displayed from the daily active users. Facebook offers three crucial sources of generating audiences; core, custom, and lookalike, which enable you to focus and determine your desired target audience. Most e-commerce brands utilize these three sources to create a successful marketing strategy across significant advertising platforms, including Facebook.

Core Audiences

The format of selecting your core audiences include a manual selection of groups according to your criterion, for instance, behavioral, likes, interests, and location characteristic. Interests and equivalents such as exercises relate to contents already existing on active user Facebook accounts and what they have interacted together. Behaviors comprise of certain activities or actions undertaken by users and stored by Facebook. Location includes specific user immediate environments while demographics entail profile information such as engineers.

Custom Audiences

Custom audiences include uploading contact lists of your current or former customers to engage with your target audience. Audience customization is one of the easiest, and your customers may provide testimonies about the physical activities of your brand. The details are then matched with users, and the ads remain delivered to target audiences directly. It, therefore, provides information about new products or product changes as well as reaching them through email addresses.

Lookalike Audiences

Lookalike audiences are ideal users you never engaged but generated from finding people similar to your existing audience. They can also be created from custom audiences selected from the specific population and may depend on location or specified criteria. Lookalike audiences increase over time from small percentages and may include new users who get into contact with your brand and access your goods and services physically.

Selecting a specific audience for your Facebook Ads ensures that your marketing strategy has a better chance of growing. More so, you can easily engage with past, existing, and targeted audiences, therefore, creating more room for converting your ads. Other categories of determining your audience include location-based, connection targeting, and demographics. The technique enables the ads to show to users both connected to your brand or not. Lookalike audiences remain the most reliable source used to attract your audience to your business website. It uses existing information to create new prospective clients.

Step 4: Choose Where to Display Your Ads

Facebook offers a wide range of platforms to display your ads for the benefit of reaching your specified audience. At the ad set level, you are free to choose where to you want your ads to show, including placements, devices, and other Facebook-owned platforms. Devices may include the ad to display on mobile only, desktop-only or both while also displaying on Instagram or messenger or both. Facebook also owns multiple apps where you can select where you want to show your ads.

However, Facebook recommends advertisers to choose an automated placement method to customize and optimize ads to produce the best outcome. You can also decide to whom you want the information to reach and select your desired audience. For example, if your target audiences are frequent mobile users, then choosing Instagram and Facebook messenger are the most reliable choices for your Facebook Ads display platforms. You may also select different groups depending on your product services while hindering your brand from showing to irrelevant groups.

Step 5: Set Your Budget Limit

Facebook provides different options for optimizing the cost of an advertising campaign. Choosing your budget includes selecting how frequent you wish your ads to display in chosen platforms. Facebook Ads may show daily, occasionally or lifetime running either indefinitely or as scheduled. Your optimization of how the ads will run will, therefore,

determine the cost you are to incur during the advertising period.

Facebook Ads performance and auctions are also other indicators of how the success and the cost may vary, especially when your audience view your adverts. However, it is crucial to set your auction into automated for those not aware of how such bids work. Similarly, you may set specific parameters in the previous steps which may exceed or overweigh what you expected. Setting some limitations during deciding your budget is essential in providing solutions to high costs during your campaign.

Besides, you can easily optimize your Ads manually as Facebook offers automated parameters which you may need to update. Thus, you can easily add, eliminate, or change some features which may alter your budget either becoming higher or lower than expected. For a successful Facebook Ads campaign, it is essential to set a favorable budget while maximizing on attracting new audiences in your brand.

Sometimes budgeting for your ads may accompany multiple challenges, but privacy and confidentiality of your information remain guaranteed of safety by Facebook. Set your budgets well to avoid additional charges as indicated in the creative dialogue. Budgeting for displaying Facebook ads is not only determined by the audience of whom your products are intended, but also depend on the following factors;

- Length of display of advertisements in the system;

- Extend of ads to related platforms;

- Cost of your products;

- Customer acquisition costs.

Step 6: Select Your Format

Displaying ads on Facebook offers a range of formats suitable for your advertisements and more so allowing you to select the right format. The forms provide Facebook among the most effective and reliable for any campaign. You can quickly choose the format fitting your objective and the targeted audience while within your budget. Some of the ad's formats provided include;

- Single image;

- Video format;

- Canvas;

- Slideshows;

- Collection;

- Carousel.

Each format comes with its benefits; for instance, photos provide a unique story for your audience compared to videos which provide a deeper engagement with sounds, images, and motions. Carousel is similar to videos but may lack sound and display in an image manner while collections display your products and the story behind it. Links ads direct your audience to your websites. Dynamics showcase your product in a more sophisticated way, and canvas ads are essential for providing full-screen displays primarily for mobile devices. Slideshows are the most affordable and offer a lightweight motion.

Slideshows, video, and carousel ads are among the best formats to market your brand and products as they have the maximum engagement and CTR rates compared to other forms. However, it is vital to select the best format for your ad to avoid increased costs of advertising while creating a broader audience. Facebook usually offer the best options of sizes while the company may guide you on some of the formats to rely on during your format selection.

Step 7: Adding Crucial Data and Placing Your Ad

Facebook ads are quite different compared to previous advertising techniques used in e-commerce marketing strategies. When using the Facebook business manager, you will need to select a business page or an Instagram account which you wish to use to present your campaign. Dynamic of products is one of the critical elements which connects your Facebook pixel and Facebook product catalog. Therefore, users or followers can view similar products you have added in your ads account. The technique enables you to retarget your advertisements through Facebook's dynamic products.

The creation of connections between your business website, ad account, Facebook pixel, and Facebook business manager enables the development of a more dynamic campaign, in achieving your objective quickly. Dynamics product ads are also essential for prospecting, enabling Facebook to display other products relevant to your brand even when not in the ad. Dynamic products campaign, therefore, increased your advertising plans while primarily connecting all your marketing platforms.

During filling of the dialogue, there may exist small details with crucial information that you miss while filling in different areas. Some include URL description and other selections at the creative collection. As such, take advantage and fill them with the CTA option and true copy playing a significant role in your advertising campaign through Facebook Ads. Then confirm all the information provided, including payments, targeted audience, and format before submitting and placing your order.

Step 8: Optimization of Your Ad Performance

Facebook Ad monitoring and measurement of its performance is an essential aspect as it enables you to analyze if it meets your objectives. Some campaigns may witness immediate CPC while others may begin to grow after the increase in the frequency of visits. Similarly, others may fail to perform as expected henceforth may demand effort. However, Facebook's ads manager will display all active campaigns within your profile. Henceforth enabling you to click and monitor any campaign you wish to analyze its progress or make changes.

Some of the activities to check to include relevant scores, actions taken by your audience after viewing the ad, frequency, and CPC value. It is also recommended that you check on your Facebook Ads daily for the benefit of analyzing your daily logs. There are situations where you may fail to experience any sale within a day or two. Hence, it is essential to be patient instead of turning off your ads or make changes. The algorithms may show a different outcome, but people may get attracted to your products over time.

Investing in Funneling

Creation of a funnel during product marketing through Facebook Ads entail an understanding that the majority of your audience will buy your product over time rather than immediately. Funnel-based strategies enable you to tailor your ad according to the audience's interests to purchase and familiarize yourself with your brand. In Facebook ads, creating a funnel allows you to reach quiet audiences of potential clients in a given campaign as well as those visiting your website without making a purchase.

The funnel also enables you to create more content-based advertisements suiting your budget, thus being intricate while covering a more comprehensive range of campaigns. Funneling, therefore, creates more prospective room to gain more sales in your brand but remains crucial in selecting a less expensive strategy. Besides, the funnel enables Facebook ads and each audience to acquire different methods of creative designs bringing prospects essential to drive purchases on your website.

Using Facebook Ads in Ecommerce Marketing Strategies

Since the introduction of Facebook business manager, Facebook advertising has created a favorable platform for different brands to grow and reach more clients. Using the account encompasses different groups of people, including those with no experience within the digital marketing sector. Facebook ads have become more attractive as reaching more targeted has been simplified significantly.

Facebook advertising is cheaper, faster, and business owners can readily check the progress of their ads and make necessary changes where applicable. As such, learning the basics of Facebook advertisement enables you to set up your account correctly and establish a successful campaign henceforth growing your business. With different forms to choose from, Facebook ads will work in your benefit as long as you have a working plan and the development of a stronger ad.

Chapter 6: Why Brands Use Facebook Ads to Maximize Sales

M odern-day marketing has shifted to digital as compared to traditional analog forms of marketing. Digital marketing techniques include blogging, affiliate marketing, email marketing, and SEO marketing. Social media sites such as Facebook, Instagram, Twitter, and WhatsApp form the platforms for internet marketing. Of all these sites, Facebook is the most popular one and boasts of over 2.5 billion users daily. Studies show that 60% of buyers are influenced by Facebook when making both offline and online purchases. This fact makes the leading site for digital marketing as it guarantees to reach a wider audience.

It is inevitable for brands not to use Facebook ads to survive in the modern market as a means of maximizing sales and targeting the right audience. The reasons for this are explained below.

1. **People spend a good amount of time on Facebook**

    Facebook is the king of all social media sites. The average Facebook user spends a little above 1 hour on

Facebook every single day just reading content and liking posts. Most of these users use mobile devices. These are your potential clients, and the fact that they spend a considerable amount of time on Facebook is really important for you to use Facebook ads. It is during this time that they can come across your brand, and depending on what you are offering and their preferences, some might just become interested! Remember, there is strength in numbers, and Facebook provides these numbers quite easily.

2. Affordability

Facebook advertising is a very affordable means of advertising. It is possible to reach a large group of people but spends very little money. It has a relatively low cost per action. For this reason, it would be wiser to utilize it as compared to placing commercials on television and radio, which could cost you an arm and a tooth. You can use as low as 50$ and reach 50000 people. You can also set a daily or lifetime budget which you can adjust at any given time.

The cost of Facebook ads is also lower than that of other digital platforms like LinkedIn and Instagram. In fact, the costs are cut down by up to 75%. This is unmatched.

3. You can gauge its results

The results of the ads will not be a mere estimation, but rather, they can be quantified. There are experts in Facebook advertising who can install conversion pixels on your site that come in handy to observe the activity. You will know how many people have visited your site, how many new followers who could be potential customers, how many clicks and conversions you have gotten. Therefore, it does not involve speculation like other traditional methods. It is also effective because you can know the reaction from your viewers since the ads provide a chance to express like, dislike or comment.

Moreover, if you do not see results, you can adjust your campaign, unlike in traditional methods where you cannot change tact immediately if you fail to see results.

4. Facebook ads can bring you to repeat clients

There are always the one-time clients and then those who come back, the repeat clients. Every business person's desire is to have their clients come back. You can use the audience features of such clients to add their emails into your Facebook advertising campaigns. This is because people who once bought from you are more likely to make a repeat purchase because they are users of your brand. One purchase should not be the end of the relationship between you and your buyer. Take advantage of the power of creating repeat customers.

5. **It can help increase referrals by word of mouth**

Tell a friend to tell a friend. This phrase is especially true when a customer is satisfied by the product or service that they got from you. A contented client will tell their friend and family in this case who might also become your clients. It may even go viral. Many fashion businesses have thrived this way. Someone orders a dress from a cloth store online and loves what is delivered. She will definitely tell her friends to check it out. The effect? A positive trajectory in the volume of your sales, which will, in turn, increase your profits.

6. **Your business rivals are also using Facebook advertising**

You definitely want to outsmart your competitors. It is business, and every entrepreneur is fighting to remain afloat. Your rivals are also using Facebook ads to maximize their sales. They are targeting the very audience that you are missing out on. To avoid being left behind, you cannot ignore the benefits that come with using Facebook advertising. Customers spend a considerable amount of time on Facebook, and that is exactly how you can get them.

Be sure to check out on the ads of your competitors. Make sure that yours are more compelling. Who knows? You might just sway away your competitor's biggest followers, and this may also result in sales conversion.

7. **Facebook ads can be a good ground to compete with bigger brands**

Start-ups can leverage internet marketing to be able to deal with competition from bigger and more established brands. You only have to make sure your ads are catchy, persuasive, and geared towards a certain audience to be able to thrive. Normally bigger brands have a bigger capital base and high profits and therefore engage inexpensive methods of advertising like television commercials and billboards, which may not be possible for new entrants.

8. **You can also get clients out of Facebook platform**

There are those clients who can know about your brand from elsewhere and then come to your Facebook. Through your ads, they may further visit your website and eventually come to your physical address if they are impressed with what you have to offer. Actually, Facebook has a tool that is able to track offline purchases that have been triggered by Facebook ads. People can be able to locate the nearest shop from the ad because this feature is able to show the estimated time of travel, address, and phone contacts.

9. Facebook advertisement can help you penetrate new markets

You can test the market at your own pace using Facebook advertisements for people who are considering introducing a new brand into the market. The platform will increase awareness about your brand, and people start getting interested in your product, translating into sales. Thus, it is very reliable for an entrepreneur in need of breaking into new markets.

10. Can be done anywhere

The mobile nature of Facebook advertising makes it very simple o reach the right target at their own convenience. Three-quarters of Facebook users log in using mobile phones. With the over 2. 5 million Facebook users, the potential audience will be reached. You cannot compare Facebook advertising with TV commercials where one has to literally schedule a time to watch TV so that they can watch your advert. It is therefore very versatile and can be used at any place, any time.

11. Time conscious

Facebook advertisement does not waste time. It does not take long to reach out to a large number of people. It is really encouraging for a business person to start receiving interested clients barely a few hours after placing an ad. It even boosts the enthusiasm of that person to continue selling their brand with more zeal.

12. Boosts brand awareness

The more people know about the existence of your brand, the more they are likely to buy from you. Facebook advertising will be a great way to inform the target audience about your brand, and they can then sample it and make a decision on whether to make a purchase or not.

You can boost brand awareness using Facebook ads by sharing superb content, using quora, and following influencers. Do not post the same tone and content across all channels. This could be absolutely boring. To make yourself stand out, use consistent branding in all parts of your website, and have a bio that is really appealing.

13. You can set up ads quite easily

Facebook ads are quite easy to set up. It is as simple as choosing the type of ad to set up, selecting your target group, choosing your budget, and the time needed to accomplish. You can opt to customize it from an array of formats and bidding techniques. You can pay per like, per impression, per click or per action.

14. You can have a specific target

Your potential customers can be gotten from filtering by connections, for example, friends of the users who follow your page or behavior and interests which entails people who have purchased a certain product recently. You can also filter according to location. This is for sellers targeting people of a specific geographical area. You can also filter based on marital status, gender, age, job description as long as it suits the service or products on offer.

A good example of filtering is in location targeting; you can target a specific country, state, or city. You can still filter for recent travelers to the location, people living in that location, or better still everyone in that location. Wow! How amazing.

15. Facebook provides video ads

Human beings are visual creatures. They would rather watch a video describing a brand than reading tons of information about the same brand. Video ads are also catchy and thus grab more attention. It is, therefore, a very useful marketing tool that is made possible by Facebook ads. In the end, Facebook ads drive more conversions. To make your video ads more result-oriented, make it short, have the right objective, and know your key performance indicators. Make sure that your call to action falls in the middle of the video ad.

16. Call buttons have taken it a notch higher

Call buttons have changed the game. Its effectiveness is much better than a click to a website. Thanks to call buttons, you see an ad, click on the call now button and guess what? The lead is captured. For someone using a mobile device, making a call is simpler than navigating through a website since it is a quicker way to get information. Call buttons have totally revolutionized Facebook advertising and can be termed as the most important feature so far. Amazing!

17. The power of remarketing

Remarketing is an advertising strategy that enables you to advertise to recent visitors to your website. This happens when you visit a website, and an add pops up a short while later. Someone can visit your website but fail to purchase or to contact you. You can leverage Facebook ads to engage and follow up on such customers, which will, in turn, lead to conversions.

18. Facebook ads can increase visits to your blog

Blogs are a great way to engage closely with your audience. Facebook can be a great tool to narrow the gap between traffic and your blog. Blogs tremendously grow with traffic hence the need for your blog to reach a wider audience. It should be as credible as possible for people to trust that the content is worth clicking on.

This means that it can also increase your social media followers on your social platforms. If you have email newsletters, your subscribers will also increase.

19. Your SEO rankings can be boosted

Social signals help to determine how to rank search engines. A higher SEO means you will get more traffic on your website than people who also similar keywords, therefore, gaining increased website referrals from search engines. The activity of social media; comments, shares, and likes on a post constitute social signals. Through Facebook, your social signals can be increased, meaning that your SEO rankings will also be improved.

SEO rankings greatly influence customer's decisions to buy since people considered brands with higher SEO rankings to be more credible and reliable. It is actually the latest PR strategy and should be invested in.

20. Effectiveness

There is evidence to show that Facebook marketing actually works. Research shows that over 90% of online marketers confirm that advertising via Facebook has been instrumental in ensuring that their business has been a success. The interesting part is that it does not discriminate but helps both startups and well-established businesses reach their audience, increase sales, and consequently increase their profits. Facebook's large global audience and the affordable costs render it the most effective and desired way of advertising.

21. Facebook users influence each other's decision to buy

Consumers get to talk about products in different groups on Facebook. Users of a product may talk about how they have found it in their Facebook pages. This will be important to you because first you can get to referrals out of this and you can also get negative feedback about your product, which will help you to improve.

For example, you are dealing with cooking oil; you might need to join cook groups where people who use cooking oils engage in following on their comments. You will also know the advantages your competitors have over you improve on the areas you need to. Another good example is a mom's group if you are dealing in diapers to where you will get to know about their various preferences.

22. Facebook organic reach is limited

Nowadays, having a Facebook page alone is not enough. Organic Facebook reach is fast declining because of the large content being created and recreated every single day. Less than 10% of your followers may actually follow up on your updates in their news feed because news feed has been designed first to show Facebook users news that is most relevant to them, for example, posts from their friends or their locality first. Facebook limits the visibility of business pages in the news feed. In paid promotion, many people will be to come across your brand because this limitation is overcome. You will have no option than to use ads to enable people to know about your brand.

23. Control burden lays on you

It is up to you to decide the content that is released in the ads and also how the budget plays out. You can also get to decide who sees your ads. This control is very dear to you because every business person's desire is to participate in decision making in their business and the type of ads to place is a very critical decision that will determine whether a business will succeed or fail.

Types of Business Models that Can Use Facebook Ads

Business Ownership Models

Before venturing into any business, you need to understand different business ownership structures. Investors usually decide on the type of business based on location, demand, and plan. While some business owners like getting attention, some prefer to go lowkey. Here are the four common types of business ownership models.

Sole Proprietorship

Most less capital-intensive businesses often start as sole proprietors. It is the simplest on the list and is owned by one person who may decide to use their name or not. All you need to have is a social security number and the necessary permits. This type of business is not subjected to many conflicts because the owner is the sole decision-maker. Besides, sole proprietors usually are taxed once and thus avoid any involving paperwork to operate. Most start-up businesses should go for this type of structure before they get more sophisticated. It gives them a chance to clearly understand the market dynamics before pumping in more capital or bringing in more investors on board.

Partnership

This usually arises when two or more people team up to form a joint business. There should be a formal written agreement that approves the union. Otherwise, it may be easy for one partner to contest for the ownership of that business. Partnerships come with advantages such as sharing the business start-up cost and losses. However, this kind of structure requires utmost professionalism because it can easily collapse when conflicts and arguments arise. All partners are 100% responsible for all the crucial decisions made. They also have unique tax requirements, and a lot of paperwork is required when filing for returns. Any tax evasions schemes are taken seriously and can lead to the closure of the business.

Corporation

For this structure, owners have limited liability and the business functions independently. This means that the owners are protected by the law from facing any personal legal action should the business be sued. Corporations have individual rights and are held responsible as a distinct entity. They have sophisticated tax requirements, and a lot of paperwork should be submitted while filing for tax returns.

Limited Liability Company (LLC)

LLCs are like corporations with the only difference being that they are owned by multiple individuals, trustees, corporations, and other LLCs. The owners have limited liability because LLCs are also treated as individual business entities. Under proper guidelines, LLCs can file taxes like partnerships only that there will be more paperwork.

Business ownership structures vary a lot, and you should do your research before investing in any business. It will give you a careful investment insight after weighing on the available exit options.

To sum it all up, it is time you accept that Facebook ads are needed to move your business to the next step. In fact, if you are not already using Facebook ads, you need to get started right away. The reason for this is because of the large number of people that use Facebook, the ability to remarket that

Facebook offers, the wonder that is the call button feature and the ability to reach a specific target of audience. Facebook will also help you increase awareness of your brand and increase customer attribution as well as enable you to track results. The affordable costs of advertising and its proven effectiveness make it desirable for businesses that want to flourish. At the very end of it all, you will experience increase leads, sales, and revenue. To ensure that you hack this well, invest in a Facebook advertising specialist who knows the ropes of the trade.

Chapter 7: The Psychology Behind Facebook Advertising and its Impact

D o you ever find yourself checking your Facebook app a few times in a day? Mostly when you are idle? Facebook dominance, as a social media platform has created incredible curiosity for researchers worldwide. Over 90% of Facebook users admit to logging in the app several times throughout the day.

From a different perspective, some could term this as "being hooked." But what could make an adult "hooked" on a social media platform? Researchers have verified that there is a psychology behind the Facebook app itself that somewhat makes the users keep going back.

The psychology behind Facebook as an app is the same concept that makes Facebook ads very successful. From the extensive research done by various institutions and organizations, the psychology behind Facebook ads can be understood from comprehensive knowledge of the psychology of Facebook users.

No matter how introverted a Facebook user might be, statistic shows that one way or another, all Facebook users participate with their accounts. It could be actively or inactively. All the Facebook users fall in either one of the personalities below depending on the content they post.

The Agreeable

- These types of people tend to good at interpersonal relationships;
- They are, in all essence, more cooperative;
- They are helpful;
- They use Facebook to maintain honest interactions;
- Their interactions are with people they value;
- They do not speak ill of other people on the platform.

Conscientious

- These people have strong work ethics;
- They are highly organized;
- Their social responsibility is high;
- They are not frequent Facebook users;
- They post discrete and controversy-free content;
- They do not make harmful posts that hurt others online.

Extraverts

- They post frequently;

- They are generally positive people who use Facebook to communicate and socialize;
- The social network is often large;
- They are talking and upbeat;
- Of all five personalities, they post the most.

Overly Open People

- They share very frequently;
- They learn new information from the platform;
- They tend to explore new intellectual ideas on Facebook;
- They barely socialize casually.

The Neurotics

- They are generally negative people;
- They exhibit traits of low self-esteem, paranoia, bipolar among other traits;
- They post on private issues like their romantic relationships;
- Constantly seeking affirmation and attention through controversial posts;
- High chances of a neurotic going off on personal rants on Facebook;
- Most neurotics and anxious and highly sensitive people.

From the above characteristics, patterns of Facebook users are bound to emerge. For instance, agreeable individuals are more welcoming than Extraverts who tend to exhibit narcissistic tendencies and neurotics who are constantly seeking validation.

Another psychological mechanism that has a major impact on how people use Facebook is the psychological rewards from using Facebook.

The Psychological Rewards of Using Facebook and How They Impact Facebook Users

People are constantly going back on Facebook throughout the day because of the psychological rewards they receive from being on the platform. There is a sense of accomplishment that comes with using Facebook. Facebook has become somewhat an irresistible platform to many because of these rewards.

People are looking to either maintain concrete relationships on the social platform or get constant attention and validation. Whichever one it is, there is a mental satisfaction that every Facebook user gets.

Advertisers use the same psychology concepts to gain the most from Facebook advertising. The psychology behind Facebook advertising can be broken down into these single factors.

- The use of colors;
- The use of images;
- The use of compelling texts.

These are the key elements Facebook advertisers consider while putting up an ad on the platform. Apart from what people look at in an ad, advertisers also consider how an ad makes the people feel. They do this by selling the ideal picture of what people need.

With constant images of people doing great in their lives, there is social media pressure for people to keep up. People want to make their lives better. Most people who shop online are purchasing the experience rather than the products. Facebook ads capitalize on ideal selling. That is why the specifics of an ideal Facebook advertisement are centered on captivating texts, colors, and images.

The Psychology of Advertising Using Colors

Color psychology significantly increases the interactions by tapping into the most unconscious part of the human brain. Colors have a different impact on Facebook users. As an advertiser, understanding the basics of color psychology can be of great help. Details in the psychology of colors are utterly essential.

There are no best or preferred colors that are used to create enable quick psychological or emotional response. However, there are a few factors you can consider to increase traffic on your ads using colors.

- For instance, you can double a Facebook Ad CTR by including a colored border on your image;
- There are a few colors preferred by the female gender to other colors and vice versa;
- Conversion rates can be increased up to 60% by contrasting colors in two different links within one image;
- Conversion rates of your page can increase by 14.5 %when the CTA color button is changed from light green to yellow.

These are some of the small but significant aspects of color psychology.

Different Colors and How They Impact Your Facebook Ads

There are popular colors used by almost all the advertisers on Facebook ads. These colors represent different situations and convey specific messages depending on how they are used. Here are few of them and what they represent in advertising

Green

- Green, in most cases, signifies affirmation or positive action;
- It is associated with environmental themes;
- It is the easiest color that the brain processes;
- Green is at the top of the list for most popular colors with men;
- It is associated with shoppers who are on a budget;
- It can be used for social offers;
- Different types of greens are effective as color contrast;
- Greens are vibrant and at the same time mild to look at;
- The color green attracts the eye on an advert while at the same time, achieves certain emotions;
- You can say green is subtle and at the same time a vibrant color perfect for advertising.

Blue

- Blue is a multi-gender color perfect for advertising;
- It symbolizes security and trust;
- Darker blues signifies professionalism;
- Lighter shades of blue sooth the eyes and have a calming effect;

- On a Facebook Ad, blue can be used with another color contrast to avoid the Ad blending with the theme color of the app itself;
- It barely works for food items since people associate it with illnesses;
- It also depicts intelligence, logic, and competence;
- It can be used as a good primary color in a case where bold colors are included.

Purple

- Purple lies on the feminine side;
- It is also associated with wealth;
- According to statistics no men like the color purple;
- It is a great Facebook Ad color for a women audience;
- Purple makes a great color for ads that converse the message of wealth and abundance;
- It can be used on a demographic of senior women from the age of 60 years.

Black and White

- Black and white is safe colors;
- They both convey sophistication;
- They also signify power, intelligence, and sincerity;
- Black and white go together in most cases;
- The colors can be used to create professionalism in ads and bring out the sophistication;

Other happy colors like red, orange, and yellow are also used in the ads. They are intentionally used to attract the reader's attention.

The Psychology Behind Facebook Ads Using Texts

Specific words cause certain responses when used on Facebook Ads. For a successful Facebook Ad, well thought out texts are essential. Texts in Ads are used to bring out emotions or create psychological reactions.

Savvy Facebook advertisers take advantage of connotative words and phrases to achieve high responses. Connotative words and phrases have a much deeper meaning. Most effective words are short and precise but carry connotations. Here are some specific words that will make your Ad successful on Facebook.

Using "You"

"You" is a simple word, but when used appropriately, it can have such a major impact on Facebook users. The use of 'you' in an Ad commands attention. The word portrays that a product is built specifically for the person reading the advertisement.

- It can be used to compel your readers to purchase a product;
- It can be used to create curiosity of a product for a reader;
- Can be used to bring awareness to the specific reader about a product.

The Word "Save"

Who does not want to save some money or time? Facebook Ads are a perfect way to give discounts and offer coupons. Discounted products have better chances of penetrating the market and creating great profits. Using the word 'save' instantly grabs a lot of attention from Facebook users and will automatically create high conversions for you. A few examples of how to effectively uses the words 'save' are:

- "Save on eating out this holiday with these simple homemade food tips";
- "Increase your savings by up to 60% with these tips";

- "Save 40% buy making purchases in the next 12 hours".

Using the Word "New"

The word 'New' is crucial in advertising. With the production of new products every day, people are purchasing new. More people are moving away from the culture of minimalism and purchasing second-hand items to buying new and affordable items. A tip for bringing home when advertising the new products is advertising to the previous clients.

The Word "Proven"

The word proven in your Facebook Ad text conveys trust. It is an effective name on Facebook Ads as its meaning heavy. The valuation of a product can be recognized through the use of the word 'proven.'

You will largely increase conversions by the use of 'proven' as it portrays a guaranteed efficacy of a product or service.

The Word "Free"

The word 'free' has been proven to increase the efficiency of adverts by 30%. People all over the world, like products or services with free offers. You must, however, make sure you use the word free authentically with honest intentions to fulfill the free offer.

Offer free items or services and include them in the advertisement. For instance, you can offer free shipping to first time buyers of a product.

A text in your Ads brings out the intended emotions of a potential buyer and propels them to make a purchase. Conversations grow through how well your Ads capture the Facebook user's emotions.

Emotional language on the Ads brings out feelings and makes the Ad more effective. You can use emotional language to evoke fear, happiness, pity, humor, or encouragement. All these emotions will result in a reaction. Depending on how well you use the words, they can create amazing conversions for your business or product.

Chapter 8: How to Use Facebook Ads Manager and Setting Up Ads Account

How to Use Facebook Ads Manager

Facebook continually introduce new features in the ad manager to make the campaign platform more intuitive. However, understanding how to use Facebook ads manager is one of the steps in creating a decent and more successful Facebook ad. Henceforth a successful implementation of a successful marketing strategy ensures that you reach more audiences while growing your brand and products.

As to create the most attractive and successful ad on Facebook and its subsidiaries, you need to understand how to get started with the Facebook business manager and the creation of an ad account. The two are the beginning of creating great ads while determining where and when to show to your target audiences. The chapter highlights step by step of how to use Facebook ads manager and the process of creating an ad account under Facebook business manager profile.

Guide on How to Use Facebook Ads Manager

Step 1: Create a Facebook Business Manager Account

After you decide that you want to advertise via Facebook ads, you are required to set up a business manager account and set your preferences about your brand and product. The ads manager is an essential tool as it provides you access to various areas such as your business pages and apps. Besides, it allows your team or other people to manage your accounts as well as optimize your ads and analyze performances.

As a beginner, personal Facebook account, business pages, and Facebook ads manager account possess significant differences, especially when it comes to business marketing strategies. Similarly, opening a business manager account and creating your advertising access also differ. Setting a Facebook ads manager includes providing your registration requirements, including your name, email address, and brand. When creating advertisements, the tool asks for details on your payments and billings, details about your product and company to display to the audience.

Step 2: Explore Your Facebook Ads Manager Account

Facebook ads manager comprises of all your needs in creating, editing, and making necessary changes to your advertisements. Facebook ads manager functionalities provide immediate impact to your ads, but Facebook enables you to set your parameters manually when you want. Some of the benefits of Facebook ad manager include the provision of management and modification of ads, monitoring of your existing campaigns, and setting of your target audiences.

After the creation of your business manager account, you may readily access the Facebook business manager dashboard after clicking a drop-down arrow on the right top corner of your page. The ads manager comprises of your account overview, campaigns, ad sets, and ads as well as other options including ad performance, breakdown, exports, filters, and charges on advertisements. You are then ready to set your standards and begin creating your marketing campaigns.

Step 3: Choose Your Objective

The Facebook business manager initially asks for users to set their objectives when considering utilizing Facebook ads when creating campaigns. Selecting the purpose of your ad is the first process of creating your advertisement by clicking on Create Ad at the top right corner. Facebook offers several categories of objectives to suit all e-commerce marketers via its platform. The types include:

- Awareness campaigns;

- Consideration campaigns;

- Conversion campaigns.

Under awareness campaigns, it involves reach and brand awareness, which creates knowledge and interest of your audience towards your products and brand. Consideration campaigns include traffic, engagement, app installs, video views, and lead generation, primarily attracting your audience to engage with your brand and products. Conversion, on the other hand, prompts your audience to purchase your products through product catalog sales, conversions, and store website visits.

Select the most convenient and sophisticated objective to meet your marketing goals, especially under the subcategories. Facebook will eventually create your ads through the set objectives after the successful creation of your campaign name. As such, you are ready to move to the next step as the advertisement is officially created. However, it is essential to select the most preferred option as it determines the performance of the following steps and the success of your campaign.

Step 4: Determine and Select Your Audience

Facebook comprises of over two billion active users who visit the platform daily, but they are not all your target population. As such, your target capabilities should solely focus on your audience, who are your potential clients. Facebook captures and records massive data about their users, including age, gender, location, education, interests, language, and behavior, among others. With such a large population, your target audiences are the crucial elements of your campaign.

Fortunately, the Facebook business manager offers the best filters to acquire your specific audience intended for your information. Some of the ways used to receive a new audience include lookalike, custom, and core audiences. Lookalike audiences are individuals generated from the existing audience as they possess similar features. Core audiences are obtained through setting your criteria manually and filtering the general population within Facebook. Custom audiences are created from your list of

Facebook friends and contact lists as well as from former and current customers.

Lookalike feature of acquiring new audiences is one of the best as it primarily targets users with similar qualities to your existing audience. When creating a lookalike audience, you either choose your filters and criteria or select your preferences and Facebook create your audience automatically. More so, lookalike audiences play a significant role in expanding your market from your existing population to a broader range and equipped with similar features. According to Facebook, it is essential to upload a contact list of between one thousand and fifty thousand to guarantee the quality of your ads.

Step 5: Set Your Budget

Advertising in all platform charges a fee while growing your brand to reach a wider audience. The same applies to Facebook ads but provides different forms henceforth enabling users to take control of their budgets. If you have multiple active ads running, you can readily display each ad separately at alternating fees as you decide how much you spend on campaigns. Again, Facebook offers two methods of displaying your advertisements; daily and lifetime media spend, which also alter your charges.

Daily Media Spend

Daily media spend are regular fees charged from a given ad set at a default of $20.00, but you can readily adjust when the campaign is running. The charges may vary depending on how many times it displays on each audience or the platform in general. However, it is vital to spend as few fees as possible, for instance, $5 daily and make your ads run for about seven days continuously to enhance your performance. You may also decide to start with a $100 charge enabling the ads to display for at least two weeks for complete analysis for effective initial optimization and management.

Lifetime Media Spend

You may choose to display your ad for a longer duration charged somehow cheaper compared to daily fees. Lifetime media spend may range from a few weeks to months while considering aspects such as CPM and CPC. The two also affected regular media spend where CPM are costs charged per every one thousand impressions while CPC charged for every click on your ads. CPM is the most important when creating awareness of your brand and products. While CPC promotes your business as people click and visit your website or app and make a purchase.

Step 6: Choose Where to Display Your Ads

Since the acquisition of Instagram, Facebook has increased its advertising platforms hence enabling you to choose your desired areas to run your ads. Among them include mobile and desktop news feeds, Instagram, and Facebook messenger. Facebook ads manager offers several placements where you can select one or more categories where your ads will show and reach your audience.

Desktop and Mobile News Feeds

When you select your ads to show on news feeds of desktops, mobile, or both devices, they will run embedded in news feeds. It is, therefore, essential for brand and product awareness as well as engagement. When running ads with links or apps, ensure they are compatible with both or one device to avoid becoming annoying when clicked by your audience. The ads should remain responsive to both mobile and desktops, accompanied by a seamless experience.

Column Ad Displays

These are ads running on the right-hand column of Facebook and among the first designs of advertisement in e-commerce. The design is consistent with desktops users only and suitable for ads that promote your brand and products. Therefore, it prompts customers to purchase or click and learn more about what your business offers.

Facebook Network Audiences

Facebook has created multiple joint partnerships, and the same applies to create a network where your ads may show and attract new audiences. Some include mobile apps and websites henceforth maximizing exposure by displaying advertisements to viewers outside Facebook. Besides, Facebook networks enable ads to run in video views effectively while reaching people on other platforms, especially while browsing on websites.

Instagram

Instagram is another platform with millions of followers to different accounts, therefore, creating a favorable environment for ads. With Instagram being an asset to Facebook, you may choose to extend your ads to Instagram under all formats provided by Facebook. Like other platforms, Facebook enables you to expose your brand to Instagram to reach more audiences to come on board and purchase your products.

Step 7: Create Ads

After setting up your campaign, audience, and placement, now Facebook ads manager requires you to create your ad. First, you will select the mode of your creative display available in different formats, which include the carousel, single image, single video, slideshow, and collection. Each form accompanies varied ways on how your ad shows. For instance, carousel ads have scrollable images between two and ten, while collections comprise of both pictures and videos displayed on full screen.

After setting your format, choose your image, videos, or slides that stand out and focuses on your brand and product and grabs your target attention instantly. Check your thump stoppers by trying different images, slides, or videos to acquire the best ones. Upload the desirable one and populate and later make a preview to see your outcome. Other factors to watch out during ad creation include main ad text, headlines, and your brand link description. The main ad text has up to ninety characters, headlines not more than twenty-five while link descriptions should have a maximum of ninety characters.

Step 8: Add Your Campaign to Facebook

Once you have developed your ad accompanied with a call to action, sweet and straightforward thump, now it is time to click on Place Order option. Facebook will then screen your advert to ensure it complies with Facebook's Advertising Policies. If it meets, Facebook will approve, and your campaign will become live to your target population.

Step 9: Ad Monitoring

Another significant benefit provided by Facebook ads manager is the ability to monitor its performance, especially on the Return on Investment of your campaigns. During the monitoring process, the ads manager enables you to make changes where applicable while noting the performance on metrics. Clicks are one of the parameters to check to determine the number of times the ad has received clicks. Impressions are the number of times the ad has been viewed, and the conversion rate is the measure of the percentage of people who see, click, and make a purchase.

Facebook ads manager also enables you to set a reminder at specific times of the day where you will check and optimize your campaigns. As such, Facebook offers the best possible ways to ensure your receive customers despite the competitive marketing techniques in e-commerce. Tweaking the information provided including creative display, copy, your budget, and billing as well as your target population may alter performance. The technique is vital if you are receiving low traction on your ads.

How to Setup the Account

Creating a new Facebook ads manager account or claiming an already existing account provides a similar procedure for developing successful e-commerce marketing campaigns. Setting up an ad's manager account is conducted under

Facebook business manager dialog essential for maximizing permission management of your brand.

Step 1: Create a Facebook Business Manager

Before setting up a Facebook ads manager account, you need to create a business manager profile found by clicking business.facebook.com and click Create Account. Enter the name of your business or brand, name, email address, and business page. In other fields below, add the necessary information correctly and submit your data to open Facebook business manager profile.

Step 2: Open Ad Account Setup Wizard

In the business manager profile, go to Business Manager Settings and click on Ad Account under People and Assets for already existing ads account. For newly created Facebook ads manager accounts, you will see a drop-down menu under People and Assets and select Add New Ad Account. Opening ad account setup for creating new accounts applies to both those with existing profiles or when new in the Facebook ads manager.

Step 3: Enter Your Details

Type your name to use in the ad account, choose your time zone, and the currency of your region, state, or country. Please ensure that the currency you submit is consistent with the coin you will use for your payments during the billing process of creating your advertisements. Facebook uses your time zone and currency to run your ads with an effort of displaying campaigns consistent with your region or country. Also, note that false information, especially on the money, may result in account closure. Add yourself as the account admin as well as your team participating in different roles in the ad account.

Step 4: Add Payment Methods

With all the above information provided, adding a payment method now activates your ad account. Select Payment Methods button and choose your preferred option and set it correctly for a successful account activation process. Once done, select billing country using either Credit or Debit Card with the previously indicated currency. Besides, ensure Credit or Debit Card information is consistent with your name as the admin as Facebook does not accept different titles of the same.

Step 5: Confirm and Submit Your Details

After placement of your information correctly, submit your data and your account will be activated almost instantly. Go back to the Ad Account option, and you will see Add New Account option indicating that you have an active account already existing. In your Facebook business manager, you may create a maximum of two ad accounts under as an admin as well as claim your account anytime in any profile.

Adding an Active Ad Account to Facebook Business Manager

Facebook Business Manager also helps when you have more ad accounts and wish to add them to your current profile. Readily select settings and click on Ad Account under People and Assets and select Claim an Ad Account. Provide your current ad account ID for campaign accounts or personal ID if using personal ad accounts. Claim the account and add it to your existing Facebook business manager and manage them with ease in one place.

How Technology Impacts Business Efficiency

To start and run a successful business without the input of technology these days is almost impossible. The possibilities of the business becoming a success are almost NIL. In a world that has nearly all the companies in various industries moving in the digital space, embracing technology is the only way to compete effectively. Many technology platforms are allowing business owners to gain maximum profits by integrating them into their businesses. From business websites to social media handles to applications meant for more natural service delivery, tech options are extensive.

The most modern technology is machine learning and artificial intelligence. It is completely changing the phase of many businesses and bringing about a revolution of efficiency and profit in minimal time. The TabSquare digital platform has embraced AI to fully maximize efficiency in its systems and service clients all around the world.

Tabsquare Machine Learning Proficiency in Running the Business

As a business operating with massive assistance of Tech, keeping up with the current tech trends is essential for the growth of the business. Consumers are the number one priority in any business. Ensuring their needs are met most professionally and effectively will undoubtedly result in a successful business. With the help of AI, TabSquare provides smart solutions that guarantee the profit and ensure quality and reliable customer service delivery.

The best part about the use of AI in TabSquare is the multilingual factor. A well-fed AI system can quickly detect thousands of languages across the globe. Limitations, in this case, become a thing of the past since business can reach out to a massive audience. The accuracy of AI in handling multiple languages is again a factor that screams efficiency in technology. With such a broad audience in business, the profits are bound to scale higher.

AI again wins in the world of advanced Tech since it enables businesses to take up data that is useful in future reference of the direction of the company. For instance, the broad information of the consumers fed in the AI system can detect future problems and trends. As a business, the ability to foresee an awaiting business calamity or progress can be extremely beneficial in future decision-making processes.

Time Saving Factor

The time-saving factor is the number one reason companies would consider while including artificial intelligence in their systems. The use of AI in TabSquare has substantially achieved this aspect. The system can provide fast and effective solutions that an average customer care agent would instead take time resolving. Also, it has been able to eliminate the inconvenience of a personal customer care agent when they have days off or when they have emergencies that prompt their unavailability. AI runs throughout the seasons and timings. It could serve your clients 24/7 as per your desired preference. The level of efficiency experienced in the time-saving factor of artificial intelligence system is worth investing in as a business.

Tech advancement creating efficiency in businesses is more than evident. The digital era is here and considering many enterprises are moving in the direction of technology and its advancements, entrepreneurs can only get excited about the possibilities of even better business operations. The success of any business in this new era solely relies on its technological versatility. More companies should embrace new technological advancements to make an impact in their space. Otherwise, they risk being thrown out of business by competitors who have already embraced technology and are willing to research more on the current business trends. Don't be left behind in this technological era.

Chapter 9: Types of Facebook Ads that you should avoid

The Facebook business manager offers several types of ads essential for you while considering e-commerce marketing campaign. However, each type accompanies varying specifications, benefits, and detriments hence vital to select the ones desired for your campaign. As such, we are going to discover different types of Facebook ads you should avoid during the creation of your advertisement. The ad formats are from all Facebook audience networks, mobile and desktop, and Instagram platforms.

Dynamic Ads

One of the top Facebook ads types to avoid is the dynamic ad, which includes your audience viewing a similar production Facebook, previously saw on your website. Despite the product being more personalized and relevant to your target audience, the campaign displays the same information already perused by the user. On the other hand, if you decide to use dynamic ads to run your advertisement, Facebook enables you to save between thirty and fifty percent on costs for acquisition

Dynamic ads as well only apply on instances where you have more than ten images you wish to display in the form of carousels. However, they are only essential when in need of posting more than ten photos as carousels only allow a maximum of ten. Similarly, dynamic ads run at higher costs while solely providing similar outcomes compared to carousel ads type. Besides, dynamic ad displays are a modification of carousels with the ability to display more scrollable pictures.

Subsequently, when utilizing dynamic ads, they enable you to accomplish several e-commerce marketing objectives. Also, you readily select your desirable audience categorized as upselling and cross-sell products and viewed or added to cart but non-purchased audiences. This type of Facebook ads is among the best when it comes to the promotion of your brand and product by enticing your viewers to buy your goods or services. It, therefore, improves your campaign performance while delivering the intended information to your audience.

Features of Dynamic Ads

- Headlines have a maximum of 25 characters;

- The image size encompasses both 1200 x 628 and 600 x 600;

- The Ad text uses up to 90 characters while link description has 30 characters.

Canvas Ads

Canvas ads are another type that is interactive and engages your audiences about your content on Facebook. However, the canvas is only applicable and compatibles to mobile devices limiting desktop users to miss out on your ad. This type of Facebook ad may utilize any format of your campaign and people can swipe to view products. You can also tilt, zoom in and out to see the product or brand correctly as they load much faster compared to other types of ads. The ads display in full-screen mode, making users to readily watch, click, tap or swipe and engage with your brand.

As a type of Facebook ads to avoid, canvas advertisement hinders your access to the general audience found in the platform. This is because almost half of your target population may miss an opportunity to view your product or brand while using desktop devices, Facebook networks, or Instagram. Like most ad types, the primary function of Facebook as an e-commerce marketing platform is to reach more audiences henceforth maximizing your sales. With such presence of limits or restriction to mobile use only, then you are missing out on other clients fond of using desktops and Facebook web pages.

However, some of the benefits of using canvas ads include lifetime view of your products on mobile, delivery of complete immersive, and interactive campaigns online. This type also ensures that your audience readily accesses your business website or while viewing details within the mobile app. Canvas ads accompany different components and features which include;

- Headers with logos;

- Button to be redirected to offsite links;

- Autoplay options;

- Characters on headlines are 45 while ad copy text has up to 90;

- Text block;

- Image carousel.

Lead Ads

Lead ads are Facebook campaigns that focus on collecting user's email addresses for the benefit of creating mail lists to alert your audiences about your brand and products. The advertisement urges your prospects to sign up with your page enabling them to share or like your business. However, Facebook plays a significant role as it automatically populates fields where your prospects quickly sign up and grow your email list. Unfortunately, not all your target population would love the process of providing their details.

Your audience's data are then stored within your ads account and later moved to a CRM system which immediately automates the general process. Like other types of Facebook ads, lead campaigns also comprises of specifications which are paragraph format of context cards with headlines box up to 60 characters and Privacy Policy of website links, among others. New email addresses from prospects are added to a list already connected to service provider equipment with leveraged automated amenities.

Lead ads are important for advertisers who wish to create a long list of prospect's email addresses and set parameters on sending automatic them alert about new products, changes, or discounts. This type of Facebook ads is, therefore, not recommended for beginners interested in creating awareness while promoting their products and businesses. More so, lead ads are most suitable for established brands who wish to expand their market. Besides, it enables their prospects to remain updated on the trending products through newsletters or occasional notifications.

Page Post Text Ads

Page post text ads are among the ones you should highly avoid as they have limited evidence about your product or brand. This type primarily engages your audience with plan texts posted on your Facebook business page but likely to deliver poor outcomes. Page post text ads typically show on right columns of your feeds on both mobile and desktop devices. Plan texts possess numerous disadvantages compared to its benefits. Some of the negatives are poor attention generated from prospects; it lacks eye-catching features to attract your audience and limited room to monitor and optimize its performance.

On the other hand, page post text ads have benefit, for instance, direct interactions with your audience despite deteriorating your engagement practices. However, direct contact has a limited area to click, scroll, or even tap to view the products being advertised. That said, ensure you avoid using this type of Facebook ads to as it is among the classes with the low-performance outcome despite being the cheapest method of Facebook advertisement. Page post text ads may even become one of the worst choices for you, especially when they lack boosted page posts from Facebook.

Single Image Ads

Single image ads are among the most common today and involve quality photos displayed on both Facebook and Instagram. The images are of 1200 x 628 pixels, therefore, enabling you to run quality photos in marketing your products. However, single product pictures may seem bias and sometimes overlaid with multiple texts. Despite being among the most used formats today, it is important to utilize other types to show your prospects more about your business and in detail through various images.

Ads containing single images are suitable for displaying funny or happy people or customers as well as beneficial ones such as when offering discounts. However, you may choose other options for new businesses to showcase several elements of your business. For instance, newly established enterprises require descriptions of the brand and products as well as some information about your company. As such, one image ad becomes a challenge to highlight all the information. Beginners should henceforth avoid single image ads while creating Facebook ads to run.

Page Likes Ads

Page likes ads are campaigns to grow likes within your business page with an effort to reach more prospects and build a broader fan base. A page like ad is essential, especially when you need your fans to view any notification about your brand or product. Facebook enables you to reach between two and three percent of your audience with an immediate call to action button after your placement. Facebook also provides you with an opportunity to set your parameters on whom to attract to become your fan. That is, you can choose your target audience from the filters and advertise the message to the desired individuals.

However, page like ads has minimal impact during the creation of campaigns to enhance awareness and product promotion. For beginners, the development of advertisements with excellent features accompanied by well-detailed descriptions encourages your audience to purchase your products. With Facebook settings, the low audience reaches while using a page like ads, seek other types of ad formats to reach a broader target population, and create a more considerable margin of prospects. Subsequently, page like ads may attract unintended individuals; therefore, may involve people not interested in your brand or products.

Abandoned Carts Ads

Abandoned cart ads are another Facebook format campaigns which are necessary, but you should avoid during the creation of your e-commerce marketing strategies. In a study conducted by the *Baymard Institute*, about seventy percent of all shoppers globally abandon their carts while shopping in different firms. As such, abandoned cart ads tend to let these shoppers back to the store and continue shopping or complete their purchase. Facebook launched an abandoned cart ad with personalized features crucial for targeting these individuals.

You may use funny videos or well-illustrated images to make them go back to their carts and complete the purchase. Nevertheless, such ads tend to contain low engagement and seductive nature suing the individual to really continue shopping. More so, the shoppers may view the ads and ignore while others may not abandon their carts but have an intention of keeping with shopping later. We would, therefore, recommend that you avoid this type of ads as they have minimal impact on driving shoppers back to your store when they abandon or halt their shipping.

Facebook Messenger Ads

Facebook messenger ads primarily focus on targeting Facebook messenger mobile application for those who like chatting with friends. The ads run in the main tab enabling a user to view it while in the messenger inbox between different conversations. If interested, the user may click on the ad, and it may redirect to either your brand's website or view the products. The ads can only be considered neither by those using their inboxes or asset during campaign creation.

Features of Facebook Ads

- Maximum image size is 1200 x 628;

- Image ratio 1:9:1;

- Characters include 30 for the description, 125 for the text and 25 for the headline;

- Minimum width of images 254 x 133.

Viewing the ads in the conversation is an excellent option for you, but more prospects may not use Facebook messenger frequently hence limiting your audiences. Similarly, the platform may show a limited number of ads compared to the main page or other platforms vital for your campaign. As such, Facebook messenger ads format should be avoided. That is because you may choose to run your ads in the news feeds or Facebook audience network and reach a broader audience. It, therefore, increases your advertising performance while increasing your fan base as well as your prospects.

Choosing the Best Facebook Ads Format

Facebook's tens of Facebook ad formats may create a challenge, especially for beginners in determining which to use when creating their e-commerce marketing campaigns. Deciding which form to use may primarily depend on the stage of your products or brand, nature, and objectives. When in need of creating awareness, then the ads should solely deliver the message intended. Beginners may end up selecting formats resulting in lower performances, therefore, leading to failure in Facebook ads marketing.

Similarly, different types of Facebook ads remain introduced to achieve a particular objective, as such, always check on your goals before deciding on your factorable format. The real purpose, audience, and formant go hand in hand in the creation of the most successful Facebook ad essential for your campaign. Before selecting your desirable format, understand the different types of Facebook ads. Learning about these formats ensures that you can readily optimize and make necessary changes in the right form collected.

Chapter 10: Facebook Pixel and Business Ad Manager

Facebook business manager is made to help users, and business owners manage and organize their businesses. For users to create a Facebook ad with the business manager, they must first create a Business Manager account. This is a simple process that has clear guidelines. However, you should first create a Facebook profile. Facebook allows a maximum of two business accounts; you cannot have more than one business manager account.

Here are the steps you should follow when creating a business manager account;

1. Ensure that you have a personal Facebook account which helps in identifying the user;

2. Link the account to the website of Facebook, i.e., business.facebook.com;

3. Click on the create account icon;

4. Write a unique business name to avoid conflicts and confusion with similar businesses. You should conduct a name search with a professional before

settling on the final business name. This is also the right time to attach your work email as well as any other important address details. Where you will also have to select its primary page and enter your name and work email.

Once users are done with setting the business manager account, they can now send invitation links to their friends. To reach a wider audience, you can start the advertising campaign.

Adding an ad account in the business manager account is very easy. Here are a few steps that you should follow for better results:

Step 1. On your business manager's home page

Click on the add ad account button. Once you have clicked it, you will have two options of either adding an existing ad account or creating a new ad account.

It is important to note that if you are creating a new ad account, you should use the name of the business when asked to name the new account. When done with the process, you will then click create an ad account. This step gives users the ability to have a brief idea of how their ads will look like.

Step 2. Installing a Facebook pixel

For a user to be able to set up an advert on Facebook, he or she needs to install the Facebook pixel on their website. It comes with greater benefits and attracts more potential customers to business websites.

But what does it entail? A Facebook pixel is a tracking code that enables Facebook to identify people who visit their customer's website. It creates a customized audience and creates ads for a potential market. It can also help businesses to identify potential and future customers based on the data that they collect from those who visit their website.

Step 3. Setting up the target audience

After installation of the Facebook pixel for the ads, you should now set up the target audience. This involves selecting the audience that you would like to reach out using the ad. It enables business owners to get optimum results from the ad that they have shared with the audience. It also ensures proper usage of resources for the user will not use excess budget while the product is reaching the wrong audience.

In choosing the right audience, factors such as age, gender, location, and demographics should be put into consideration. To access the audience tool, the user should log in the business manager account under assets and select the audience option. The audience can be categorized into; lookalike audience, saved audience, or custom audience.

The customize audience is that audience that is already familiar with the user's product and engage now and again with the user through Facebook page and website.

The saved audience, on the other hand, is the audience that shares a common interest with your line of product. The saved audience is a good start for a first-time marketer who is advertising his or her product to a new market.

A lookalike audience is that which resembles the same interest as those of the customize audience that the user has already interacted with.

Step 4 Creating your ad.

After you are done with all the above steps, you will be in a good position to create the ad and run it through the business manager account via the Facebook page. Before running the ad though, the user must most importantly not forget to categorize his or her ad campaign into three levels i.e., the objectives, conversions, and sales or clicks. With all these in mind, the user or the marketer will be ready to run a very successful ad campaign that will yield optimum results.

In conclusion, we do realize that the most important thing even as a user runs an ad through the business manager is always to have his or her objective set right. In everything that a person does even in our normal day to day life, objectives are what always guide us to success. For example, when a marketer wants to advertise the product, he/she should be well aware of the benefits that will accrue from that campaign. When advertising a product, the user should always make sure that he considers the interest, age, gender, location of his or her target market before running an ad on Facebook via the business manager account. A marketer must also have a reasonable budget so as not to be constrained so much when running an ad campaign.

Facebook is a global platform that is used nearly by every person in the world, has proven to be a great place where many businesses have managed to grow through advertisements. This is because business owners can target the right market and audience in line with the products that they are dealing with.

How to Use the Facebook Pixel?

Facebook pixel is an analytical tool that is used to find out the performance of a user's advertisement. It enables business owners to understand the actions that visitors take when they visit their website. Every time potential customers visit their preferred website through a Facebook ad, Facebook pixel analyzes, measures, and reports the action. This will help business owners to know the type of actions visitors perform when they visit their site. It, in turn, helps in creating a customized audience or a target market. Through Facebook pixel, the social media giant can know people who are most likely to take similar actions if they visit your site and can help set for a user lookalike audience. Some of the actions that Facebook pixels perform include the collection of information and data that will help a user in tracking conversion from Facebook ads and building a target audience to be used in the future.

The use of Facebook pixel for marketing is very important for it plays a crucial role in providing information that a marketer can use to help in creating an ad that will have an optimum return. The information gathered can also help the user to get the right target audience for his or her ad. This informs the business owners on who is most likely to take any action, for example, purchasing a product after seeing the advertisement. As a result, this would eventually increase the rate of conversion from a Facebook ad.

How Facebook pixel can help you with marketing

1. It helps you know how many visitors visit your website after seeing the ad on Facebook. It also helps in tracking your visitors and enables you to see which device they mostly use to visit your website. For instance, you can check if most are using their mobile devices or their personal computers.

2. After visiting your website, the Facebook pixel can help you retarget your audience. It allows you to see the type of product a visitor was interested in. For instance, a customer can select a product on your website and leave it in the chart without finalizing the transaction. With Facebook pixel, you can be able to re-advertise the product to the specific client as a way of enticing the client.

3. Facebook pixel also allows a user to create a lookalike audience. Besides, its groups those who already visited the user's website and those who might tend to have the same interest as those who already visited the site. It will consider the interest, location, gender age, and demographics of the look-alike target group.

4. Facebook pixel also helps business owners to optimize the conversion rate of their Facebook ad. With the data gathered the user can focus his or her ad to a specific audience which will, in turn, enhance the conversion rate to the maximum. It does this by increasing the possibility of the audience visiting the website and taking various activities such as purchasing a product.

5. As visitors visit your website and do purchases, the Facebook pixel can help the user to group his audience

according to the value of the product they purchase or which they are interested in. For example, it can help a user to know the audience that is most likely to purchase a product of high value and those that are interested in products of low value. This will help the user to group his or her audience per their level of income.

Facebook Pixel Standard Events

Events are actions that always take place when people visit your site through Facebook ads.

Facebook has 17 Facebook pixel standard events;

1. **Purchase** - this is when a visitor visits your site and completes a purchase and makes the required payments for the product.

2. **Contact** - this is when the targeted customers visit your website and make a telephone call, sends SMS or email to contact your business regarding a specific product or service.

3. **Donate** - this when a visitor in your website donates to your organization or event that had been advertised on Facebook

4. **Customize product** - this is when a customer picks a specific product, e.g., a product of a specific color or size.

5. **Schedule** - this is when a customer books or schedules for an appointment with your business.

6. **Find a location** - when a customer searches for the physical location of your business.

7. **View content** - when a customer lands on a specific page or category of the products on your website.

8. **Subscribe** - when a customer pays a subscription fee for a product or service on your website.

9. **Add to chart** - when a customer adds a product that they are interested in their shopping cart on your website.

10. **Add payment information** - a customer adds his or her payment information during the purchasing process on your website.

11. **Lead** - a customer signs up for a product trial in your website or identifies themselves as leads in your website

12. **Complete registration** - when a customer completes registration form or subscription form on your website

13. **Search** - when a customer uses the search engine in your website to search for a product or service.

14. **Initiate check out** - when a customer starts the checkout process after buying a product on your website.

15. **Start trial** - this is when a customer signs up for a free trial of a product or service on your website.

16. **Apply** - when a customer applies for a product or service in your website

17. **Add to Wishlist** - when a customer adds a to a Wishlist on your website.

Here is the step by step procedure of creating Facebook pixel in the Facebook manager account;

Step 1. Visit your business manager business account. On the top of the business manager, the home page, click on the menu at the top (it has three lines) then select create pixel from the asset column.

Step 2. Click create pixel to begin the process.

Step 3. Select your business name

Step 4. Select the + add button

Step 5. Insert the name for your pixel

Step 6. Enter your optional website URL

Step 7. Select create

The final step is installing Facebook pixel on the user's website. Here the user must choose the option he or she is going to use to install the pixel. There are three options that a user can choose to install the pixel. One can either copy-paste the pixel code manually or if he or she is using a third party, then the user may use a tag manager plugin to install the pixel. The other option is emailing the pixel code developer or a trusted friend who can help with the installation process.

If the user decides to use the copy and paste option, he or she will see the install pixel base code page. He or she should click on the code box to copy the code in the clipboard. After this, all the user has to do is to paste it in the header tags of their website under the SEO (Search engine Optimization) settings. If a user is using a third-party service, he or she should just do it the same way in the header tags of his or her page.

Next, the user should be free to install the Facebook pixel code. The user should then click next to get a snippet of code they install on specific web pages to be able to track actions taken on those pages.

The final step in the installation process is testing the pixel status. To do this, the user should go to the Facebook business manager account and select pixels. If the pixel status is active, it means the Facebook pixel was installed correctly. It may take between 20-30 minutes before the status of the pixel is updated.

In conclusion, Facebook pixel's main objective is to help a business or a marketer to get to know more about the people who are always engaging with its(business) content. A user can use this valuable information to create content and product that has a better appeal to the target audience.

Chapter 11: Advert Mistakes that Facebook Marketers Should Avoid

Facebook ads are one of the best tools to use for both new and existing businesses. However, for the ads to give satisfactory conversion, every marketer needs to select the best ad type for their trade wisely. To decide which the best type of ad to use is, some things should not be overlooked. The business owner should first consider setting up the goals they intend to achieve as the beginning stage of ads creation. These goals should be tangible so that they will assess and know when they need to change their ad type. There are four primary goals for every business. These are;

- Creating their brand awareness;

- Generating leads to their products;

- Customer care;

- Converting traffic to sales.

These are general goals basically for most businesses. However, every business should set their own more specific goals and decide on how to meet them. Once the goals are set, the next step will be to understand the different types of Ads available. With different types of ads for different marketing goals, your specific goal will help you decide which one of them is best for your business. You will then customize the ad type you choose to use and create it in a way to suit your business. When the time to assess progress comes, you will know if the add was helpful. If you don't meet your goals, you will know what did not work and try a more suitable ad type. Experimenting with different types of ads will give you lots of information regarding what works for you to meet which goal.

In this chapter, we shall look at some types of ads that should be avoided at all cost by any Facebook marketer.

Page-Like Ads

These are Ads that focus on increasing the number of likes on your page. Having high traffic on your page could increase your sales. It's good to note, however, that it's not guaranteed that everybody who likes your page likes your products. Such ads will rise the likes on your page drastically, but in most cases, the conversions will not pace up. This is because someone may have liked the page without necessarily even looking at what is displayed on it. Instead of targeting likes that might not give your business, it will, therefore, be better to have a few likes from people who genuinely like your products. Others, like the engagement ads, would instead help you gain likes, comments, and shares on your post. This is likely to give awareness and at the same time, convert traffics to result in sales.

Facebook Stories Ads

These are ads that will appear for 24 hours and then disappear. If you want them to appear longer, you should make sure to save them. People who may miss Facebook for a period of more than 24 hours may not see the ad because it will have disappeared when they go through their app account. More so, Facebook stories ads alone will not effectively work alone.

Untargeted Ads

General ads that do not target a particular group of people may end up as a waste of time and money. This is because people who will not get interested in your products will be seeing your ad and may not respond to it. For example, if an untargeted ad is able to reach one thousand people, half of them may not get interested. Targeted ads do better because they seem to appear to a specific group of people. The groups are defined either in a specified age group, a particular region or with a specific shared interest. Targeting ensures that 100 % of the people who see it will in one way or another connect with the ad.

Pop Up Ads

These have proved to be the most annoying type of ads among most Facebook users. Mobile surveys have also seen most people disliking and disapproving them. If people do not like these types of ads, chances are they will not even click on them to know what they are advertising. Bad enough, most people will block them from appearing. It's good, therefore, to use Ads in a way that will not annoy people to avoid giving people a negative attitude towards the product. Instead of getting interested in knowing more about the product or your business at large, potential buyers may get irritated by the site of any advert from your store.

Ads with No Set Goals and Objectives

The first step in the creation of an advert is supposed to be the setting of goals to be achieved. The goals help you with determining what kind of advert you need to create. Some Facebook marketers encounter difficulties making any positive progress because of not setting their objectives. This occasionally leads to losses that could not have been encountered if they had a clear intention before setting the advert. Having set goals also enables you to assess the progress of your business. It also helps you understand how each type of advert has assisted you in meeting the marketing funnel stages' goals. With no goals, Some Facebook marketers choose wrong adverts for their products. This, at times, confuses the minds of their audience since they find the advert irrelevant. Consequently, part of the audience will drift away from the product.

Ads That Target the Wrong Objective

Some Facebook marketers want to sell as soon as they post their first Ad. This does not catch the audience that just found out that you exist. Like every other engagement, it's wise to consider giving before asking to receive. It is always good to consider the marketing funnel stages and create ads considering the different kinds of people likely to view it. For an extremely new seller, it will make more sense if they create an ad that gives awareness before they start their sale. Once you have an already engaged audience selling to them will be easy altogether. At the same time, having more people recognize your brand and liking your page and website should be the first thing in your mind. Once you have more followers, you can then try converting the viewers to buyers. Most marketers rush into conversion ads while they have no audience to convert. This mistake makes the advert to end up making zero achievements.

Lack of Using Facebook Pixels for The Ads

Pixels are important units to all Facebook marketers for them to build a custom audience. Facebook pixels optimize adverts for conversions and also track conversions on every Facebook marketer's website. However, some Facebook marketers tend to ignore this vital unit. As a result, they miss getting views from their viewers. Clients' opinions are an essential aspect of the growth of any business. They help every business owner to assess and understand how people feel about their products and the business as a whole. This will help them decide on changes they need to make either in their targeting or their ads type. They will also understand the market trends as potential buyers tend to compare you with your competitors. Evidently, anyone who does not use Facebook pixels will be missing a lot.

Adverts with Irrelevant Headlines

Most people either don't like reading a lot of content or are lazy when it comes to reading. Long complicated headlines in an advert will most probably put off such people since they will view it as a boring post. Some other headlines are too wordy that even some Facebook users who may want to read may not understand what is being advertised. The many words make the advert seem irrelevant to people who view it, and it may cause a lack of interest to Facebook users. When people lose interest in the advert, most definitely they will not take time to think about the product leave alone considering buying it. The business will most probably not achieve its main goal as per the advert and may also incur losses since the ads could be paid advertisements.

Advertising Multi-Products at One Time

Many Facebook marketers tend to advertise many of their products at the same time. When such adverts may give excellent results, they require a lot of consideration on how they are set. When put in slides or videos with clear descriptions on each slide, they can be the best kind of ads for awareness. However, the marketer must have the best of professionalism to create beautiful and organized ads. Photos are not ideal for such adverts unless put in a slide. People will not scroll down on a post whose first photo is not of something they are interested in, which leaves some products unnoticed. Some marketers also market with so many products in the same post, giving links that direct viewers to the website. When traffic moves to the site, it can be overwhelming, and some inquiries may not be well responded to, which can put off impatient buyers. Such adverts are also time-consuming since it takes time to refresh your creativity. In the long run, some products may lack your attention on your website such that even clients may notice you are inconsistence. Inconsistence is very dangerous as it can lead to people doubting your credibility, which can cause a downfall in the business.

Poorly Targeted Ads

Some marketers tend to focus on a small number of audience or a very large number. While targeting a large number can increase their sales, it's not guaranteed. A large number can cause too much congestion on your website with ninety percent of your audience's not interested in your product. Some marketers target a very small group which is not healthy for the business. For you to increase sales, you need to have a high number of people who are viewing it. However, the target population must be the relevant people who need the product, and in a locality that you can efficiently deliver. For example, if a seller is marketing cartoon themed school bags, it will be useless to target youths aged 12 – 20 years. As much as they are very many on Facebook, the cartoon-themed bags may not make sense to them. If the same person targeted young parents aged 20- 35 years, they would most likely have convertible traffic on their website. If they targeted the population of 12 – 35 years male population, they also might have so much useless traffic on their wall. The cartoon-themed school bags will catch the attention of people shopping for kindergarten and primary children. Most shoppers will be women and not men.

Ads That Concentrate on One Form of Advertising

Many Facebook marketers focus too much on one type of advertising. While the video form of advertisement can be catching, it may not be suitable for every Facebook user. Videos may be discouraging to some people who may not have time to watch but prefer short descriptions. Other people go through Facebook when they are in the office working or waiting to be served. Watching videos in such a place may cause disturbances, and so they pass the advert without opening to see what it is about. In such a case, a written advert featuring pictures of the product will be the best to catch such an audience. Some people also tend to think that videos are edited to create an impression to the viewer and hence ignore video adverts. It's important for everybody to concentrate on different forms of advertising to attract more of the audience who have different preferences and advertisement beliefs.

Monotonous Adverts

Your audience gets used to your ad in a few days or weeks. It's advisable therefore to keep refreshing them with new ads so that they will not get used to one and get bored. Even though you do not have different products every few weeks, there are still things you can do to show changes in your advert. This means you have to be creative every time you make an ad, or else people will start ignoring them. You can refresh your adverts by

- Turning statements in the previous ads to question forms;
- Change the personification;
- Edit images to change some features like filters, edit texts, add or remove logos, use gifs instead of photos;
- Change background colors;
- Increase or decrease words in the description.

Through the edits, it will make the audience want to see what you have for them every time they see your adverts. It keeps them wanting to see more of what you have, and this helps keep your audience engaged.

Unproductive Paid Ads

While paid Ads are more productive, they are also the riskiest type of ad that any Facebook marketer should be careful when using. This is because the ads require one to invest real money for you to run your advertisement. Facebook paid ads can lead to a significant loss to the marketer if he or she does not have a clear guideline on how it should be created. They are one reason why many Facebook marketers tend to make loses other than the expected profit. When you realize your ad did not deliver per your expectations, it's wise to consider revisiting it before investing more on the same. Try to check where you went wrong and make the necessary changes before giving it a second shot. When paying for your ads, it's also good to consider a reasonable budget. A meager budget can allow your competitors to outdo you while a very high budget can increase your losses. When your advert starts performing well, you can gradually begin increasing the budget. If you realize that your paid ad is performing poorly, it's wise to stop running it and work on improving it. By doing this, you will be controlling your chances of incurring heavy losses. When running paid ads, it's advisable to be diligent so that you don't pause or stop ads before your target population gets to see them.

Bonus: Split Testing as a Way to Maximize Your Impact

As promised, I wanted to offer you a special ***bonus*** chapter that would help you do even better at creating strong performing advertisements. This special bonus chapter discusses split testing and the power of split testing as a way to maximize your impact and increase the value you gain from your advertising budget.

What is Split Testing?

Split testing ads essentially means that you run two or more advertisements, each of which are slightly different, to see which ones perform the best. When you use split testing properly, it allows you to accumulate a large amount of information about your audience in a relatively short period of time. Through that, you are able to begin understanding your audience in a deeper manner which means that future ads are more likely to convert with great success *and* you know what types of products or services to offer your customers to boost sales. While this particular method for getting to know your audience will cost money, it tends to be faster and far more accurate than nearly any other method out there.

Facebook itself has a split testing feature built in, which is also known as A/B testing. This feature enables you to make your two separate advertisements and run them, and it will use Facebook's built in analytic trackers to ensure that you are getting the results you desire from your advertisements. Plus, it will allow you to compare the productivity of both of the ads to see how well they performed.

What Should You Split Test?

Split testing can be done on any number of things in your Facebook advertisements. When it is being down, however, it is more useful to do it on smaller differences rather than larger differences so that you know exactly what your audience is and is not responding to. For example, you could split test with things like:

- Colors of the call to action button;
- Images vs. videos;
- Words in copy;
- Specific call to actions ("Sign Up!" vs. "Learn More!");
- Audience targeting;
- Element positioning;
- Landing page design.

By split testing with these subtle differences in your advertisements you can get specific information regarding what works best and what doesn't. This way, you can begin to construct advertisements that reflect the findings of your A/B split test practices.

The key to making sure that your split testing practice works is to create two advertisements that are almost identical, except for subtle differences. If you attempt to try too many different aspects all at once you will find that you struggle to identify what was working and what wasn't. As a result, you may not be able to duplicate your success because you have not gotten a clear understanding as to what it was that your audience really wanted.

How Much Of Your Budget Should You Place Into Split Testing?

At first, your entire budget should be placed into split testing so that you can start to get more specific findings on your audience. You should take your entire budget, set the goal for how many different advertisements you are going to try, and then allot your budget accordingly. This way, you have enough money to run each of your split tests.

If you are new to Facebook advertisements, you should try running each split test for at least five days before cancelling it to see your results. If your results seem highly obvious much sooner than that, though, then you can take action accordingly.

If you were to try one split test at a time, for five days, then this would get you 12 advertisements per month. This means that if you had a budget for $1000 for advertising, then you should allot about $83.33 per advertisement so that you can begin to see what your results are like.

If you are not new to Facebook advertising and you already get generally decent results from your advertisements, then ideally you should only use split testing when you are unsure about what will work. If you find that your current ads are not getting you the results you desire and you want to try expanding into making more money through Facebook advertisements, then at this point you might want to start allotting some of your budget to split testing. In this case, you should keep at least 50% of your budget for your ads that are already working, even if they are not working exactly how you wish, and use the other 50% of your budget to conduct split testing. This way, you can see what is likely to work and you can start improving the quality of your standing ads according to your findings, without excessively disrupting your existing results with your advertisements.

What Should You Do When The Results Start Coming Back?

As you begin running your split tests, you will find that in some cases the advertisements receive fairly similar results whereas in other cases the results are completely different. How you manage your advertisements will ultimately depend on your findings in this case.

If you find that your advertisements are performing fairly similarly, you should let them run all the way through the entire five days, or whatever allotted time period you have provided them with. This way, you can get conclusive findings from your results. If the results are incredibly close, you may want to make a few more tweaks to the split test before running it again to get a more conclusive finding. Or, in some cases, you may find that people do not particularly care more or less in one way or the other for the shift that you are making.

If you find that one ad clearly outperforms the other ad to the point where one is barely performing at all, you should pause and cancel the advertisement that is not performing well. Rather than spending money waiting to see if it does better, you can invest that money into prolonging an advertisement that is already working well, instead. This way, your budget is spent wisely *and* you learn about your audience through the power of split testing.

Refrain From Overtesting Your Audience

As helpful as split testing can be, it is important that you do not over test your audience as this can lead to wasted money, confusion around your brand, and poor results from your ad budget. Ideally, split testing should be used sparingly to ensure that you are still creating consistency in how you show up and that you are able to turn great results from your advertisements.

As well, make sure that you avoid hyper-segmentation, which ultimately means that you run a split tests where you are getting far too specific on who you are advertising to. If you find yourself getting too specific, you are going to end up wasting money because you will not turn any results from your audience.

When you run split tests, make sure that you have an audience of about 500,000+ people to advertise to, depending on your budget and who your actual target audience is, so that there are plenty of people to collect numbers from. This way, your budget will still turn you back with some results from your tests that will enable you to make greater success with your Facebook advertisements overall.

Conclusion

Facebook adverts are with no doubt the best tools for any marketer to reach their audience on Facebook. However, wrongly chosen ads can lead to losses for the same business. Worse still, the right ads done incorrectly can lead to the downfall of any business. Therefore, wisdom dictates that every marketer should first understand their product well enough to know which population to target. Once they have understood the product, the marketers should then set adverts for their products, following the advert funnel tips to ensure the audience is covered at all levels. The adverts should be created considering already set strategic goals. Once the adverts are posted to run on Facebook, it's the job of the marketer to follow up and see how they are doing, as they make necessary adjustments. Finally, when the marketer is sure they have the best ad for their product, it's time to run them on Facebook. They should be sure to set their budget reasonably and maximize their potential to maximize their profits.

www.ingramcontent.com/pod-product-compliance
Lightning Source LLC
LaVergne TN
LVHW051219050326
832903LV00028B/2163